THE CANADIAN
PROTESTANT
EXPERIENCE
1760 TO 1990

THE CANADIAN PROTESTANT EXPERIENCE 1760 TO 1990

Edited by G.A. Rawlyk

McGill-Queen's University Press
Montreal & Kingston • London • Buffalo

© G.A. Rawlyk 1990
ISBN 0-7735-1132-6

Legal deposit first quarter 1994
Bibliothèque nationale du Québec

Printed in Canada on acid-free paper
Reprinted 1999

Canadian Cataloguing in Publication Data

Main entry under title:
The Canadian Protestant experience, 1760 to 1990
Includes index.
ISBN 0-7735-1132-6
1. Protestants – Canada – History. 2. Canada – Church
history. I. Rawlyk, George A., 1935–
BR570.C36 1994   280'.4'0971   C94-900112-0

CONTENTS

Acknowledgements

A generous publication subvention for this book has been provided by the Dean of Graduate Studies and the Dean of Arts and Science, Queen's University. For this grant I am very, very grateful. I also appreciate the financial assistance provided by the Jackman Foundation.

Editor's Preface

Early in 1987 I had come to the conclusion that there was a great need for a book dealing with the Canadian Protestant experience from 1760 to the present day. There was no such book available and, like other scholars in the field, I very much wanted to see this embarrassing historiographical void filled. There was so much new and exciting historical work recently published which needed to be disseminated to a wider audience. I therefore approached five leading Canadian religious historians to see whether they would contribute chapters to this book. The first chapter was to cover the 1760 to 1815 period; the second, 1815 to 1867; the third, 1867 to 1914; the fourth, 1914 to 1945; and the last, 1945 to the present.

Each author was encouraged to base her or his chapter largely upon available secondary literature and recently written theses. I also emphasized that each chapter was to be strongly informed by what the author considered to be major underlying themes. The influence exerted by key personalities was to be noted, as well. In other words, I expected each chapter to be stamped with a distinctive organizational and conceptual framework that recognized the interplay of individuals and social movements. Each author was to take into account:

(1) the importance of both the "evangelical" and "liberal" traditions of Canadian Protestantism;
(2) the impact of ethnicity on the Canadian Protestant tradition;
(3) the way in which British and American forces have shaped the Canadian religious landscape;
(4) the symbiotic relationship between regional religious life and national religious life;
(5) where relevant, the importance of popular and elite religion, secularization, and the changing character of Canadian Protestant religiosity; and,
(6) where available, census and public opinion survey data (which was to be carefully integrated into the text).

Instead of using footnotes, I requested that a cogent bibliographical essay be added to the end of each chapter. These essays would provide a carefully considered list of further readings on a variety of topics and also clearly show which key sources had been used by each author.

Nancy Christie's Chapter I, " 'In these Times of Democratic Rage and Delusion': Popular Religion and the Challenge to the Established Order, 1760-1815," is a boldly conceived chapter which underscores the importance of the "Evangelical tradition" as well as "Church/Sect" tensions within early Canadian Protestantism. In Chapter II, "Protestantism Transformed: Personal Piety and the Evangelical Social Vision, 1815-1867," Michael Gauvreau carefully and sensitively traces the changing face of Canadian Protestantism during these formative years. Phyllis D. Airhart's Chapter III, "Ordering a New Nation and Reordering Protestantism 1867-1914," examines in both a sophisticated and empathetic manner Canadian Protestantism at the peak of its influence and the begining of its decline. The weakening and fragmentation of Canadian Protestantism during the 1914 to 1945 period is confidently described and analyzed in Chapter IV by Robert A. Wright. In the final chapter of *The Canadian Protestant Experience*, John G. Stackhouse Jr. presents a controversial thesis concerning the ways in which the forces of change and continuity flowed through Canadian religious life during the forty-five years after the end of the Second World War.

It is clear that Protestantism exerted its greatest influence on Canadian life in the nineteenth century. As the twentieth century unfolded, however, Canadian Protestantism, battered by demographic change, profound inner doubt, so-called modernity, and secularization, was gradually pushed to the periphery of Canadian experience. Here it remains in the 1990s with the Evangelical tradition becoming increasingly significant once again and American influences noteworthy. In 200 years many things had profoundly changed in the Canadian Protestant experience. A few, however, apparently did not and this, too, is part of the story.

G.A. Rawlyk
Kingston, Ontario
November, 1990

"IN THESE TIMES OF DEMOCRATIC RAGE AND DELUSION"

POPULAR RELIGION AND THE CHALLENGE TO THE ESTABLISHED ORDER 1760-1815

Nancy Christie

I

In 1760, when New France was captured by the British, there was only a small number of Protestants in what is now Canada. Gradually, however, the Protestant population grew to the point that by 1776 less than ten percent of Nova Scotia's estimated 20,000 residents were Roman Catholic (Nova Scotia then included all of present-day New Brunswick, Nova Scotia, and Cape Breton Island). Well over half of the Nova Scotia Protestants were recently arrived Congregationalists from New England. There were also sizeable numbers of newly-settled Methodists and Anglicans from the North of England; German Protestants; and a smattering of other sects, including Quakers. Outside of the capital of Halifax, the Yankee Congregationalists set the religious tone of the colony; in Halifax, however, the Church of England would dominate. At the outbreak of the American Revolution in 1776, there were fewer than a dozen Protestant ministers in Nova Scotia, most of whom were Congregationalists. They served widely scattered and isolated communities and they, to a man, realized that during the settlement years of the 1760's and 1770's, they had made very little religious impact on their congregations. The weakness of the Congregational

9

appeal among the humbler classes who formed the majority of the population opened the door to a wave of popular evangelicalism in the form of New Light revivalism after 1775.

To the west, Quebec, in 1776, had a population of some 90,000. Only a tiny percentage were not French-Canadian Roman Catholics. Protestantism would never make any real inroads into the French-Canadian population. Despite the fact that many English-speaking Loyalists settled in Lower Canada, it was apparent by the beginning of the nineteenth century that Protestantism was destined, in that province, to be a minority religion. There were only a handful of Protestants in the rest of Canada west of Quebec in 1776 — most were connected with the fur trade.

Over 50,000 American Loyalists arrived in Canada during and after the American Revolution. Most of these Loyalists settled in the Canadian Maritimes. Soon after 1784, they were joined by thousands of American and British immigrants, most of whom made their way to Upper and Lower Canada, present-day Ontario and Quebec. And just before the outbreak of the War of 1812, hundreds of Scots emigrated to what is now Manitoba. The post-Revolution influx of immigrants profoundly altered not only the demographic shape of Canada, but also its religious contours. By the time of the outbreak of the War of 1812, the population of the Maritime colonies had grown to over 100,000 — approximately 70,000 in the present-day Nova Scotia, 25,000 in New Brunswick, and some 10,000 in Prince Edward Island. The Protestant population of the region, well over half of the total number, was divided into two major denominational groups — the New Light evangelicals, mostly rural Baptists and Methodists, largely American in origin — and the Established Churches — the Anglicans and Presbyterians, with strong demographic ties to Great Britain and particularly important in the urban centres.

In Lower Canada in 1812, the population was in the neighbourhood of 300,000. Less than ten per cent were Anglo-Americans. Anglicanism and Presbyterianism had some strength in the urban centres of Montreal and Quebec City but, as was the case in the Maritimes and neighbouring Upper Canada, the Methodists, the Baptists, and other evangelical groups were particularly strong in the Eastern Townships where settlers from neighbouring New England had pressed their unique Protestant stamp.

In Upper Canada in 1812, over eighty per cent of the estimated population of 80,000 were Americans — either Loyalists or so-called "late Loyalists." Though the Anglican Church received considerable state support, it could claim the adherence of only a tiny minority of the population, and they were found in the garrison centres of Kingston, Niagara, and present-day Toronto. There were indeed two Protestant worlds in British North America — that of the Anglicans and Presbyterians and that of the Evangelical denominations. These, in turn, were defined by two rival world-views: the Anglican which saw society in static terms of hierarchical corporate bodies and social ranks, and the Evangelical, which stressed the dynamic role of the free individual in transforming society based on a more inclusive and egalitarian concept of human relations. The two dominant evangelical groups, the New Lights in the Maritimes and the Methodists in Upper Canada, can thus be viewed as two facets of a common popular religious impulse which sought to redefine British North American society in contrast to the established authority.

II

The Reverend Charles Inglis was the first Anglican Bishop of Nova Scotia, serving in this capacity from 1787 to his death in 1816. He believed that in the 1790's and the first decade of the nineteenth century he was indeed living in what he described as "these Times of Democratic rage and delusion." Unlike many modern historians who separate politics, religion, and society into discrete categories of meaning, Inglis and other members of the Protestant religious elite during the years immediately following the American and French Revolutions were fully aware that evangelicalism, as a popular expression, was the dominant vehicle by which established notions of an orderly, stable, and hierarchical society were being challenged and transformed. Likewise, by referring to religious revivals as a "reformation," evangelistic preachers such as the Methodist Joseph Gatchell contended that evangelicalism was indeed a popular mass social movement which was reshaping individual values and human relationships. What these historical figures understood, and what some modern historians have generally ignored, was that this era of democratic revolution, the period from 1776 to 1815, had engendered more than a political "stir." The age of democratic revolution was a manifestation of more general changes taking place within eighteenth century societies whereby notions of an organic, homogeneous culture defined by rank and deference to authority were giving way to ideals of individual self-expression, social equality, and democratic consent.

For the ordinary British North American Protestant whose world was defined not by the written word but by oral communication, rituals and mass events were important expressions of these transformations in values and consciousness. The account of the first mass camp meeting held at Hay Bay on the Bay of Quinte, Upper Canada, in 1803, recorded by the Methodist itinerant preacher, Nathan Bangs, evokes the various ways in which evangelical popular culture functioned as a direct rival to the polite, literate, and mannered world of the British North American gentry. Apparently, some 3,000 Upper Canadians attended this mass religious gathering. Bangs highlighted the fact that the meeting was removed from civil society by clearly establishing its rural location. More importantly, however, by stressing its natural setting, Bangs was confirming that there were no artificial mediators between the individual and God. Again and again, Bangs described how God immediately communicated with the converted by sending "shocks" to the people. The relationship between the communicant and God was both direct and personal: "The power of God descended upon a Travelling preacher in such a manner that his shout pierced the heavens, while his body was sustained by some of his friends. He was at length carried out of the Camp into a tent where he lay speechless, being overwhelmed for a considerable time with the mighty power of God." More importantly, God imbued the humble with personal authority, for "when his strength came, and his tongue was unloosed his song was 'Glory to God in the Highest.'" Not only was the camp meeting defined by popular participation whereby both the preachers and the converted laypeople exhorted and sang to bring about new conversions, but it also represented a form of religious experience in which, as Bangs himself noted, "old and young, male and female were now employed in carrying out the work of God." A new sense of an inclusive community which overcame both class and gender divisions was fashioned throughout the four-day vigil. Progressively, those who had hung about on the outskirts of the camp, viewing it merely as spectacle to jeer at, were brought into the "square" throng of the redeemed.

Such open-air meetings were occasions for popular and equal expressions of frank and personal religious experience. They were perceived as boisterous and emotional, thus symbolically challenging the elite conception of a rational world of polite behaviour. Throughout his narrative, Bangs unabashedly described the shoutings, crying, singing: one backslider "roared aloud for mercy" until 10 o'clock the next morning for God was in him "like fire in a dry stable." Often it was difficult to distinguish between "shouting and revelling." Here was a religious culture which encouraged the free expression of the humble and marginal people who possessed little power in colonial society, and in which the very power of God was associated with popular revelry: "It might be said of a truth, that the God of the Hebrews is come into the camp for the noise was heard far off. The groans of the wounded, the shouts of the delivered, the prayers of the faithful, the Exhortations of the courageous penetrated the very heavens, and reverberated through the neighborhood." Its associations with eighteenth century popular culture were obvious —such as Bangs' recounting of exorcising a young boy — but popular evangelicalism was also a catalyst in nudging their world towards modernity. Learning gave way to the authority of popular persuasion, ecclesiastical homogeneity to evangelical pluralism, communal status to individualism, and elite control to popular consent. As with American evangelical preachers, the once narrowly defined political language of liberty and egalitarianism suffused the Canadian evangelical scene, nourishing a pervasive cultural republicanism. It was with conscious pride that Bangs, the American evangelical preacher of prominent anti-Tory origins, proclaimed that with conversion people moved with a new "boldness," for through their relationship with God they had been "delivered from bondage," and "brought into liberty."

Until recently, influential historians of early Upper Canada have sought to highlight a single climate of opinion which was anti-democratic, anti-American, and wholly prescribed by the conservative values of the political and social elite. This uniform portrayal of the social world of Upper Canada has been challenged by Jane Errington's *The Lion, the Eagle, and Upper Canada*. Her analysis of Upper Canadian politics has clearly demonstrated that even among the gentry there was a diverse spectrum of attitudes towards the United States and England. One of the central contributions of Errington's study is its portrait of ethnic and cultural pluralism in early Upper Canada. Our attention is implicitly redirected away from simplistic notions of a fully-formed and hegemonic counter-revolutionary tradition immediately following the American Revolution, towards a recognition that post-revolutionary British North America was a new society in which ideologies were pluralistic, dynamic, and still unformed.

If we are to accept the Loyalist conservative imperative in early Canada — and certainly such a conservative ideology did exist — we must conceive of ideology not simply as reflective of a social reality, for values and ideas are refracted and transmitted through an extremely complex social world. In other words, Bishop Inglis' Tory views and those of many of his Anglican and Presbyterian supporters — particularly those of the Reverend John Strachan, the powerful voice of Anglican Toryism in Upper Canada in the 1800-

1815 period — did not represent a total culture, rather they were part of a larger dialogue of two ideals of society. Their evangelical rivals were vigorous participants in this dialogue. Even the exclusivist mind of Bishop Inglis and that of Strachan appreciated that the defence of a Tory, Anglican establishment had to share its voice both in the Maritime colonies and the Canadas with a cacophony of religious dissenting persuasions. Errington's pathbreaking work and the very observations of the gentry themselves implicitly directs the historians to recognize that one must look beyond the rarefied world of politics to the social world of popular culture to fully understand the voice of dissent within colonial society.

David Mills has observed in *The Idea of Loyalty in Upper Canada* that before the War of 1812 there was no organized political dissent in Upper Canada. In his work on early Saint John, David Bell has shown that within this Loyalist settlement there were initial expressions of political opposition which utilized the language of political dissent similar to that of the Patriots during the American Revolution. However, he also notes that these attempts to found politics of faction were soon squelched by the Tory elite which in turn imposed political consensus. Mills' quiescent attitude towards political dissent, however, raised the question of how to account for the Tory obsession with religious enthusiasm. What, for example, do we make of John Strachan's pre- 1812 comment that he had "serious political objections" to Methodist itinerant preachers? One could perhaps conclude that Tory commentators were simply alarmists who were rashly fulminating at a non-existent challenge to their social world of orderly government and reasonable religion. But if we are to take seriously Strachan and Inglis' remarks that evangelicals were "to a man" violent Republicans and Democrats, we must likewise accept that in the late eighteenth century there existed an intimate and causal relationship between religious expression and political ideology. From very different historiographical perspectives, J.C.D. Clark, the British Tory historian, and Nathan O. Hatch, the American interpreter of early American Republican culture, have concluded that religion has not always existed to buttress the status quo, but that in this period evangelicalism functioned as the fulcrum of dissent which anteceded political debate. Religious liberty enjoined the concept of civil liberty in opposition to established churches and gentry dominated politics.

This intersection of political and religious ideologies was duly noted by contemporaries both within patrician and plebeian cultures. Tories in post-revolutionary Upper Canada and the Maritimes sought to root out "novel doctrines" of liberty and equality not in the realm of politics but in evangelical religious movements. In Upper Canada, they targeted Methodism while in New Brunswick and Nova Scotia, Baptists, New Lights and some Methodists were the concern. Bishop Inglis noted in the 1790's, his sensitivity to radicalism having been heightened by the French Revolution, that the New Lights were effecting "a general plan of total Revolution in Religion and Civil Government." In a similar vein, John Strachan declared in 1806 that Methodists did not follow the "rational doctrines" of the Church of England, and therefore were suspected of "republican ideas of independence and individual freedom." Further, although evangelical pietism stressed the withdrawal of the converted individual from the sinful world of politics, evangelical preachers such as Henry Alline, the charismatic Nova Scotia preacher during the American Revolution, were no less attuned to the reality that their religious movements represented an assault upon the established order in church and state. As an outsider to elite politics, Alline employed his vital religion as a vehicle for social critique: "The Hypocrite and Pharisee can no longer deceive the World with their Cloak of Religion; they have nothing now to hide Shame and Pollution of the guilty and despairing Souls; neither dare they any longer mock the Searcher of all Hearts with their Lip service, or plead their close Conformity to the Externals of Religion." As was the case in Britain and the United States, all ranks within colonial British North America experienced the overwhelming tidal force of the age of democratic revolution. The upsurge of egalitarian cultural expression forcefully challenged and eventually wore down the central ideological stronghold of gentry privilege, namely the established church.

III

The Church of England had been established in Nova Scotia in 1758, and although it claimed a privileged position under the patronage of both the British government and the Society for the Propagation of the Gospel (both of whom somewhat reluctantly contributed financial support for the Anglican clergymen), its dominance was from the beginning limited by explicit decrees for religious toleration which were intended to attract New England settlers into the colony. Thus, despite its official status as the national church, the Church of England never garnered substantial popular support in the Maritime colonies, nor was its position buttressed by political favour due to the persistent strength of the liberal and dissenting flavour of the House of Assembly. The House offset any proclivities governors might have had to replicate the British equation between executive rule and an Anglican oligarchy. Before 1776 the Church of England had little social influence in Nova Scotia. After the American Revolution, in a flurry of concern, the Colonial Office erected the first colonial episcopate, appointing in 1787 Charles Inglis, a well-seasoned defender of the Tory establishment in New York and a devout Loyalist. Nevertheless, the Anglican church was challenged by the New Lights and the Methodists. The British government under the Whig Prime Minister, William Pitt, desired to curtail the "democratic element" in the British colonies in order to stave off future ruptures in her empire. It saw the Church of England as an active partner in upholding the principle of executive rule within the British constitution and in cementing the imperial connection. However, with the British Empire's "swing to the East" following the American Revolution, when British defence interests turned toward unholding trade interests both in India and China, the Colonial Office did little to sustain the Church establishment in British North America.

Moreover, the Church of England foundered in the Maritimes largely because of the smug assumption among both Inglis and many of his SPG missionaries that the traditions and rituals of the Anglican church need not be adapted to colonial circumstances. When Inglis did recognize the virtual necessity for local support once the SPG withdrew its financial commitment, individual missionaries who were largely trained in England were unaccustomed to promoting their church or travelling in order to evangelize new adherents. Consequently, they were very reluctant to shoulder the responsibility for the growth of the Anglican missions. The intransigence of the Anglican clergy, together with the fact that far fewer Loyalists were Anglicans than was assumed by British officialdom, meant that the arrival of post-revolutionary settlers contributed surprisingly little to solidifying the church's claim to be a national church; the Anglican church would therefore have to be satisfied with a minority status in the Maritimes. Furthermore, whatever rights the Church claimed under the constitution — such as the exclusive right to perform marriages — were whittled away in Nova Scotia and New Brunswick after 1800 by assemblies which tended to decide in favour of non-Anglican ministers who chose to challenge church authority.

In Upper Canada the privileged position of the Anglican church more accurately reflected the reciprocal relationship between church and state in England. Exclusive rights for the Anglican church were entrenched in the Constitutional Act of 1791, which established clergy reserves, gave the Lieutenant-Governor the power to appoint clergymen, and set aside provincial funds with which to support the clergy. A lucrative source of income was accordingly alienated from evangelical ministers in 1793 when the restrictive Marriage Act conferred the right to solemnize marriages exclusively to the Anglican clergy. As an extreme example of the exclusivity of the Church of England, the Rev. John Langhorn, the Anglican incumbent in Ernesttown, near Kingston, demonstrates the inflexibility and lack of understanding of the needs of the wider population. Langhorn, known for his obesity and obsessive daily cleansing in the waters of Lake Ontario, was almost a caricature of the overbearing and arrogant Anglican clergyman. He allowed no deviations from the formal liturgy even to the point of not giving communion to two women who would not kneel in his church; he also stubbornly refused to comfort the sick unless they held the Anglican prayer book. Langhorn refused to walk on the same side of the street as a dissenter, and finally held the whole of the Anglican community up for ridicule by writing rude and satirical poems about the Methodists, who outnumbered Anglicans by a substantial margin in the colony. As he himself stated when even his own parishioners, who were Americans familiar with a more informal and democratic Episcopal church, finally ousted him in 1806: "The great objection people here have against me is, that I will not model my religion to their fancy, but adhere to the Church of England."

IV

In 1791, Lieutenant Governor Simcoe articulated the desire to make Upper Canada's political and social structure "the image and transcript" of Britain in as far as the Church of England functioned to support the State in upholding the distinction of ranks enshrined in the English constitution. In practice, however, the Church suffered severely from the overwhelming competition of extremely popular evangelical societies, most notably the Methodists. Their centrally organized circuits and reliance upon tireless, cheap preachers and local lay exhorters, allowed this denomination to thrive in a sparsely settled frontier and in turn dominate a religious landscape refashioned in its own image. It was with a note of despair, then, that John Strachan, who believed that the survival of a hierarchical society and a political order defined by executive rule depended less upon the venerable constitution than upon the rational traditions of the Anglican church, entreated his fellow-clergy in Upper Canada to "outpreach and outpractice our opponents." Likewsie the embattled Church of England in the Maritimes resorted to intimidation, particularly in New Brunswick, to quell the rapid and spontaneous expansion of evangelicalism by invoking the 1786 Act for Preserving the Church of England thirteen times between 1791 and 1812.

Inglis and Strachan, the two most influential Anglicans in pre-1812 British North America, conceived of the Church as an instrument of allegiance. They saw government and religion as the pillars upon which society rested. It was common, of course, for eighteenth century British leaders to view "manners" as the tempering ethical glue which held together those prescriptive customs and obligations which defined proper relations between superiors and inferiors. Thus the Church of England, which encouraged the taming of passions and inculcated rational religious values, was the most important vehicle for ensuring public order and unity of belief. Any formal recognition of other religions outside the established Church would be, in Strachan's words, a "contradiction," for in the ideal hierarchy of rank, power devolved from God, through the church and constitution to the people. No room was left for plurality of belief. According to Strachan the ideal Christian society can flourish only when "the waywardness and selfwill of individual caprice is subjected to the restraints of wholesome and enlightened authority." Strachan believed in a providential social order, in which the Anglican church, the British constitution, and the separation and subordination of classes were ordained by God and therefore unchangeable.

These doctrines voiced by Inglis and Strachan, and by other Anglicans and Presbyterians before the War of 1812, reflected an interpretation of social and political relations commonly held by the British gentry who upheld rule by tradition. These two Anglican leaders did not put forward these ideas as unquestioned verities, for it is significant that these statements were made during and after the important decade of the 1790's when it became clear that all through the western world established churches, and thus the once solid notion of a prescriptive constitution and social order, were under siege. With the upsurge of the democratic critique, the Church was seen as a man-made, voluntary institution, which individuals could join at their will. Moreover, the evangelical impulse, by placing greater emphasis upon individual assertion, and by viewing piety as a personal rather than communal exercise of authority, tended to undermine the priority granted the civic community in Whig political thought. This, in turn, undermined the idea of obedience which sustained the close ties between Church and State. Charles Inglis experienced at first hand the American Revolution. John Strachan, for his part, witnessed the particularly fierce Scottish Tory backlash against the republican and individualistic tenets unleashed by the French Revolution. Consequently, both of these colonial leaders exuded a brand of Toryism which, fearful of Revolution, had become hardened and inflexible towards the idea of legitimate opposition and constitutional reform, the hallmarks of the anti-Tory, Whig political tradition. They abhorred the notion of the church as an institution responsive to social change or popular will and obdurately held to a concept of Church government founded solely upon tradition and precedent.

For John Strachan, who eventually became Bishop of Toronto, the Church was hierarchical, and thereby reflected and sustained a similar natural and social order: "It is evident that there is a subordination in the Natural World. We may extend the analogy and suppose that it is the intention of nature that the like subordination should prevail in the Moral World." This assumed, therefore, that the humble individual could not have a direct and personal relationship to God, for this must be mediated by an educated clergyman, a representative of the government elite, itself providentially ordained. Like the evangelicals, Strachan accentuated universal sin, but in contrast to their conception of universal salvation, Strachan posited that man was spiritually ignorant and must be tutored from above. The "mysterious truths of God," in Strachan's view, could be revealed only "by Messengers especially commissioned for that purpose." Not only was the Church thus averse to popular participation, but what more dramatically placed it in opposition to evangelical religious temper was the evisceration of any notion of sudden individual conversion whereby the emotions served as the vehicle of direct contact between the sinner and God.

For Anglicans, emotions were suspect in that they led to personal and social disorder. Only the rational doctrines purveyed by educated minds could properly dispose the individual towards goodness. Strachan's Church was intent on preserving distance between the social orders, and more importantly, it stressed the infinite distance between man and God, thus ensuring that authority was encompassed solely within the corporate institution, and was not within the grasp of the individual. God, declared Strachan, was present in "no one man, but in his new body, the Church" for there was an "infinite distance between the Creator and the highest created being." Anglicanism, therefore, was an institution which sought to preserve social rank and wealth, eschewing any concessions to the common people or the principle of equality. Clearly this was a church which served the needs and aspirations of the colonial gentry, for as the Rev. G.O. Stuart commented about his church in York, present-day Toronto, in 1809, a balcony was built by necessity for the garrison and the poor, because pews were purchased solely by "persons of rank." But if the Anglican church in Kingston was representative, the poor were soon pushed out of these quarters by the large garrison.

While the established Anglican church was the only Protestant church to be formally and legally recognized in British North America during 1760-1815 period, this elite institution was certainly in no way indicative of the popular religious landscape following the American Revolution. In terms of demography, the sacred landscape of Upper Canada, the Martimes, and Protestant Lower Canada more closely reflected the American experience of extreme religious pluralism and competition, what George Rawlyk has termed a "fragmenting religious ethos." In the aftermath of the American Revolution, when established religious authority was severely constrained and in some areas virtually non-existent, popular theology flourished and spread at a remarkable pace, unimpeded by the rigid distinctions of eighteenth century polite culture. As Nathan O. Hatch has argued, the democratic revolution broke down standard theological categories, and, as a consequence, unleashed upon all of North America a vast range of self-proclaimed preachers, who, by emphasizing the primacy of individual conscience, were instrumental in producing a multiplicity of religious options. In this period Christianity was totally reconstructed by unlettered popular preachers, who explicitly voiced the concerns of the poor and marginal, exalted the idea of free, individual choice in religious belief, and championed egalitarianism and religious ecstasy over education and social gentility. In this period of religious and social ferment, a new pattern of religious diversity based upon evangelical fervour and conversion took root in North America.

This striking diversity of the Protestant religious experience was immediately translated to Upper Canada and the Maritimes after the American Revolution when an array of religious denominations formed new local pockets of settlement. Quakers settled in Prince Edward County and Newmarket; Mennonite communities were established in the Niagara Penninsula in 1786, and in Waterloo and Markham Townships in 1803; while Scots Presbyterians settled in Glengarry. Many former Lutherans and Congregationalists founded Presbyterian churches, although this period of settlement brought with it much instability, and only in 1798 was a

Presbyterian ministry established at the Bay of Quinte. There were relatively few adherents to the established church among the Loyalist migrations into British North America for these American settlers had for many years been exposed to a culture in which the Episcopalians and Congregationalists had long been retreating before the groundswell of evangelical pluralism. To the horror of Loyalist Anglican clergymen, they soon found themselves leaders of a minority church in a society divided into many dissenting religious sects. The social unity which the established church was intended to cement in this new British society was severely undermined. As one Anglican clergyman commented his was a "settlement made up of foreigners bred in other churches." In Upper Canada there were only six Anglican missionaries in 1812. Although the Church fared better in the Maritimes, at Cornwallis, Nova Scotia there were in 1790 only 30 out of 400 families who attended Anglican service. At Horton, where Henry Alline's New Light revival was in full swing in the late 1770's, a mere 4 families were devout Anglicans, and even in Loyalist Shelburne in 1785, only 1 in 3 Loyalist families were Church of England.

In both the Maritimes and the Canadas, popular evangelicalism was clearly dominant by 1812, with the New Lights, Baptists, and Methodists clearly on the rise. During the 1770's and 1780's the religious landscape of Nova Scotia was completely reshaped by the New Light stir led by the charismatic revivalist Henry Alline. As George Rawlyk has clearly demonstrated, the Congregationalist presence was all but eliminated after Henry Alline swept the colony with his highly emotional, mystical revivalism which concentrated on the individual's personal spiritual relationship with God, sudden conversions, and an anti- Calvinist belief in universal accessibility to conversion. After Alline's death in 1784 the New Lights were split into the Free Christian and Calvinist Baptist and New Light Congregational churches. The evangelical fervour of the New Lights also invigorated Methodism. For example, the Methodist intinerant preacher, William Black, at first worked very closely with Alline, and Alline's New Light Evangelicalism significantly affected Methodism in the late 1770's and early 1780's. However, in 1785, the Methodists split off from the New Lights when Freeborn Garrettson, the remarkable American Methodist led a series of revivals in Nova Scotia between 1785-1787. Although Garrettson was extremely effective in bringing about a widespread Methodist revival, Methodism in the Maritimes always suffered from competition from the New Lights, especially since Francis Asbury, the leader of the American Methodist Conference was reluctant to send itinerant preachers to isolated Nova Scotia. After Garrettson quit the colony in 1787, Methodism was relatively weak in the Maritimes when compared to its strength in the Canadas. Nevertheless, the evangelical ethos had been firmly established in the region. Alline's powerful and extensive revivals, which had inspired and given comfort largely to farmers, artisans, and fishermen, had brought about a complete transformation in the way in which most Nova Scotians experienced religion, and had therefore made his brand of emotional evangelicalism the dominant form of religious expression in the Maritime colonies after 1770.

V

Methodism in Upper and Lower Canada formed a northern extension of the New York Methodist network of preaching circuits and camp meetings. Since almost all the itinerant preachers who served in Upper Canada were American-born, Methodism represented a very direct importation of American republican values through the culture of popular religion. By 1812 Methodism formed the largest Christian denomination in Upper Canada, with 2,550 active members and thousands of adherents who broadcast the egalitarian and individualistic message of the Second Great Awakening. Methodism also made up the largest group of Protestants in Lower Canada. Unlike Methodism in the Maritimes, which experienced setbacks both from the New Lights and Anglicans, Methodism in Upper Canada experienced much less competition. From the reminiscences of frustrated Anglican clergy, the popular revivalist preaching by itinerant preachers such as William Losee, Lorenzo Dow, Nathan Bangs, and William Case initiated a series of revivals between 1790 and 1810 which allowed Methodist teaching to take firm root along a string of widespread settlements. Methodism was much more unstable in the Maritimes, in part because the most acclaimed preachers such as Freeborn Garrettson hastened to return to the United States where they could feel much more immediately immersed in the exciting growth of the Methodist movement. Moreover, Methodist leaders in the Maritimes sought to seek the cooperation of the governing elite much earlier than those in the Canadas. As a result, after 1800 the Maritime Methodists associated themselves with the less radical Wesleyan Methodists in Britain. This in turn further diverted the support of American settlers toward the more socially egalitarian New Light Baptists.

Such problems of leadership and personnel did not plague Upper

Canada in part because of its proximity to one of the most dynamic frontiers of American Methodism, New York. As well, because Francis Asbury viewed Upper Canada as a field of greater potential for the growth of Methodism, he ensured strong leadership. Although immediately after the outbreak of the American Revolution Methodism in the United States found itself on the defensive because of Wesley's conservative opposition to political revolt, the American movement was revitalized in 1784 when Wesley created the Methodist Episcopal Church in America. Through Francis Asbury's authoritarian but dynamic leadership, Methodism was reorganized along a "travelling plan" of itinerant preaching which was peculiarly suited to a largely unsettled frontier of isolated communities. Both efficient and adaptable, it relied upon a combination of mobile ordained clergymen, the famous black-frocked circuit riders, and local lay exhorters. These lay exhorters enhanced the spirit of Methodist piety in local class meetings between the often flamboyant exhortations of the visiting preacher. Although Methodism grew more slowly in towns where it often had to compete with other churches, they were without rivals in rural Upper Canada and the Eastern Townships of Lower Canada. Although recruits were usually youthful and highly individualistic, Methodist itinerants under Asbury's firm hand became a highly efficient corps of disciplined individuals. Its intense evangelicalism engendered personal conversions in even the remotest quarter of the colony.

Once the first circuits were established by William Losee in 1791 in the Bay of Quinte area and by Nathan Bangs in Niagara in 1804, Methodism grew unimpeded as these and new circuits (10 by 1810) were sustained by a constant procession of Methodist intinerants. By 1812 Methodism had become the largest Protestant denomination in Upper Canada. The Methodism of Francis Asbury, however, veered sharply from British Wesleyanism which, under the leadership of Jabez Bunting, sought to shore up traditional authority. In the United States and in its Upper Canadian and Lower Canadian satellites, American Methodism challenged constituted authority and overtly fostered democratic values by extolling the universality of spiritual perfection and equality in religious communion. As such it became one of the most active cultural vehicles for transplanting the anti-traditionalism and reformist spirit of the new American republic particularly into Upper Canadian society outside the rarified stability of the Tory elite.

The post-revolutionary settlement of British North America was characterized by a vast movement of peoples; nearly 20,000

Loyalists arrived in present-day Nova Scotia, 15,000 in New Brunswick; and by 1791, 10,000 had arrived in Upper Canada. In turn these Upper Canadian Loyalists were followed by a similarly large number of so-called late Loyalists who took up Lieutenant Governor Simcoe's offer of free land. Not only did this dislocation entail considerable economic hardship, but, except for those ethnic groups such as the Moravians and Mennonites who recreated homogeneous communities in the new frontier, old bonds of parish life were broken apart. With the breakdown of familiar community structures came the disintegration of traditional bonds of social control and order, social rank, and networks of personal communication. Although speaking in a disparaging tone, Strachan accurately observed the complete absence of unifying social codes and values and likewise conveyed the still unformed nature of Upper Canadian community life. As late as 1803 he stated: "Every parish in this country is to be made; the people have very little or no religion, and their minds are so prone to low cunning that it will be difficult to make anything of them." The lack of religious feeling was often commented upon. The Baptist missionary Asahel Morse toured the province of Upper Canada in 1807 and described it as "a dismal region of moral darkness and the shadow of death." Even the prominent Methodist revivalist Nathan Bangs called the capital of York "a town of people as wicked as the Canaanites of old." In this case, however, we should not accept at face value Bangs' condemnation. York was, after all, a leading centre of Anglicanism, and many of the attacks upon the irreligiosity of the colony were part of the anti-establishment polemic.

Modern Canadian historians preoccupied with the institutional growth and presence of the Victorian church have all too readily believed these descriptions of the lack of religion in early colonial society and have used these as evidence of social backwardness. In fact, it appears that colonial British North America conformed to a larger North Atlantic pattern of religious experience and commitment. Because the evangelical ethos gave prominence to an otherworldly pietism and the necessity of individual conversion marked by a spiritual "New Birth," the very rhetoric of revivalism entailed an exaggerated disapproval of the social divisions and moral conduct of the sinful material world prior to a successful revival. Such a critique served to highlight the distance between the integrated world of the converted and the unregenerate. The reformist nature of the evangelical revival which had restored an ideal Christian purity was dramatized. Evangelicalism performed a much needed social reorganizing function in these new societies whose members had undergone severe cultural dislocation. As

George Rawlyk has forcefully argued, Henry Alline's emotional evangelicalism was particularly effective while Nova Scotians were experiencing the trauma of the American Revolution. Moreover, American historians have illustrated that revivals were particularly frequent in either those areas which were in economic decline, such as certain areas of New England prior to the American Revolution, or in peripheral frontier areas which were economically deprived and institutionally impoverished.

The conjunction between the obliteration of familiar social landmarks and the rapid and spontaneous spread of new forms of popular religion are well illustrated by the life-story of Duncan McColl, a Methodist preacher. McColl served in the Argyllshire Regiment during the Revolutionary War and during this period of stress and insecurity became concerned about his religious state, and converted to Methodism. Having overcome his own sense of personal waywardness, he naturally described his new post of St. Stephen, New Brunswick as a fractured community in need of a unifying spiritual "reformation": "I found a mixed multitude of people from many parts of the world, without any form of religion."

Although the social instability engendered by the American Revolution might explain the rapid spread and mass popularity of evangelical revivalism, the theory of community breakdown downplays the real continuities and incremental change brought about in part by the rise of popular evangelicalism. The gradual replacement of communal values with the tenets of individual self-expression, the erosion of hierarchical views of the social order by more inclusive and egalitarian values, and the reversal of educated authority by that of the vernacular, all of these currents were encapsulated within evangelicalism. The evangelical movement was a thread in these great social and cultural upheavals which transformed the traditional and static eighteenth century conceptions of social rank and authority and hastened the dissemination of these modern ideas.

Historians such as Joyce Appleby, Rhys Isaac, and Gary Nash have generally agreed that the period between approximately 1760 and 1820 in the United States was one of constant cultural ferment and negotiation whereby old formulations of what constituted virtue, liberty, and the public good were slowly being redrawn. Whether we refer to this process of a bourgeois or middle class outlook, the period between the late eighteenth and early nineteenth centuries marked an increasing emphasis upon individualism, optimism, linear interpretations of history, and the experience of the lower orders. As Joyce Appleby has persuasively argued, the older view of society embodied the idea that government was a providential institution which protected men against the irrationality of economic events and thereby ensured that society would be orderly, rational, and civilized. Increasingly, however, men and women began to view the economy as an orderly and natural system which of itself could create social harmony. Not only did this view subtly eliminate the need for authoritarian social institutions, but it also gave priority to voluntary associations as the fulcrum of progress. These associations, in turn, were founded upon the very new and important concept of individual self-interest. Where a traditionalist would have conceived of the individual *within* society with its concomitant web of social obligations, a 'liberal' or modern person would begin with the individual's needs and conclude that all people, even ordinary people, could make rational decisions and therefore participate in the polity.

While Appleby's picture of ideological change is largely concerned with economic thought, her observation of the initiative of ordinary people could just as easily apply to the changing ways in which they experienced religion. Although the father of Methodism, John Wesley, has correctly been associated with political Toryism in England, his views of society were essentially very radical. Wesley rejected the notion that social behaviour was formed by rational and external institutions. Further, he believed that God could be known by the heart and not the intellect. Such an interpretation of human relations immediately gave priority to the individual conscience. It also emphasized that social reform must begin with the individual conscience, and that, because all individuals were capable of seeking salvation, they could share equally in determining both the direction of church and civil government. Certainly Wesley was a conservative in that he championed civil government as the bastion of public order; he did, however, assert a concept of liberty based upon individual free choice and conscience, thus allowing Methodists the freedom to withdraw from a government of which they did not approve. Wesley's espousal of religious experience founded upon universal salvation, emotional fervour, and the individual's personal interaction with God, challenged the traditional concept of social relations. According to the new evangelical ethos, social order was sustained not from the coercive forces of external institutional authority, but was the natural result of mass inner discipline achieved through the individual's spiritual efforts working in conjunction with God's grace. In such an ideal world, authority devolved not from one's social betters or man-made government institutions, but was granted to each individual directly from God.

These radically new ideas were given impetus in the Thirteen

Colonies by <u>George Whitefield in the 1730's and 1740's</u>. <u>The great</u> <u>charismatic evangelist helped inspire a series of revivals generally</u> <u>called the First Great Awakening</u>. This period of intense religious piety has been viewed by many American historians as a cultural and social watershed because it unleashed among the lower orders — small farmers, traders, artisans, and labourers — a form of emotional religion which allowed direct experiential knowledge of Christ. This was the first mass popular religious movement that cataclysmically confronted the traditional parish church and its institutional foundations. As Harry Stout has argued, the religious revivals inspired by Whitefield's powerful preaching were important outlets which allowed the common people to assert themselves against the often coercive authority of their social betters.

Symbolically, Whitefield held his mass meetings in field and squares outside regular meeting halls. Through his emotionally charged sermons in which he sang, wept, prayed, and told colloquial stories, Whitefield encouraged individuals to appeal directly to God. Although like Wesley, Whitefield did not overtly exhort the people to challenge the established government, his call for a purer, otherworldly pietism, with its insistence upon spiritual equality, ultimately led ordinary people to disparage worldly standards of greatness and the legitimacy of constituted power. In telling people to be instruments of their own salvation, Whitefield helped inspire a new form of popular religious experience which, quite unlike the Wesleyan evangelical movements in England, activated a more thorough radical assault upon traditional centres of civil and religious authority. It is of some significance, therefore, that Henry Alline was referred to by his contemporaries as Nova Scotia's George Whitefield, and that even during the period of Victorian religious respectability Canadian Methodist preachers still placed themselves within the more populist "dissenting" tradition of George Whitefield than within the more socially quiescent British tradition of John Wesley.

The observation made by the historian of revivalism, William McLoughlin, that the unfettering of tradition and hierarchical institutions begun by the First Great Awakening was carried forth during the <u>Second Great Awakening (1800-1840)</u> has been reinforced by Nathan O. Hatch's groundbreaking work on popular religion. However, Hatch pushes back McLoughlin's time frame, viewing the immediate post-revolutionary decades of the 1780's and 1790's as the dynamic period of social and cultural ferment, when republican values became clearly dominant. These decades saw an ever increasing sharpness to the democratic social critique as its language of individual liberty and equality permeated the darkest recesses of American culture. The democratic impulse renewed the well-springs of popular religion. These years saw an explosive burst of evangelical activity which even more consciously challenged church establishment and elite orthodoxies. In short, religious practice throughout North America during this period was effectively made over in the image of popular culture: it emphasized the vernacular in language and song, encouraged popular participation in religious rituals, denigrated the values of educated society by defining cultural authority in terms of emotional persuasion and dramatic demonstration and taught the common people to place their individual spiritual convictions on a higher plane than that of the material world still defined by social privilege.

why?   In the wake of the American Revolution, when leadership in the traditional churches was unstable, membership in the Baptist and Methodist churches exceeded all other Protestant denominations. This marked the triumph of evangelical Protestantism which, by identifying the common people with the will of God, placed the democratic ideal at the forefront of American culture. Those very preachers who assertively set about reconstructing American social ideals along egalitarian and republican lines, extended the popular base of Methodism into the Canadas and the Maritimes. In doing so, they directly transplanted the ideology of equality and liberty into British North America, where their radical religious tenets found a sympathetic hearing among the American Loyalists who were largely common folk, small farmers and artisans. For more than a generation already, these people had experienced the slow but insistent assault upon elite culture wrought by popular evangelicalism.

VI

That evangelicalism had become an integral aspect of popular culture after the 1780's may be demonstrated by the social origins and leadership style of both the Baptist and Methodist itinerant preachers who flooded into the newly settled British colonies following the disruptions of the Revolution. For the most part these preachers came from humble backgrounds similar to that of their audience. The historian of Canadian Methodism, Goldwin French, has concluded that among the first generation of Methodist preachers there were nine schoolteachers, three farmers, two blacksmiths, two carpenters, one soldier, one sailor, and one surveyor. Most were very youthful and unmarried, attributes which ensure maximum mobility and the stamina to endure hazardous journeys across a largely unbroken frontier and the frenetic pace of preaching up to 400 sermons in one year.

Nathan Bangs (1778-1862) had only rudimentary education and was a surveyor and, later, a schoolteacher in Niagara when in 1800 he underwent a conversion and became a Methodist itinerant preacher. His father was a blacksmith and a staunch anti-Tory. As he himself recalled, Methodist preachers in the United States were generally ridiculed because of their lack of education. Similarly the young Methodist preacher, Duncan McColl, who had been a pay-sergeant in the army, was threatened by the magistrate in St. Stephen, New Brunswick, for this lack of theological learning, despite the fact that he inspired much emotional ecstasy in his congregation. He described the effect of one of his sermons: "During one his mind was carried up from the world and a power came down like an earthquake: some fell on their faces. . .Others adored the Lord." Henry Ryan was best known for his "hearty manner" and for such stirring exhortations as: "Drive on brother! Drive on! Drive the devil out of the country! Drive him into the lake and drown him!" Ryan left professional boxing to battle on behalf of the Lord. Similarly, the famous New Light Yankee preacher Henry Alline was a farmer and tanner, and thus was clearly outside the dominant social order. Alline himself was aware of his humble social station and lack of education, and for a time was drawn to the Congregational ministry which would have conferred him with social status, but he curbed his "proud heart that aspired after a public station in the world, to make a great show and court the applause of men." By becoming a New Light preacher, Alline was equally conscious of the fact that he was rejecting conventional forms of religious as well as parental authority, and that he was choosing to immerse himself in the world of plebian culture. Even though Joseph Gatchell came from a prosperous and educated family, his social condition nevertheless placed him at the margins of his community. His father's decision to fight for the Patriots during the American Revolution had resulted in his expulsion from the Quaker church and a consequent loss of social prestige. Another example of this change in social status is the charismatic Methodist revivalist Freeborn Garrettson. He belonged to the Southern plantation gentry, but, upon coverting to Methodism in 1775, he freed his own slaves and pursued a life of poverty, often preaching to prisoners and inmates of the local poorhouse. This renunciation of wealth forcefully symbolized that evangelicalism rejected distinctions of social rank and consciously framed an egalitarian world.

That the Church of England and evangelical denominations

occupied very different social terrain is suggested by statements from clergy on both sides. Methodist William Case observed that after church services the Anglican clergy regularly joined their congregation in dancing and playing cards which "renders them very popular, especially in the higher circle." Anglican clergymen were likewise conscious that evangelical itinerants —"illiterate rambling preachers" (to use Bishop Inglis' phrase) — were very popular and that "their acquaintance with the tastes and pecularities of the Canadians" was allowing them to gain a somewhat disturbing "ascendancy over our infant population." Certainly these young, disciplined, and dedicated evangelical religious leaders were proclaiming the gospel in new ways. They diverged from religious norms characterized by the learned sermon and a familiarity with the subtlety of theological argument, relying instead upon popular appeal and emotional persuasion. It is also apparent from the constant vituperative attacks against "Enthusiastic Teachers" and religious "infatuation" by Anglican leaders that their "serious and sober sense of Religion" was under considerable threat.

Bishop Inglis recognized the degree to which the authority of personality, wrought by the transforming nature of popular evangelicalism, had pervaded Maritime society: "here, people must be persuaded, and won by address, to do what in Europe is done by habit, and by virtue of Established Laws." What Anglican leaders such as the Reverend John Strachan in Upper Canada and Bishop Inglis in Nova Scotia feared most of all was that the cultural norms established by this tumultuous and disorderly religion would attract not just the "lower classes" but would soon become the norm for all the "ranks of the People." This explains why Anglicans so obstinately adhered to "that outward mode and form" of the Anglican liturgy. Any concessions to the evangelical style, in their view, would be tacit approval of the cultural ascendancy of popular religion. Thus the Anglican clergyman for Cornwallis, William Twining, was severely reprimanded in the 1790's for adopting some of the preaching techniques familiar to Methodists. If the Anglican Episcopacy had reluctantly recognized that British North America had become a cultural battleground, they were nevertheless unwilling to participate on any terms but their own: "If New Lights and Methodists are only to be brought round by adapting the Church Service to their ideas, it is not worth the Sacrifice."

The constant barrage of criticism from the Established Church indicates that the evangelical outlook was dramatically transforming social norms and values at an uncontrollable pace. Within one generation the genteel traditions of Anglicanism and much of Canadian Presbyterianism had been forced into a defensive, even impotent, position. Venerable Anglican traditions might have been preferred by the small colonial elite, but the vast majority of settlers in British North America were being won over by the emotional zeal of the barnstorming evangelical preacher. Samuel Coate, who was acclaimed as a marvellous speaker, was said to have "swept like a meteor over the land and spellbound the astonished gaze of the wondering new settlers. . .He was the heaven-anointed and successful instrument of the conversion of hundreds." As this quote makes clear, this style of preaching was both novel and effective. A preacher's success was measured in terms of the number of conversions he was able to bring about. For example, Nathan Bangs made frequent references to the number of conversions made in order to measure the success of the first camp meeting in Upper Canada. Since the spread of evangelicalism was based upon popular appeal, it followed that the successful preacher had to adapt his style to that of his audience. His sermons, therefore, had to be the antithesis of the learned written sermon. The best known Baptist, New Light, and Methodist preachers were defined largely by their highly charged, emotional preaching. Henry Alline was noted for his "Wild and Extravagant Gesturing" and as the Congregational minister from Harvard, Aaron Bancroft, recalled, Alline "by this popular talents made many converts." William Losee, the first Methodist itinerant preacher in Upper Canada, endeared himself to the people of Cataraqui largely because of his "fervent sermons" which conveyed the evangelical message in a manner accessible to the ordinary citizen. Despite the fact that after contracting tuberculosis he could speak in but a whisper, Calvin Wooster preached in a "bold and pointed" fashion. His straightforward terms were persuasive because they were unencumbered with the heaviness of theological debate. According to Wooster himself, after his sermon the wicked "would either flee from the house, or, smitten with conviction, fall down and cry aloud for mercy." If Calvin Wooster used language which would make "the ear tingle," other preachers attempted to convey their message of free salvation to as wide an audience as possible by telling stories of their personal voyage towards spiritual reformation. In the case of the Methodist Robert Perry, "homely analogies" were used to render his sermons "bearable." Often preachers shouted aloud, lay prostrate, or wept openly in order to convey the intensity of spiritual conversion and to thus inspire and penetrate to the listener's deepest emotions. Theatrical displays of the supernatural were improvised in order to awe the sinful audience with the power of God. For example during a Methodist meeting at the Bay of Quinte a man swore volubly during a sermon to which the preacher responded "My God, smite him!" This prayer duly caused the sinner to fall as though "shot by a bullet." Many conversions followed. The dramatic trick most favoured by the Methodist preacher Calvin Wooster involved ascending a ladder to a window. With the people assembled below, he would then descend like Moses on the mount.

Here was a style of preaching which, in Asbury's words, consciously attempted "to condescend to men of low estate." The use of dramatic, lively, and emotional exhortation appealed to the popular audience. Evangelical preachers adapted the language and style in order to break down the walls of deference between the preacher and the audience. Methodist preachers, for example, abandoned clerical dress and wore simple homespun. They lived a simple life, carrying all their possessions in their saddlebags.

Preachers used all of their personal attributes in order to persuade and convert, including their youthfulness and attractiveness. The very successful Upper Canadian Methodist preacher William Case was remembered as "youthful, beautiful, amiable" — with a charming personality and a singing voice which "first spell bound and then melted his audience." The power of hymns and popular song contributed much to the rapid expansion of evangelicalism. In this way it functioned as a form of popular spectacle which endeavoured to attract a crowd whose interest had been peaked enough to make them open to the emotional appeals of the preacher.

Nathan Bangs noted the frequent use of popular "ditties" at Methodist services. The fact that most popular hymns of the post-revolutionary generation were Henry Alline's *Hymns and Spiritual Songs* (1786) clearly illustrates the immersion of the evangelical ethos in popular values. These hymns were based upon folk songs orally transmitted for generations in Nova Scotia and New Brunswick. With their powerful voices, the handsome William Case and the six foot former boxer Henry Ryan would collect about them a large assembly by singing down the streets of Kingston. In a similar vein, one contemporary noted how Henry Alline's sermons were "interspersed with Poetry calculated to excite and raise the Passions" in order to convey his message of "individual liberty" and hope.

One senses that the function of the evangelical preacher was not to authoritatively teach people to know God, but, through often boisterous and charismatic preaching, to inspire each individual in the audience to directly participate in their own spiritual renewal. It appears from George Ferguson's comments in 1813 concerning the

Methodist Rev. T. Hamon, that the experience of religious conversion was shared equally between preacher and his audience: "His voice I think might have been heard a mile. He uncovered the depravity of the human heart and thundered the terrors of sin. . .There was a shaking among the people." The evangelical ethos fostered ideas of equality and democracy by encouraging lay participation. In the following excerpt from William Case's 1808-1809 journal we see that the role of the preacher following his sermon was clearly subordinate to the spontaneous emotional ecstasy of the lay converted: "The people continued praising the Lord in shouts of glory until 10 o'clock at night, about seven hours without intermission, or very little." The democratic impulse — what one Methodist commentator called "popular freedom" — was championed among the first generation of itinerants. Descriptions of Methodist meetings emphasize an extremely informal manner of worship with people meeting in fields, barns, or local houses. Some were sitting, others were standing, even some were "thronging the overhanging trees." At a Methodist meeting a period of preaching and praying by the visiting preacher was followed by a much longer session of audience interlocutions and personal confessions of spiritual waywardness. One preacher recounted that his insistence upon popular participation eventually involved the whole assembly in a long evening of earnest debate.

VII

In his reminiscences, Nathan Bangs declared that he was well aware of his "deficiency in qualifications" when he chose to become a Methodist preacher, but that his authority to preach had been personally received from God. The Lord wanted him to break away from the "dogmatic prejudices and ecclesiastical traditions" and to proclaim "the radical doctrines which are essential to it" [Methodism]. Moreover, as a confirmed anti-Calvinist, Bangs believed that each individual was imbued by God with "personal power" in order to choose spiritual salvation. It was entirely legitimate, therefore, that Bangs described his evangelical outlook as the "new moral economy," for it represented a challenge to traditional definitions of authority. In a society in which virtue implied public outward conduct, the social fabric was defined in terms of hereditary estates, and authority devolved from the gentry through a fusion of constitutional and ecclesiastical law. The watchwords of the 'ancien regime' were veneration and custom, hence the Nova Scotian Anglican minister Roger Viets' admonition in the 1790's to "guard with greatest Care against Innovations and

Changes." Evangelical culture, on the other hand, was recreating a social world in which spiritual authority was vested no longer in the outward, man-made institutions of church and government, but in the inner spirituality of the individual resulting from the personal encounter between the converted and God. While Strachan stressed duty, obligation, and moral government, all of which pertained to institutions, evangelicalism extolled liberty, freedom, and moral economy, concepts which underscored the importance of the individual in the new social order.

Similarly, the New Light preacher Henry Alline consciously pitted his evangelical ethos against the mores of traditional gentry society. In his treatise of 1781, *Two Mites*, Alline proclaimed the radical intent of his emotional piety and called upon his readers to break cleanly with the past by converting to the New Lights: "Let me entreat you to divest yourselves as much as possible of the strong Ties of Tradition. By no means embrace or retain any Practice or Principles as Right or Scriptural, only because it was a precedent set up by your predecessors." In stating that he was "fighting for the new and spiritual Man," Alline meant that his religion of the heart was redrawing the social order. Community and social harmony were to be founded upon voluntary association between individuals who shared a common intimacy with God. As George Rawlyk has argued, Alline combined a communitarian form of religious experience with William Law's emphasis on the individuality of the religious experience and Wesley's principles of freedom of will and universal salvation. Alline's was a highly personal religion. He did not give priority to an intellectual familiarity with Christian doctrine. Rather, he instructed his followers to feel God's grace and to "rejoice in Jesus Christ their friend." The individual's bond with the Highest Being was intimate and emotional in the extreme. As Joseph Dimock, a follower of Alline, described his conversion experience in the 1780's, he "felt a weight of truths that flowed from the eternal God into my soul, which has enabled me to communicate to others a sense of God and eternal things." Although evangelical preachers often spoke to masses in open fields or town squares, they just as frequently joined small groups in private homes where the preacher could more intimately attend to the spiritual needs of particular individuals. Alline related how he often "laboured with distressed souls" until the small hours of the morning. He described the personal nature of his brand of revivalism: "when I take persons by the hand and speak to them they know that I mean this, while preaching in public may be turned on others, and I have thought that God blessed this particular addressing of individuals more than all the preaching."

By making individual testimony, the outpouring of emotional fervour in the form of weeping and shouting, and introspective prayer the centrepiece of the evangelical experience, New Light, Methodist, and Baptist preachers contributed to a redefinition of the individual as a private being. A person's aspirations and goals were no longer prescribed by the authoritarian social codes of a remote and impersonal polity. Within the terms of evangelical culture the men and women were free to pursue their own goals because they were empowered by their very relationship with God. In a society still defined by rigid social codes between masters and servants, by shifting the notion of virtue away from the public domain to one's personal spirituality in communion with God, evangelicalism instructed even the humble that they had a voice in determining their own destiny. As Freeborn Garrettson pointed out: "I know the word of God is our infallible guide and by it we are to try all our dreams and feelings." If people could have direct access to God and if God's authority was the predominant voice, then the individual was persuaded to listen to their own conscience and to no longer defer to the authority of their betters. It was not surprising that those evangelicals who were viewed by society as "despised New Lights" whose names have been "cast out by men" saw in their religious experience a new found freedom of expression. Thus Edward Manning, the Nova Scotia Baptist, recorded in his journal that the act of directly experiencing God's grace allowed him for the first time to "tell his mind freely" and feel "a good Deal of freedom."

Apparently, obeying God rather than one's social superiors was a new experience for many Nova Scotians, for, as Alline stated of one of his religious revivals, "many dared not open their mouths, for it was new and strange to them and to the whole town." Methodist preachers often recognized the conjunction between civil and religious liberty, for they witnessed that as evangelicals took responsibility for their own salvation "the people appeared as just awakened from the sleep of ages." Although Alline was usually referring to religious freedom when he said that he "enjoyed great liberty in the gospel," the very act of releasing individuals from the bonds of tradition by encouraging them to speak aloud itself was meaningful. Evangelicalism was overturning accepted social authority by urging the ordinary individual to transform their society through their special relationship with God. As "'A People Highly Favored of God' to use Henry Alline's ebullient phrase" — evangelicals were placed in an equal, if not superior, position to the educated clergy and political elite. As Alline's testimony on August 12, 1781 suggested, it was God's direct immersion in the Christian soul which gave the individual a sense of self-assertion and the right to speak aloud as one wished: "May Christians rejoice in great liberty. . . O how my soul travailed, while speaking, when I beheld many groaning under almost unsupportable burdens, and crying out for mercy. . . O the power of the Holy Ghost that was among the people this day."

Evangelicalism eschewed involvement in political debate. During the late eighteenth and early nineteenth centuries, evangelicals rejected the contemporary relations between church and state in which the ecclesiastical body buttressed the power of the hierarchical political edifice. Others, like Henry Alline, remained neutral during the American Revolution because they objected to war and political revolt. Although professing an other-worldly faith, both Methodist and Baptist evangelicals offered a persuasive critique of established ecclesiastical and political institutions by erecting a renewed spiritual and egalitarian social order. Ordinary people naturally sought to use religion as the primary vehicle for their dissenting viewpoints because, in the world of elite political jurisdictions, their political participation was out of the question. For most people then, religion, and, more particularly, the society of evangelicalism, provided the one forum in which the opinions and aspirations of the lower orders were given free reign and the complementary causes of civil and religious freedom could be articulated. Indeed, the very act of declaring your religion to be other-worldly implied a rejection of the convention of elite political authority.

In a world which took precedence and tradition for granted, removing oneself from the civil community to a new "society" defined entirely by evangelical spirituality powerfully challenged the notion the governmental institutions were providentially ordered. Even though he had ostensibly withdrawn from gentry politics, — Henry Alline's radical evangelicalism effectively relativized all civil laws and institutions in light of the evangelical experience. His tendency towards antinomianism, in which individual experience takes precedence even over Scripture and the moral law, allowed inquiry into what had been viewed as incontrovertible truths.

Henry Alline was fully aware of the radical implications of his religious outlook. When in 1777 Alline's right to preach was queried by two educated Presbyterian ministers, Alline replied that his "authority was from heaven." Later he observed that, by ignoring the constituted social codes of an educated clergy, he was "breaking through all order." Others also saw the unsettling consanguinity between religious and political dissent. The British Dean of Gloucester, Josiah Tucker, drew a direct parallel between

Enthusiasts and Republicans, describing those who resisted established political authority as "new-light men." A religion which upheld the individual's right to decide upon his or her own spiritual salvation and allowed free participation in religious rites might lead all too easily to the exercise of individual judgements in matters of civil government in a society with a close relationship between Church and State. What traditionalists like Strachan and Inglis feared about evangelicals was not that they might immediately incite political revolt or mob rule, but that the democratic spiritualism of the evangelical ethos might unleash upon the embryonic society a host of newly assertive individuals. "Consenting to Redeeming Love" might divert people from the priorities of the Constitution of 1791. As Alline himself prophesied in one of his hymns:

'Tis not a zeal for modes and forms
    That spreads the gospel-truths abroad;
But he whose inward mien reforms,
    And loves the saints, and loves the Lord.

From the point of view of the conservative elite, once a "feeling of endless power" was engendered in the ordinary citizen through evangelical Christian fellowship this reformed inward "mien" might lead to a thoroughgoing reformation of social values. For example, William Black wrote to John Wesley in 1783 about a Methodist revival in Liverpool, Nova Scotia. He reported that once people were "set at liberty" after "an astonishing outpouring of the spirit" the "manners of the people are entirely changed." It needs to be realized that, in the language of the late eighteenth century, 'manners' was shorthand for general social conduct. The precepts of evangelicalism, and particularly the notion of popular consent, led directly to the spread of democratic values. Such values can be discerned in Henry Alline's conception of a participatory spiritual republic: "For you may remember, that it has been sufficiently proved already, that the very Nature of God, and his high Decree among all his Creatures is a Freedom of Choice, therefore GOD cannot redeem those, that will not be redeemed, or save them without their Consent. . ." This was not John Strachan's conception of God as an arbitrary moral governor, for here God was an intimate person whose spirit, though resting in every individual, depended for its power upon the human desire for conversion.

VIII

During the period 1776-1815, the evangelical movement was

throughout North America a prime mover in transforming traditional social relations. It overturned the culture of genteel dominance by challenging the very core of social deference: the passivity of the common people. Even when outside God's grace, the ordinary individual was deemed the direct agent of his or her own eternal destiny. In Alline's words: "that the Creature tho' fallen was not passive, but still an active being, and now acting and raging in Contrariety to God."

By becoming an integral part of the emerging culture, appealing progressively to both the lower and middle orders, as the Anglicans so grudgingly conceded, evangelicalism threatened to elevate the tenets of popular culture to the position of arbitrating the future direction of British North American society. It seemed to the colonial elite that these youthful itinerants, who were not residents of any particular parish and therefore immediately open to suspicion, were attempting to completely reverse the partriarchal social controls of the gentry. The evangelical revivals were feared by the elite not simply because they offered a critique of traditional cultural values, but because they were also very effective in forging bonds of social unity. However, their sense of community was defined by the distinction between the converted and unconverted. Moreover, it was built upon personal bonds rather than the impersonal agencies of the established Church and State. It was difficult to ignore the powerful effects these often charismatic itinerants had in transforming the daily life of local parishes.

In 1807, for example, the Baptist Manning wrote to his wife that after a revival in Chester, German and English-speaking settlers were brought together for the first time. Likewise, in his Westmoreland mission the Methodist Joshua Marsden preached to both white and black, and declared that with his 1804-05 'stir' in the St. John valley "old differences in the society were composed and the contending parties reconciled." The degree of social stability wrought by evangelicalism may have been overestimated by evangelical preachers. However, as George Rawlyk has demonstrated in his account of Henry Alline's career as a New Light preacher, though religiously innovative, the evangelical ethos provided a high degree of ideological coherence. This was especially true for the disenfranchised and economically marginal converts in a new society marked by economic and social uncertainty. By visiting virtually every locality in Nova Scotia and New Brunswick, for example, Henry Alline broke down the barriers of parochialism and geographical isolation, and his mystical pietism drew together the poorer settlements in a new sense of identity which could effectively offset the ideological control of colonial office-holders in

Halifax.

Evangelicalism defied the constituted social order in many ways: the camp meeting at Hay Bay allowed the classes to mix, and, in fact, it even allowed the humble folk to exhort and convert two upper class sisters who were thus brought into the world of popular religion; in Nova Scotia New Light and Baptist revivals were particularly successful in encouraging the young people and women, those particularly without power in the wider patriarchal society, to openly express their sense of spiritual rapture; and, more generally, revivalism brought people together in mass demonstrations of piety — the New Light Baptist preacher Thomas Chipman noted that "almost the whole town assembled together" and "a vast concourse of people" listened to his preaching. Anglicans were thus prompted to comment that evangelicalism encouraged the common folk to "neglect their temporal concerns," namely working for their masters. For the ordinary settler, revivals obviously provided a much needed break from the routine of work and often inspired a renewed sense of community togetherness.

John Payzant, the brother-in-law of Henry Alline, in 1807 described the sense of community fellowship and harmony engendered by an evangelical meeting: "There was no business done that week and but little victuals dressed. The people were so many for there was old and young, rich and poor, male and female, Black and White, all met together and appeared as one. At night they came into the meeting House in that manner; the meeting House echo'd with their Praises and rejoicing. So that there was no publick Singing or Prayers but the whole night was Spent in that manner. It was judged that there was above 1,000 people." As Mrs. Anna Jameson observed, in a society bereft of social amusement, it was no wonder that whisky and camp-meetings assumed a dominant place among the common folk. The first camp meeting at Hay Bay in October 1803 enabled the farming community a release of emotional energy following the completing of the autumn harvest. Such forms of amusement or social outlet, however, were deemed to be dangerous by the local elite because they encouraged unnatural social interaction. Furthermore, they induced the lower orders to disregard their subordinate role by allowing them to establish their own rhythms of work and leisure. In 1799 the Rev. Jacob Bailey, an Anglican, accused evangelicals of inciting civil disobedience during a revival at Annapolis: "The former for several weeks before & after Easter held their Meetings four times on Sundays & had a lecture every evening, which frequently continued till 3 in the morning. During these exercises, ignorant men, women & children under twelve years of age, were employed to pray &

exhort, calling aloud, Lord Jesus come down & shake these dry bones. Groanings, screamings, roarings, trembling, & faintings immediately ensue with a falling down & rolling upon the floor, both sexes together. . ."

The evangelical critique of elite ideology and traditional social codes was effected largely through the more overt demonstration of spiritual holiness in the venue of the camp-meeting or meeting house. On the other hand, the degree to which the democratic underpinnings of evangelicalism challenged the established order is revealed by the frequency with which itinerant preachers were violently attacked. As has been demonstrated, episcopal leaders like John Strachan and Charles Inglis communicated in often highly coloured language their annoyance with the success of the evangelical movement in the young colony. But generally speaking they and their clergymen adhered to a policy of tolerance respecting the dissenting sects. This was not because they were unusually tolerant Christian souls, but as the ever pragmatic John Strachan put it, until Anglicanism could win the war of numbers of church adherents, the Church of England would have to bide its time and quietly endure the evangelical juggernaut. Writing in 1819 in the recently inaugurated Anglican journal *The Christian Recorder*, Strachan outlined his strategy for Anglican supremacy: "I will gradually lead my readers in favour of the Church taking care to insert nothing particularly offensive to Dissenters; as the work gains ground, we can be more explicit, but caution is necessary as the whole of the population not of our Church is ready to join against us."

At times, however, the social conflict which was obliquely expressed through the principles of evangelicalism flared into the open. Despite the establishment's policy of tolerance, the local military was often used as a policing agent of the Anglican church. Freeborn Garrettson was attacked by the militia in Loyalist-dominated Shelburne and in Halifax. In 1785 Garrettson recorded that, again in Shelburne, 400 local citizens attempted to push the house where he was preaching down the hill. Attacks against this Methodist preacher were frequent enough that he was advised to seek refuge with the local magistrate should disorder break out at one of his meetings. Henry Alline was also set upon by soldiers while travelling in Nova Scotia. Henry Ryan, the former boxer, and William Case must have come to view attacks of violence as a common occurrence, for when describing their visit to Kingston to preach, they made particular mention of the fact that there they were allowed to preach with no disturbance or interruption. Nathan Bangs best conveyed the degree to which leading citizens of many local communities readily interpreted Methodism as a form of civil disobedience: even though the local schoolteacher Bangs was well known by the other settlers in Newark, as soon as he converted to Methodism, and symbolically shed the trappings of worldliness — his hair queue and his ruffled cuffs — he was threatened with personal violence.

Local authorities also employed legal means to forestall the spread of evangelical culture. In Nova Scotia and New Brunswick especially, Baptist preachers were jailed for illegally performing marriages. One Baptist preacher continued to defy local authorities by professing his faith to a crowd gathered beneath his prison window. Although we still do not know enough about local responses to travelling Methodist and Baptist preachers, it appears that violence against them was sporadic and unorganized, in contrast to the ritual mob attacks initiated by the local gentry in England against Methodist preachers. In the newly settled colonies of British North America where the governing elite was still small and the institutions of social control underdeveloped, popular evangelicalism flourished unchecked until the arrival of a new wave of British immigration in the 1820's.

IX

The spectacular expansion of popular evangelicalism was abruptly curtailed, especially in Upper Canada, by the War of 1812. In Queenston, the Baptist congregations were permanently dispersed, and, more importantly, the very life-line of early Methodism was cut off when the Upper Canadian border was closed to all American denominations. The War of 1812 also served to galvanize the Upper Canadian elite around a coherent ideology which prescribed a more active defence of loyalty to the British crown. By linking anti-republicanism and anti-Americanism with the patriot defence of one's native soil in the minds of all those who fought in the militia regiments, the War of 1812 became one of the greatest stimulants for spreading what had previously been merely the ideology of a conservative elite to the wider population. By invigorating and unifying the Tory elite, the war also led to a strengthening of those government institutions which could ensure public order and social stability. Conservatism spread its tentacles well beyond local pockets of control by creating its own machinery of popular education, benevolent societies, and commercial institutions such as banks and land companies. In this way, conservatives assertively courted the popular mind of Upper Canada.

Similarly, as evangelicals in the Maritimes became more prosperous, they also tried to temper the more disorderly components of popular religion, and progressively allied themselves with the more conservative elements there. It is indeed significant that by the 1840's, the Baptists played a leading role in the formation of the Conservative party in Nova Soctia. The very constituency of evangelicalism was being challenged for the first time. Moreover, the impetus of this anti-American campaign was sustained by the British government, which was financially instrumental in entrenching the politically conservative British Wesleyan Methodist Society in both the Maritimes and Upper Canada. As Nathan Bangs correctly recognized in a letter to his brother in 1818, the Methodist church was becoming fractured by the infiltration of Methodism by what he disparagingly termed the "British Spirit of division." Bangs personally resisted these interlopers by contributing one hundred dollars to finance Irish local preachers who would ensure the persistence of a radical spirit.

While in Europe and the United States the instruments of the 'Ancien Regime' had been in constant retreat after the 1790's, in Canada the doctrines of traditionalism were ironically given a new lease on life after 1812. Popular evangelicalism, which had become so well integrated into the very essence of British North American life, was stifled. The sudden revival of conservatism at this particular juncture, just as the more prosperous evangelicals were pushing their faith into the political and social mainstream, resulted in making the Methodists and the Baptists, both in the Maritimes and the Canadas, much more conservative denominations than they might otherwise have been. In order to escape the tincture of radicalism, Methodists, and to a lesser extent, Baptist congregations, were divided. The respectable majority was all too effectively coopted by Toryism, leaving the radical fringe at the margins of early Victorian culture.

The more radical dimensions of early evangelicalism, however, were not wholly lost, for the popular legacy survived much longer in rural communities which continued to enjoy spontaneous religious revivals well into the 1840's. Not only was there a division between the respectable and popular forms of the evangelical as British North American society became more prosperous and social divisions more dramatic, but there was an increasing gulf between the rural and urban church. Although the War of 1812 and the cult of British respectability, which occurred as early as 1800 in the Maritime colonies, compelled the expansiveness and eglitarianism of popular evangelicalism to go underground, such republican cultural ideals probably continued to nourish the social outlook of many.

As Jane Errington has argued, some of the chief vehicles for the continued transmission of American cultural values [wre]ᵍᵖ˒ agricultural societies whose members no doubt enthusiastically participated in the remnants of popular revivalism. Later movements of republican political dissent, such as the Rebellion of 1837 and the Clear Grit phenomenon of the 1850's, were built upon a base whose population had long experienced in both religion and economic life the democratic impulse. It is also not inconsequential that new interpretations of loyalty which argued against conformity to external institutions such as those expressed by the new Methodist leader, Egerton Ryerson, emerged from similar evangelical quarters where the individual's inner spiritual sense was given priority and viewed as the fulcrum of social change. In a larger sense the questioning of established institutions launched by the early evangelical critique was not totally submerged after the War of 1812 but, as many evangelicals moved into positions of political power, they transformed what had been a more diffused assault upon social convention into post-1820's reform politics. There was a direct continuum, therefore, between the popular and radical evangelicalism of Alline and Bangs and what have been conceived of as the exclusive and rarified debates over the role of church and state in the 1820's. The social conflict of an earlier generation, by presenting a clear cultural alternative to the old hierarchical society, created the basis of ideological debate around the issues of voluntaryism in religion and education, loyalty, and ideas of reform which undergirded emerging political parties between 1820 and 1860.

SUGGESTIONS FOR FURTHER READING

A very useful general study which outlines the growing religious diversity in both the United States and Canada after 1760 is Robert T. Handy, *A History of the Churches in the United States and Canada* (New York, 1972). While Handy's work emphasizes the institutional framework of religious experience, William McLoughlin's *Revivals, Awakenings and Reform: An Essay on Religion and Social Change, 1607-1977* (Chicago, 1978) was a groundbreaking work in exploring the social, psychological, and broadly cultural implications of revivalism. In the Canadian context, George Rawlyk's extensive work on the religious revivals of the New Light preacher Henry Alline in the Maritimes has opened the question of the influence of religious revivals upon social and cultural change in early colonial

British North America, and in particular has argued for the importance of charismatic leaders in bringing about religious revivals. See Gordon Stewart and George Rawlyk, *A People Highly Favoured of God: The Nova Scotia Yankees and the American Revolution* (Toronto, 1972); George Rawlyk, *Ravished by the Spirit: Religious Revivals, Baptists, and Henry Alline* (Kingston, 1985); George Rawlyk, *Champions of the Truth: Fundamentalism, Modernism and the Maritime Baptists* (Kingston, 1990), especially chapter 1 "Revivalism and the Maritime Religious Experience" in which the importance of both Henry Alline and Freeborn Garrettson are highlighted. See also, George Rawlyk, "Freeborn Garrettson." *Dictionary of Canadian Biography* (Toronto, 1987). For a particularly remarkable description of religious conversion among early evangelicals, see George Rawlyk, ed., *Henry Alline: Selected Writings* (Mahwah, 1987). For a very fine analysis of the transition from the New Light to Baptist traditions in the Maritimes, see D.G. Bell, ed., *The Newlight Baptist Journals of James Manning and James Innis* (St. John, 1984).

The literature on the relationship between evangelical religion and popular culture is much less developed for Upper Canada in the period between 1776-1812. The first chapter of John Webster Grant, *A Profusion of Spires: Religion in Nineteenth Century Ontario* (Toronto, 1988) provides an overview of the religious diversity in Upper Canada following the American Revolution. Still one of the best studies of Methodism in Upper Canada is Goldwin French, *Parsons and Politics* (Toronto, 1962) in which much serious consideration is given to the early itinerant preachers. The finest portrait of the Methodist itinerant preacher and his role in spreading Methodism throughout Upper and Lower Canada remains John Carroll, *Case and His Contemporaries*, 5 Vols. (Toronto, 1867-1877). Although an older classic whose perspective was somewhat limited by the dominance of the frontier interpretation, S.D. Clark's *Church and Sect in Canada* (Toronto, 1948) is still extremely useful in uncovering the social meaning of evangelicalism. Clark is particularly attuned to the social conflict inherent in the evangelical and Anglican religious traditions.

The religion and social thought of the Anglican minority in both Upper Canada and the Maritimes has received some scholarly attention. For an examination of the relationship between Maritime Anglicanism and British Imperial policy, see, Judith Fingard, The *Anglican Design in Loyalist Nova Scotia, 1783-1816* (London, 1972). More recently, the career of the first Anglican Bishop, Charles Inglis, has been more extensively discussed in Brian Cuthbertson, *The First Bishop: A Biography of Charles Inglis* (Halifax, 1987). Turning to Upper Canada, the best biography of Bishop John

Strachan remains Alexander Bethune, *A Memoir of Bishop Strachan*
(Toronto, 1871). For a thorough compilation of Strachan's sermons,
see Norma J. MacRae, "The Religious Foundation of John
Strachan's Social and Political Thought as Contained in His
Sermons, 1803-1866," M.A. thesis, McMaster University, 1978. For a
very fine discussion of the Anglican church's place within Upper
Canadian society and its reaction to the constant threat from
evangelicalism, see Curtis Fahey, "A Troubled Zion: The Anglican
Experience in Upper Canada, 1791-1854," Ph.D. thesis, Carleton
University, 1981. For primary documentation, largely concerning
the Anglican church in both Upper Canada and the Maritimes, see
John S. Moir, *Church and State in Canada, 1627-1867* (Toronto,
1967).

For the intersection between religious and political thought
throughout the transatlantic world in this period there are a range
of monographs which have explored the broader intellectual
transitions both within the conservative and radical Whig
traditions. Indispensable for a knowledge of the complexities of
political debate during the late eighteenth century both in Britain
and the United States, see J.G.A. Pocock, *The Machiavellian Moment*
(Princeton, 1975) and Pocock's, *Virtue, Commerce and History*
(Cambridge, 1985). Particularly engaging on the importance of the
Anglican church in British political life, but written from a strongly
Tory perspective, is J.C.D. Clark, *English Society 1688-1832: Ideology,
Social Structure and Political Practice during the Ancien Regime*
(Cambridge, 1985). For an analysis of the breakdown in the
influence of Anglicanism upon political commentary, see Robert
Hole, *Pulpits, Politics, and Public Order in England 1760-1832*
(Cambridge, 1989). An excellent discussion of the rise of broadly
republican values is given by Joyce Appleby, *Capitalism and a New
Social Order: The Republican Vision of the 1790's* (Cambridge, 1984).
For a treatment of the transition from Whig dissent to Loyalist
conservatism among political elites, see D.G. Bell, *Early Loyalist St.
John: The Origins of New Brunswick Politics, 1783- 1786* (Fredericton,
1983), especially Chapter Four, "The Origin of Discord." David
Mills postulates the hegemony of conservative Upper Canadian
thought in *The Idea of Loyalty in Upper Canada: 1784-1850*
(Montreal, 1988). The most important revision of the standard
interpretation of Upper Canadian conservatism which idealizes the
homogeneity of political culture is Jane Errington's *The Lion, the
Eagle, and Upper Canada: A Developing Colonial Ideology* (Montreal,
1987).

For a stimulating and broad synthesis of the Protestant
experience in early America and its European context, see Jon

Butler, *Awash in a Sea of Faith: Christianizing the American People*
(Cambridge, Mass., 1990). A similar treatment of the institutional
church prior to the American Revolution is offered by Patricia U.
Bonomi, *Under the Cope of Heaven: Religion, Society and Politics in
Colonial America* (New York, 1986). There has been extensive
scholarly debate over the role of the Protestant churches in the
American Revolution. Bonomi has argued that both the evangelical
and established churches equally supported the patriot cause, while
Ruth M. Bloch, in *Visionary Republic: Millenial Themes in American
Thought, 1756-1800* (Cambridge, 1985), similarly posits a greater
unity within Protestant thought. See also, Ruth Bloch, "Religion
and Ideological Change in the American Revolution," in Mark
Noll, ed., *Religion and American Politics* (New York, 1990). Stephen
A. Marini, in contrast, has seen the revolutionary experience as
crucial in reshaping and fragmenting evangelicalism into a diverse
range of sects. See his *Radical Sects of Revolutionary New England*
(Cambridge, Mass., 1982). Likewise, Nathan O. Hatch has viewed
the Revolution as a fundamental watershed in so far as it was a
major social catalyst in creating a culture defined by individualism
and egalitarianism. In perhaps the most seminal work dealing with
the relationship between popular evangelicalism and the rise of
democratic values, Nathan O. Hatch has redefined the
circumference of debate by arguing that the fundamental religious
experience in the early republic was not shaped by theological
differences between sects and churches. Rather, the evangelical
experience was homogeneous by virtue of its relationship to
popular culture. For Hatch's revisionist interpretation, see: Nathan
O. Hatch, *The Democratization of American Christianity* (New Haven,
1989); Hatch, "The Democratization of Christianity and the
Character of American Politics," in Noll, *Religion and American
Politics;* Hatch, "In Pursuit of Religious Freedom: Church, State and
People in the New Republic," in Jack P. Greene, ed., *The American
Revolution: Its Character and Limits* (New York, 1987). On the other
hand, see Bonomi's rejoinder to Hatch, "Religion in the Aftermath
of the American Revolution" in Greene, *The American Revolution.*
For two excellent articles which also reinterpret religion as a vehicle
of social dissent against established church authority, see: Rhys
Isaac, "Evangelical Revolt: The Nature of the Baptists' Challenge to
the Traditional Order in Virginia, 1765-1775," *William and Mary
Quarterly,* Vol. 30, third series, July 1974 and Harry S. Stout,
"Religion, Communications and the Ideological Origins of the
American Revolution," William and Mary Quarterly, Vol. 34, third
series, October 1977. In a similar vein, Gary B. Nash has outlined
the populist and radical components of evangelicalism, in *The*

Urban Crucible: Social Change, Political Consciousness, and the Origins of the American Revolution (Cambridge, Mass., 1979). For a study of the incremental rather than revivalistic spread of evangelicalism in the rural community, see Curtis D. Johnson, *Islands of Holiness: Rural Religion in Upstate New York, 1790-1860* (Ithaca, 1989). Leigh Eric Schmidt has published a very important book *Holy Fairs: Scottish Communions and American Revivals in the Early Modern Period* (Princeton, 1989).

For the most extreme characterization of Methodism in England as a form of "psychic exploitation" of the working classes, see E.P. Thompson's leftist, *The Making of the English Working Class* (Harmondsworth, 1963). For a resurrection of the Halevy thesis, see Bernard Semmel, *The Methodist Revolution* (New York, 1973), who has, in opposition to E.P. Thompson, viewed British Methodism as a broadly socially progressive force which staved off political revolution in England. More recently David Hempton, in *Methodism and Politics in British Society: 1750-1850* (London, 1984) has argued for wider working-class participation in English Methodism, presenting a more diverse picture of Methodism which was often divided into conservative and radical wings. Deborah M. Valenze renders an even more complex interpretation of English Methodism in *Prophetic Sons and Daughters: Female Preaching and Popular Religion in Industrial England* (Princeton, 1985). She highlights the importance both of female religious leaders and the common practice of domestic preaching as opposed to mass revivalism. For a very stimulating discussion of the social conflict engendered by Methodism, see John Walsh, "Methodism and the Mob in the Eighteenth Century," in G.J. Cumming and Derek Baker, eds., *Popular Belief and Practice* (Cambridge, 1972).

PROTESTANTISM TRANSFORMED

PERSONAL PIETY AND
THE EVANGELICAL SOCIAL VISION,
1815-1867

Michael Gauvreau

Looking back in 1883 upon a distinguished career in the Methodist ministry and in the Canadian public service, Egerton Ryerson vividly remembered his conversion experience in 1815, when he was only twelve years of age. "My consciousness of guilt and sinfulness," Ryerson stated, "was humbling, oppressive and distressing," and was finally relieved when he "simply trusted in Christ, and looked to Him for a present salvation; and, as I looked up in my bed, the light appeared to my mind, and, as I thought, to my bodily eye also, in the form of one, white-robed, who approached the bedside with a smile, and with more of the expression of the countenance of Titian's Christ than of any person whom I have ever seen." For this young Upper Canadian, the joyful, liberating vision of Christ and the personal assurance of salvation which it conveyed marked a decisive moment of transformation in his own life, one which conferred upon him "new views, new feelings, new joys, and new strengths." Indeed, so powerful was Ryerson's personal encounter with Christ that the experience induced him to defy his father, a prominent member of the Tory Anglican oligarchy of Norfolk County, and join the Methodists, whose itinerant evangelists and enthusiastic camp-meeting revivals earned the contemptuous scorn of the ruling elite and the clergy of the established church of Upper Canada.

The young Ryerson's decision to abandon the traditions of the

48

established church for a revivalistic or "evangelical" type of belief
serves as a lens through which the historian can study the very
process by which society and culture was created in British North
America between the end of the Napoleonic Wars and the
achievement of Confederation. For many inhabitants of the
colonies, as well as for Egerton Ryerson, personal conversion and
the subsequent commitment to a life of holiness was an experience
with revolutionary implications. The conversion dictated a
deliberate rejection of an inherited model of religious, social, and
political organization, founded upon traditional notions of rank,
status, and social subordination. For men like Ryerson's father,
authority was divinely established and patriarchal, and was
anchored upon a legally established "Church-State," the sole
repository of true belief and the social order itself. To the defenders
of the old order in both Britain and her North American colonies,
the connection between church and state was vital to the building of
a stable and loyal society and was explicitly enshrined in the
colonial constitutions as a bulwark against the revolutionary
republican experiment of the United States. In the late eighteenth
century world, political loyalty was endowed with a divine sanction
and was thus merely the obverse of religious orthodoxy: any
criticism or dissent from the church establishment carried with it
the stigma of political radicalism.

Four decades after the end of the War of 1812, however, the
religious and cultural pattern of British North America had evolved
in a direction not anticipated by the colonial governing classes.
Historians have cited environmental factors such as the
"democratic" influence of the American republican tradition and
the early nineteenth century reform impulse in Britain itself, and,
more critically, the vast transformation of the colonial political
economy occasioned by massive immigration. Environmental and
demographic factors alone, however, cannot account for the
emergence of a new cultural pattern in the colonies. What was
perhaps the most significant force in the transformation of society
and culture in nineteenth century British North America was the
evangelical impulse itself, the very consciousness of sin and
redemption which changed the life of young Egerton Ryerson. As
Donald G. Mathews has explained in his important study of
religion in the antebellum American South, the "revolutionary
quality" of the evangelical movement "was not its assault upon
power, for it made none, but its weakening of the cultural, religious,
and psychological constraints upon people of relatively low estate
by elevating them in their own esteem and giving them the personal
discipline to use their lives as best they could in Christian service."

Immigration, the formation of communities, the new market forces of capitalism, and the new ideas of political and social democracy were influenced by the new concepts of individuality and community forged by the evangelical movement.

As Owen Chadwick has remarked in his magisterial study, *The Victorian Church*, "evangelicalism" was the strongest religious force in British life, and fundamental to the shaping of early Victorian society. It may be argued that in the colonial setting, evangelicalism exercised a more decisive formative role than in Britain or in long-settled parts of the United States such as New England. Outside the colonies, the evangelical movement, which was shaped by the First and Second Great Awakenings, acted upon religious institutions and traditions of belief which were well established and which, for centuries, had been woven into the very fabric of national life. By contrast, in 1815, many parts of the British North American colonies lacked not only the institutional apparatus of churches, schools, parish organizations, and municipal institutions, but there was no consensus over what type of religious organization, social forms, political institutions, or public values ought to prevail. In a relatively impoverished culture, evangelicalism, as perhaps the most vital cultural force acting upon colonial society, secured a much wider field of action. Through the new model it presented of the relationship between the individual and God, it provided not only a theology, but also an ideology. Concepts of order, respectability, and the patterns of personal and social behaviour which were to prove most influential in forging the values and institutions of the maturing English Canadian society were provided by evangelicalism. By 1867, it had secured an intellectual, institutional, and social preeminence in a society which defined the very core of its identity as British, Protestant, and progressive.

The Evangelical Creed: A Problem of Definition

To the modern mind-set of English Canada, the term "evangelicalism" conveys a number of largely negative images and impressions. Students of the novels of Roberston Davies, Hugh Maclennan, Margaret Laurence, and Margaret Atwood are doubtless familiar with the portrait of the oppressive sense of sin, guilt, emotional repression, bigotry, narrow-mindedness, and obsession with sexual purity. Unfortunately, historians, by equating "evangelicalism" with intellectual conservatism and narrow dogmatics, have themselves unwittingly contributed to reinforcing the literacy image created by these paragons of Canadian culture. Thus the mental universe of nineteenth century evangelicals emerges from these works as something of a caricature of Calvinism, a closed, inflexible system of "orthodox" theological doctrines, a brittle mind-set destined inevitably to shatter after 1860 under the hammer-blows of "Darwinism" and the higher criticism. And, to further confirm the validity of the literary and historical revolt against "Victorianism," Canadians in the 1970's and 1980's have witnessed the scorn directed towards the resurgence in North America of a politically active, conservative "fundamentalist" Protestantism which has appropriated the designation "evangelical." The word "evangelicalism" thus incarnates not only the opprobrium raised against "Victorianism" by a self-proclaimed literary and cultural "avant-garde," but raises the spectre of a militant anti-modernism engaged in a successful undermining of scientism, pluralism, and tolerance, the supposed hallmarks of liberal society. For most English Canadians, "evangelicalism" is thus viewed as a Victorian skeleton best hidden in the closet.

Against the novels of Davies, Laurence, and Atwood with their gloomy reflections on sin and guilt, must be juxtaposed the vision and the subsequent rebirth of the young Egerton Ryerson, the more passionate and mystical sense of personal communion with Christ recorded by the Nova Scotia New Light preacher Henry Alline, and the countless moments of joyful, liberating release from sin through encounter with their Saviour experienced by so many ordinary British North American colonists. Although in the nineteenth century, evangelicalism acted as both ideology and social ethic, its central core of meaning was provided by a specific moment of personal encounter between the individual, who believed that he or she stood radically convicted of sin and guilt, and Christ, the personal Saviour, whose death and resurrection offered the divine grace of forgiveness and salvation. As John Mocket Camp (1796-1881), a prominent Baptist, preacher, educator, and President of Acadia College (Nova Scotia) remarked, the "correct view of the essentials of religion" was founded upon the view that it was "a transaction between the soul and God."

The "conversion experience," however, marked only the beginning of the path of salvation. Evangelicals were acutely aware of the dangers of antinomianism, the belief prevalent among certain radical religious sects that the infusion of divine grace superseded the moral law. To the challenge of antinomianism, evangelicals like Cramp replied that the sudden infusion of divine grace enjoined a constant commitment on the part of the Christian believer to holy living, diligent study of the word of God, prayer, and avoidance of worldly thoughts and amusements. After the death of his first wife and his own serious illness, Cramp recorded in his journal:

May my renewed strength be given wholly to God. Perhaps he

has laid me aside awhile, because I did not do his work at night, nor aim sufficiently at His glory. Now that I am about to commence again, may I go in the strength of the Lord God, with humble, holy fervor and active diligence. I have heretofore wasted many precious hours, and sometimes exhausted my strength in pursuits scarcely worth of it. May it never be so again. My time, my strength, my talents, are not my own, but God's. There are some things of which I see the importance more than usually great, and which I hope specially to guard should the Lord spare me and again employ me in His work. These are more personal intercourse with God, and more diligent reading of His word; a more spiritual manner of stating the whole truth, with more prayer for the Holy Spirit on myself and the people, and a more diligent attention to my private pastoral duties.

The recurrence of words like "diligence" and "humility" in the letters of preachers and ordinary believers capture the prevailing evangelical mood which stressed the acute dependence of the believer upon God and the necessity of constant self-scrutiny in order to avoid a relapse into sinful ways, and a forfeiture of God's offer of salvation.

It was precisely the emphasis placed on this personal, experimental quality of the individual's encounter with God, rather than the mediation of church traditions, priests, and sacraments, which distinguished evangelicalism from alternative forms of religious belief and expression. Significantly, however, it is this same quality which renders "evangelicalism" resistant to definition and classification according to modern ideological categories. The evangelical impulse was the product of the cultural climate of the late eighteenth century. At that time, the customary opposition of liberal and conservative, academic and popular, individual and community, which the modern mind takes for granted, simply did not apply. For the historian of ideas searching for systematic or original thought, such a portrait of the mind-set of evangelicalism must prove a major disappointment. Early nineteenth-century evangelicalism was, first and foremost, a passion, a living force, a pulsating energy infusing the individual soul and human communities. Descriptions of its power often took the form of medical analogies in which faith assumed the character of a "remedy" for the "disease" of sin.

As Professor Goldwin French correctly observed over twenty years ago, "evangelicalism" was not so much a fixed, philosophical system of doctrine as a much looser, and consequently more

pervasive, body of beliefs and assumptions. Thus, it might best be
described as a "creed," rather than as a formal system of thought. To
the modern mind, "theology" is nearly always equated with an
abstract, university discipline, taught as an esoteric, metaphysical
body of knowledge closed to all but professional initiates who
intend a career in the ministry of a particular church. To Protestant
Christians of the nineteenth century, however, theology was the
concern of the many, rather than the few, and it thus occupied a far
more central place in culture and society. According to Cramp,
President of Acadia College between 1851 and 1869, theology was
"the most sublime of all sciences." Its task was "not to collect and
compare many various opinions, nor to hew and square the divine
revelation by the measure of any human standard; but, first of all, to
ascertain, by assiduous and reverent inquiry, the truth of God, as
contained in his own word." For this prominent Baptist, "theology"
in effect meant "the word of Christ," derived "from the Bible and the
Bible only," which, he reminded his students, was "the authority
from which there is no appeal."

Of fundamental importance to evangelical preachers and their
congregations was the conviction that all human beings were
sinners who stood in need of redemption through God's grace. In
the words of the Presbyterian leader Principal Michael Willis of
Knox College, Toronto, "the central place should be given to the
doctrine of 'Christ crucified,' as that around which, as from the sun
in the natural world, all light and heat radiate." The ramifications of
this important conviction have been masterfully summarized by the
English scholar Boyd Hilton in the following vein:

A sharp discontinuity exists between this world and the next.
God transcends this world, and his providence is responsible
for everything that happens in it. His creatures are all in a state
of natural depravity, weighed down by original sin, and life is
effectively an 'arena of moral trial', an ethical obstacle course
in which men are tempted, tested, and ultimately sorted into
saints and sinners in readiness for the Day of Judgment. Then,
souls will be despatched either to Heaven or to Hell, literally
conceived as states of eternal felicity and everlasting torment.
The all-important contractual relationship is directly between
each soul and its maker, and such intermediaries as priests
and sacraments are of relatively little significance. The organ
of redemption is the individual conscience, and the means are
provided by Christ's Atonement on the Cross, which
purchased ransom for the sins of all mankind. Justification
comes through faith in that Atonement, and through faith

alone, for though good works, sanctification, and holiness are important, they cannot precede faith.

Evangelicals were saved from the pessimistic implications of the doctrine of the Atonement, however, by the knowledge that despite the chasm between nature and grace, God was a conscious agent who actively intervened in creation; on one level, by transforming the souls, minds, and actions of individual sinners; and, on another, by directing the process of history itself; the rise and decline of nations and empires was due, not to the visible forces of wars, commercial development, or human desire, but to the divine will. Of equal importance to the evangelical vision was the fact that individual believers did not need to blindly grope for assurance of God's presence. The Bible, which all Protestant Christians regarded as a sure and trustworthy record of God's revelation, supplied the data of faith and the moral principles which directed the conduct of both Christian believers and societies.

From these beliefs flowed several basic cultural imperatives. First, although evangelicals believed that God's grace was freely given, they also maintained that human agents and institutions could assist in channelling that grace to both individual sinners and to the society at large. For that reason, preaching was of central importance in "reviving" true religion. Preaching awakened the sinner to the consciousness of sin and to the reality of divine redemption by directing the audience to the biblical "facts and doctrines" of sin and salvation. Because conversion, in the early nineteenth century, was not simply a matter of feeling, but also involved the minds and consciences of the congregation, it had to rest upon some intellectually secure foundation. Although there was wide disagreement among the churches influenced by the evangelical impulse over how to properly train and qualify preachers, all were united in their insistence that the only secure foundation for preaching, and for all other forms of intellectual activity and social organization, was the Bible itself. Young preachers, as well as the ordinary members of church congregations, whether low-church Anglican, Baptist, Presbyterian, or Methodist, were enjoined by their respective leaders to preserve a careful balance of faith and intellect by subordinating critical reason to faith. Speculative hypotheses on the nature of religious truth were to be avoided, and both secular and theological knowledge were to be acquired through the sober accumulation of "facts." Any deviation from this scheme would only question the authority of the Bible, which in turn would impair the effectiveness of the preacher's message, and thus would weaken both the spiritual life of the individual and the impulse to transform and regenerate the community.

Evangelicalism was thus an interlocking series of beliefs and imperatives concerning individuals, communities, and their relationship to God. Perhaps the characteristic feature of evangelical theology, binding together the divergent practices and attitudes of the Protestant churches touched by the evangelical current, was the notion that "theology" was less an academic discipline than a body of beliefs and assumptions which, through the art of preaching, sought to mediate between the world of scholarship and the world of popular culture. In the nineteenth century, by contrast to the present day, these two spheres were by no means mutually exclusive and, particularly in matters of religion, intersected and blended together at many points. The meaning of "theology" was thus defined not simply in the lecture-halls of the clergymen-professors like Cramp, Willis, and Ryerson. Indeed, these leading evangelicals considered themselves accountable to their wider constituency of preachers, itinerant evangelists, and the ordinary members of the Protestant churches themselves.

Without exception, evangelical leaders accepted the close identity between "theology" and the Bible, and, like J.M. Cramp, insisted on the ability of ordinary literate believers to apply the central doctrines of the Christian faith to daily life. "Theology" did not refer to a mere philosophical system or formalized doctrinal structure, but to the vital union of biblical study and the personal experience of God's saving grace manifest in Christ. Cramp's Methodist contemporary, Egerton Ryerson, forcefully illustrated the practical and accessible nature of "theology" to the students of Victoria College in an 1848 address:

A person may spend the greater part of his life in investigating disputed doctrines of Theology, and litigated questions of polity and ceremonies, and terminate his investigations in greater doubt than when he commenced them; but being master, by experience and reading the Word of God for himself, of the doctrine that 'being justified by faith he has peace with God through our Lord Jesus Christ, and the love of God shed abroad in his heart by the Holy Ghost given unto him,' he carries abroad in his heart the true antidote for the symbolism of Italy, the rationalism of Germany. . .the Puseyism of England.

Even in the Presbyterian Church, which boasted a long tradition of an educated ministry and an inheritance of several centuries of Calvinist theological disputation and speculation, college professors like Rev. Michael Willis, the principal of Knox College, Toronto, accented the biblical and practical aspects of their task. According to Willis, the best preachers were not necessarily those trained in the minutiae of systematic theology. He maintained that the discipline of systematic theology was secondary to a proper understanding and exposition of Scripture itself. Sound preaching could only be undertaken by those who were "most deeply alive to the value of the Gospel truth, and who know experimentally its value to the spiritual life," and who would thus "be the most urgent in setting forth the claims of the divine law."

The novel and potentially explosive quality of evangelical belief and culture in the context of early nineteenth century British North America can best be illustrated by noting that "evangelicalism" was not coextensive with "Protestant." The evangelical impulse dominated the Baptist, Methodist and, after 1840, the Presbyterian churches in British North America. Evangelicalism even attained considerable influence among adherents of the Church of England. There existed, however, a competing model provided by High Church Anglicanism, best defined according to the eighteenth century concept that there existed a theological rationale for an intimate connection between church and state. According to D.C. Masters, the High Church and evangelicals agreed concerning basic Christian doctrines and the idea of salvation, but differed sharply over the personal quality of the relationship between human beings and God. Speaking in 1807, the Reverend John Strachan, then principal of the Cornwall Grammar School, and later Archdeacon of York and Bishop of Toronto, perhaps the ablest defender of High Church principles in the colonies, admonished his students:

At the same time that you are animated with the laudable ambition of excelling in your profession, and rendering yourselves agreeable by your amiable manners, do not neglect to improve those correct principles of religion and virtue, which must ever constitute your most solid merit. Impress upon your minds the sublime and affecting truth that there is a God above, our Friend, our Benefactor, the Creator of all things; and that it is only by imitating His moral perfections, as brought home to our hearts and affections by our blessed Redeemer, that we can render ourselves worthy of the rank we hold in the scale of beings, and enjoy solid pleasure in this life, and in that which is to come.

When juxtaposed with the views of, for example, the Baptist John Mocket Cramp, it is clear that for Strachan, religion is less a bond between the individual and God than a complex of social duties, one interwoven with earthly concepts of rank and obedience. For clergymen like Strachan, salvation was secured through the corporate association of an established church, priests, and sacraments, and was not the result of a sudden conviction of sin and experience of conversion. Salvation was a gradual process mediated by priests and bishops whose authority derived less from preaching the word of God than from the continuity of the apostolic succession.

Here, then, was the basic religious and cultural breach affecting British North America between 1815 and 1867. Although it would be tempting to suggest that the division was one between the freedom of personal experience, represented by evangelicalism, and the restraints of tradition, hierarchy, and order, represented by Anglican High Churchism, such a characterization would ignore certain vital aspects of the evangelical creed. True, the emphasis on the relationship between God and the believer implied a potentially radical, egalitarian challenge to the corporate church and its sacraments. However, potentially more troubling to the ancien regime equation of religious establishment and political loyalty was evangelicalism's rival concept of social order, based upon a voluntary sharing of the experience of faith. As Donald Mathews has explained, evangelical thought did have individualist implications, but equally important was the insistence on "initiating the individual into a permanent, intimate relation with other people who shared the same experience and views." The polarization was thus not between the individual and the community, but between the community of believers and the rest of the world. Social integration, for evangelicals, was not based upon hereditary custom, but upon the principle of "voluntaryism," a belief which implied not only the free association of equal individuals, but social participation and fellowship for the achievement of a common purpose. And it was precisely the success of evangelicals, in the four decades after 1815, in establishing the "voluntary" model of social relations in British North America that marks the decisive moment of transition from the culture of the eighteenth century to the Victorian mental climate.

The Evangelical Achievement: The Maritime Provinces and Upper Canada

In order to understand the magnitude of the evangelical cultural achievement between 1815 and 1867, it must be realized that this great intellectual and social transformation coincided with one of the great movements of population within the North Atlantic world. At the close of the Napoleonic Wars, the population of Nova Scotia stood at approximately 82,000, and the first census of New Brunswick in 1824 recorded about 75,000 inhabitants, while the population of Prince Edward Island in 1827 was estimated at 23,000. At end of the War of 1812, the population of the inland colony of Upper Canada, the scene of much of the fighting during the war, numbered about 80,000 persons. Lower Canada, by far the largest of the colonial societies, stood at 300,000. British North America was a series of scattered, peripheral societies still in a pioneer stage of development. By the time of the 1861 census, all five colonies had attained a level of social and economic maturity as a result of heavy immigration and capital investment from the British Isles. At that time, the population of Upper Canada (or Canada West), with its prosperous agricultural frontier tied to British and American markets through transportation improvements, numbered 1.4 million, and that of Lower Canada (or Canada East), 1.1 million. The latter province, however, with the large majority of its population (943,000) professing Roman Catholicism, lies largely outside the confines of a study of the Protestant experience. Despite slower rates of growth, Nova Scotia recorded 330,000 people, New Brunswick 252,000, and Prince Edward Island, 80,000.

The Protestant churches were able, both intellectually and organizationally, not only to keep pace with this massive demographic and social transformation, but to actively lead and reshape colonial society in their own image. The early nineteenth century was also the great age of revivalist camp meetings, missionary societies, and church building. As well, it was a time for the extension of evangelical voluntary organizations such as Bible societies and temperance unions, which sought to Christianize and control individual behaviour. As John Webster Grant has noted in a recent study of religion in Ontario, the 1842 census listed 16.7% of inhabitants as having "no religion," yet by 1871, that number had dropped to 1.2%. Given the fact that historians have generally viewed the "modernization" which took place between 1750 and the First World War as a period when economic and social change gradually "secularized" Western society, the early nineteenth century stands as a great moment of discontinuity; a period where despite the magnitude of these changes, society in 1870 was more overtly religious than it had been in 1815.

In order to account for this phenomenon, it is necessary to look to the vitality of the evangelical impulse itself, which expressed itself in

British North America in several waves during the first half of the nineteenth century. As colonial societies whose cultural and social traditions owed a great deal to both Great Britain and the United States, Upper Canada and the Maritimes were beneficiaries of what historians have termed the "First Great Awakening," which occurred in Britain and America in the mid-eighteenth century. The colonial societies became active participants in the religious revivals and cultural restructuring which marked the "Second Great Awakening" of the early nineteenth century. The American historian William McLoughlin has defined "revival" as "the Protestant ritual. . . in which charismatic evangelists convey 'the Word' of God to large masses of people who, under this influence, experience what Protestants call conversion, salvation, regeneration, or spiritual rebirth." Awakenings, while closely associated with moments of religious revivalism, are defined by McLoughlin as "periods of cultural revitalization that begin in a general crisis of beliefs and values and extend over a period of a generation or so, during which time a profound reorientation in beliefs and values takes place. Revivals alter the lives of individuals; awakenings alter the world view of a whole people or culture."

The eighteenth century "Great Awakening" spanned the period 1740-1760 and was characterized by the preaching of men like John Wesley, the founder of Methodism, and the Calvinist evangelists George Whitefield and Jonathan Edwards. These men sought to re-emphasize the biblical doctrines of sin and redemption which they believed had been submerged and partly forgotten by the orderly, moderate Christianity of the eighteenth century church establishments in both Britain and America. In the American colonies, the Awakening culminated with the American Revolution, which, some historians have contended, was the secular fulfillment of the evangelical Calvinist ideas of regeneration preached by George Whitefield and Jonathan Edwards. The "Second Great Awakening," which began about 1800, further tempered, and in some cases rejected outright, the Calvinist intellectual tradition. A move was made towards a "democratization" of Protestant Christianity under a more simplified and practical evangelical creed in which salvation was open to all who would desire conversion. Even many elements within the Presbyterian Church in Scotland, the United States, and British North America found it necessary to accommodate itself to the revivalist impulse, revising the doctrines of election and predestination in light of the gospel of "free grace" and perfectionism preached by the aggressive Methodists. Of great importance to the eventual shape of colonial culture was the merging of currents of this non-Calvinist evangelicalism with impulses of political and social reform in the belief that once converted, regenerated individuals could voluntarily create a perfect society. Many believed this perfect society would be the millennial kingdom of Christ.

Revivalism, then, involved the questioning of both received traditions of theology, and prescriptive notions governing social and political conduct. For this reason, Archdeacon John Strachan could state in 1825 that the Methodist clergymen then operating in Upper Canada were "uneducated itinerant preachers, who leaving their steady employment, betake themselves to preaching the Gospel from idleness, or a zeal without knowledge, by which they are induced without any preparation, to teach what they do not know, and which from pride, they disdain to learn." Strachan's further suggestion that most of the Methodist preachers were of American origin drew an explicit contrast between the High Church vision of an orderly, harmonious religion undergirding a loyal, hierarchical colonial society, and religious "enthusiasm," which, in his estimation, could only lead to republicanism, rebellion, and social disorder.

It is one of the great ironies of the study of the past in English Canada that Strachan's High Church view of revivalism as a disorderly, disruptive process has become something of an orthodoxy among historians in a liberal society. The tendency, generally, has been to focus upon descriptions of emotional excess as somehow conveying the essential meaning of the revival spirit. The Methodist journal *The Christian Guardian* offers such a description of a revival meeting in 1841 on the Niagara Peninsula:

> This meeting is still progressing, and night after night the altar is crowded with penitents, with heart-rending sighs and tears flowing amain, declaring that they never would give up their suit until they should know that God had power on earth to save such hell-deserving sinners. O, sir, to see the chapel covered with the spiritually slain, what a blessed sight it is. Husbands and wives, parents and children, all in a kind of regular confusion, weeping, exhorting, praying and rejoicing alternately with and for each other. So graciously has God engaged the hearts of the people, in quest of salvation, that at times I have had much to do to prevail on them to disperse and go home.

As the historian William Westfall has observed contemporary descriptions of revivals in Upper Canada constantly stressed a number of themes: mass participation; the isolation of sinners from the world; the emotional nature of the religion preached by the evangelists; and the emphasis upon conflict, feelings, and passions.

The revival spirit had a double-edged effect upon early nine-teenth century Protestants, as it meant not only an intense individual conversion experience, but the dedication of entire communities to a new spirit of Christian behaviour and action. Evangelical leaders were aware, however, that the insistence upon the dramatic crisis of conversion held potentially dangerous overtones, and they were anxious to distance themselves from the criticism by men like Strachan that they advocated the revolutionary or cosmic overthrow of the social and political order. At the beginning of our period, evangelicals in Upper Canada and the Maritimes were more likely to be people on the margins of colonial society, often recent immigrants from the United States or Great Britain. Because the evangelical churches appealed to this social element which sought "independence" from the prescriptive hierarchy of the old society, the tone of early revivalist movements was often likely to stress a repudiation of the social system, with its distinctions of wealth and status replaced by the more egalitarian spirit of a shared conversion experience.

By the 1830's, however, the evangelical impulse was being gradually modified by its own successes. Baptists and Methodists, once viewed by the established church as on the extreme fringe of the religious spectrum, had established powerful and successful churches and were moving into the cultural mainstream. Thus, men like Egerton Ryerson, the Methodist "chieftain" of Upper Canada, and the Maritime Baptist "patriarch" Edward Manning, began confidently to articulate a rival vision of social order. Evangelicals were now intent on proving the political loyalty, orderly behaviour, and respectability" of their churches to the colonial authorities. Indeed, Methodist Baptist, and Presbyterian evangelists were anxious to distinguish themselves from antinomian sects like the Millerites and the Southcottians, who gained numerous adherents by predicting the catastrophic end of the world and the installation of the millennial kingdom of Christ They argued their movement would transform society by a slow permeation of Christian values and conduct expressed in the lives of converted individuals, who would "voluntarily" combine in civic associations for the purposes of social improvement. The millennium would thus be gradually realized in a non-revolutionary process, through partnership of divine and human agencies operating in the world.

George Rawlyk has explored this tightly woven individualist/ communitarian meaning of evangelical culture in a recent study of popular religion in Upper Canada and the Maritimes. He states that on an individual level, the revivalist impulse was the means by which thousands of ordinary colonists in British North America, through personal conversion experiences, were able to break away from social constraints and boundaries to reach out to a new world of self–discovery and inner freedom. The religious revival, he concludes, was the means by which "all sorts of complex and hitherto internalized and sublimated desires, dreams, hopes, and aspirations became legitimized."

Revivals not only served as a point of individual affirmation, but also provided an occasion for intense fellowship and a spontaneous flowering of community spirit. This spirit was captured in a sermon entitled "The Prosperity of the Church in Troublous Times" preached at Pictou, Nova Scotia, in 1814 by Rev. Thomas McCulloch, a Presbyterian minister soon to enjoy a celebrated career as a pioneer of higher education in the Maritime colonies. McCulloch's own religious outlook was founded upon the traditions of a popular Calvinist theology preached in the Secession churches of Scotland. It insisted on original sin and human depravity, but sought to reconcile the contradictory elements of predestination and free will. Despite the presence of pessimistic tenets of the old Calvinism, McCulloch's sermon at Pictou struck an optimistic note. Like many British and American clergymen of the time, he confidently predicted that missionary endeavour could convert and Christianize entire societies, and he looked to historical events to justify his optimism. Even in the most calamitous events of the time, this Presbyterian clergyman discerned evidences of God's care for his church and people. The wars and revolutions plaguing Europe during the Napoleonic years were, he declared, but the "times of trouble" which "an over–ruling Providence has marked out for the revival of the spirit of religion, for abundant enlargement of the prosperity of Zion." Signs of the great revival, he reminded his congregation, were everywhere: the spread of a spirit of benevolence, the abolition of slavery, and the growth of vital religion through voluntary social unions and educational societies. For men such as McCulloch, the evangelical spirit did not welcome the disorderly impulses in society. Rather, it recognized that these impulses augured a period of uncertainty in which older patterns of beliefs and values gave way to modes of acting, thinking, and believing.

Thomas McCulloch's sermons and addresses aptly captured the drama of religious and cultural transformation in early nineteenth century British North America. As a dedicated evangelical Christian, McCulloch eagerly welcomed the revival of religion and the new sense of seriousness and commitment which he observed in the Presbyterian churches of Nova Scotia. Although a Calvinist, he was concerned to downplay overt discussions of theology in favour of the practical evangelical agenda of preaching and salvation. As he declared to his first theological class at Pictou Academy in 1820, the task of the minister was that of awakening the spirit of vital religion in the heart of the sinner. His sympathies stood staunchly on the side of political reform as he championed the resistance of Presbyterians and Baptists to the Anglican monopoly over higher education. But, as a forceful defender of the Calvinist intellectual tradition, he believed that it was his duty to warn his students that it was possible to overvalue the practical and the pragmatic dictates of the revivalist temper. "Upon this continent," he stated, "there is a considerable disposition to overlook religious truth, and to reduce religion itself to mere feeling and conduct."

McCulloch feared what he witnessed happening in many communities in British North America and the United States: the devaluation of the intellectual apprehension of religious doctrine in favour of an emotional, enthusiastic revivalism. In his estimation, this brand of revivalism verged outside the bounds of authority and social respectability. Rather than attempting to abolish revivals, however, evangelical leaders sought to control them more tightly. Contemporaries described the camp meetings of this period as highly organized events, with special platforms erected for preachers, and with the desired segregation of converted believers from the world enforced by the banning of alcohol and other popular amusements from the campgrounds. The leaders of the evangelical churches also knew that the spirit of revivalism was very transitory, oscillating between times of intense spiritual commitment and relapse into worldly concerns. For the evangelical, backsliding into "sinful" ways remained a perpetual risk to both the converted sinner and the community. The permanent evangelization of communities could only be successful if a network of institutions could be created which would somehow preserve the intensity and commitment of the revival meeting in the Christian believer's daily life. Thus, beginning in the 1830's, evangelical leaders like Egerton Ryerson in Upper Canada and prominent Maritime Baptists like Edmund Crawley, John Pryor, and Isaac Chipman advanced schemes to found academies and colleges. These institutions would not only train a Canadian-born clergy, but they would educate a new evangelical elite in a setting dominated not by the polite learning of the English and Scottish Enlightenment, but by the principles of evangelical theology.

To some extent, the institutional impulse enabled the evangelical churches to downplay the centrality of revivalistic preaching, and to place a greater weight upon college learning and preparatory training. Revivals, however, remained a vital part of the evangelical culture of the period, and even in Methodist colleges like Mount Allison in Sackville, New Brunswick, and Victoria in Cobourg, Ontario, large portions of the student body were converted in local revivals which occurred in the 1850's. But even revivals, those supposedly spontaneous outbursts of religious emotion, were subject to the more dominant impulse among evangelicals to create a new social order. For example, by the 1850's, evangelical congregations increasingly relied upon professional, itinerant evangelists like the Methodist preachers Rev. James Caughey and Phoebe Palmer to periodically "revive" and stimulate the spiritual life of the community. Perhaps more importantly, as Marguerite Van Die has suggested in an important recent study of the Methodist educator Nathanael Burwash, the culture of evangelicalism began to place great emphasis upon the influence of the Christian home and the role of women in performing the all-important task of "Christian nurture." Children, from the moment of their birth, would gradually be exposed to the vital message of evangelical Christianity. This would prepare them for conversion as adolescents or young adults, and would thus perpetuate from generation to generation the vitality of the evangelical creed. Although some have seen in these subtle changes the downplaying of revivalism, it is possible institutionalization conferred even greater cultural power upon evangelical religion and its social vision. No longer content to rely upon transitory camp meetings, evangelicalism was, rather, the principal force in the day to day lives of thousands of British North Americans by 1860.

The dynamic of the revivalist impulse was also responsible for the peculiar shape of the religious demography which emerged in British North America between 1815 and 1870. One might expect that Upper Canada and the Maritimes would follow either the British or the American pattern, given their location in the culture of the transatlantic world. In Britain, the waves of evangelicalism had by 1840 substantially transformed the eighteenth century religious environment, but ultimately failed to reduce the Church of England to a religious minority. Anglicanism retained the allegiance of approximately sixty per cent of the population. Because it enjoyed continued social preeminence as a religion of the artistocracy, it dominated the rural areas and small towns of England. The tide of Nonconformity, though strong among the emerging urban middle classes and sections of the skilled working class, did not expand beyond these bridgeheads. Despite the power of the "Nonconformist conscience" to invigorate public debate in mid-Victorian England, this equivalent of the evangelical creed was forced to share power with "Whig," "Utilitarian," and "Tory-

Anglican" prescriptions of social reform. Therefore, it did not achieve the cultural hegemony of its colonial counterpart.

In the dominance by the evangelical spirit, British North America more closely resembled its southern neighbour. Even here, however, there were crucial differences. Colonial religion did not move towards sectarianism and fragmentation of religious groups, but converged towards the centre, with nearly ninety per cent of all Protestants grouped in the four "mainstream" Protestant churches: Anglican, Methodist, Presbyterian, and Baptist. In the Maritimes, for example, at the time of the census of 1861, the population of the province of Nova Scotia numbered 330,587, of which 75% were Protestant. Of the Protestant total, Baptists numbered 20.5%; the Church of England, 17.4%; the Methodists, 11.4%; and the Presbyterians, 35.1%; although the latter were divided into three denominations, the Church of Scotland, the Free Church, and the Associated Synod. In New Brunswick, the Baptist presence was, if anything, even more striking. Of a total population of 252,047 in 1861, 66% were Protestant. Of this number, Baptists numbered nearly 35%; the Church of England, 25%; the Methodists, 15%; and the Presbyterians, 22%. Prince Edward Island, the smallest of the Maritimes societies, diverged somewhat from the pattern of Baptist dominance. There, in its only pre-Confederation census (1848), out of a total population of 62,678, Protestants numbered about 35,000, with Presbyterians in the majority at 57.4%, followed by the Church of England, with 18.3%, the Methodists with 13.8%, and the Baptists comprising 8.2%. Denominations such as the Mormons, Lutherans, Quakers, Congregationalists, and Unitarians, which played such a vital role in nineteenth century American life, were almost absent from these colonies.

Perhaps the most remarkable difference between the religious demography of the Maritimes and Upper Canada in this period is the great strength of the Baptists in the former, and their relative weakness (5.8%) in Upper Canada. The Baptist dominance in the Maritimes was achieved without the support of the state, upon which Anglicans could rely, and, unlike the Presbyterian and Methodist groups, without the institutional support of missionary societies in Scotland and England. How, in light of these initial disadvantages, is it possible to account for the pervasive religious and social influence of Maritime Baptists in the early nineteenth century? In the first place, it may be argued, none of the other churches could appeal to the legacy of a charismatic preacher like Henry Alline, whose mission and activities in the early 1780's, according to George Rawlyk, became the subject to a persistent popular, oral tradition in many Maritime communities. Secondly, and of perhaps equal importance, the Baptist denomination took on the democratic characters of revivalism; that is, there existed within it a tolerance of divergent theological traditions. Beyond a few fundamentals, such as the central importance of regeneration and adult baptism by immersion, Baptists possessed an eclectic and unsystematic theological tradition. Thirdly, their most formidable evangelical competitors, the Methodists and the Presbyterians, were able only to maintain their base among English and Scottish immigrant communities. They did not fully engage the local traditions of religious belief and practice. Consequently, they remained dependent upon the support of external bodies such as the Glasgow Colonial Society or the British Wesleyans for the recruitment of clergy. Such a reliance only prolonged the immigrant character of these religious groups. Indeed, the Maritime Methodists, as both Goldwin French and George Rawlyk have noted, turned their back on the democratic currents of the revival, and sought to identify themselves as an appendage of the established church, by which they hoped to attain social respectability for their clergy and church members. It was not until 1855 that Maritime Methodists severed their institutional links with Britain in order to establish an independent conference, and it was not until 1860 that they secured the facilities at Mount Allison University for the training of a native clergy.

Upper Canada experienced a very different relationship between Protestant religion and its emerging culture. The new province, first of all, lacked the commanding influence of a preacher of Alline's stature. As well, it diverged from the "New England" model in that it did not possess an already localized Calvinist tradition as a base upon which evangelicalism could build. Powerfully assisted by the colonial government, and directed by the highly able Archdeacon John Strachan, the Anglican Church initially enjoyed considerable success. Although by 1851 it was certainly the largest Protestant church, with a sixty year history, it held the allegiance of only 28.5% of the Protestant population. Remarkably, each of the other major Protestant groups, the Methodists (27.2%) and Presbyterians (26%), were almost equal in number to the Anglicans. Ten years later, disestablishment (in the form of the secularization of the Clergy Reserves) had changed the picture. Anglicanism (26.4%) had lost its numerical preeminence to the Methodists (29.7%), while the Presbyterians had held their ground at 25.7% of the Protestant population.

Although Lower Canada (or Quebec) has been largely exempted from consideration, that province in 1861 contained a substantial Protestant minority (15.1%). A similar pattern of organization into the four largest "mainstream" churches was evident, but the evangelical impulse was substantially weakened in this older, more religiously established society. Perhaps the most revealing statistic was the surprising strength of the Churches of England and Scotland, the "established" churches of colonial society. Among the Protestants of Lower Canada, these bodies retained something of their earlier prestige, with the Church of England able to secure the allegiance of 38.8% of the Protestant population, and the Church of Scotland Presbyterians a further 14%. While the Presbyterian total stood at 26%, approximating figures in Upper Canada, it is surprising that only in Quebec was the evangelical Free Church numerically weaker than its Church of Scotland rival. A most significant indicator of evangelical strength was the number of Methodist adherents. In contrast to Upper Canada, where Methodism was the largest of the "mainstream" Protestant denominations, the Quebec census data revealed that Methodism attracted only 18.3% of the Protestant community, while the Baptists, the other pillar of the evangelical movement, mustered only 4.6%. The Baptists were unable to sustain a college in Montreal.

Further analysis of the census data suggests two main conclusions: first, that outside Lower Canada, revivalist churches such as the Baptists and Methodists were the most successful in attracting adherents. To a lesser degree, the same held true for Presbyterians, who retained the loyalty of the Scottish immigrant communities in this period. The Church of Scotland, which enjoyed, to some extent, the Anglican privileges of legal establishment, was in both Upper Canada and the Maritimes the weakest of the three Presbyterian groups. The United Presbyterians and Free Church accommodated revivalism to their theological traditions and were thus able to make very rapid inroads after the Great Disruption of 1843. The colonial situation, where the "establishment" included only about one-third of all Presbyterians, was the reverse of that in Scotland, where the "establishment" retained the allegiance of nearly two-thirds of the congregations.

Second, the churches most committed to revivalism were the first to "Canadianize," that is, to become independent of missionary societies in Britain and the United States. With their strong belief in local church autonomy, the Baptists were the first to separate. By the end of the 1840's, in moves which both paralleled and anticipated the achievement of colonial responsible government, the Upper Canada Wesleyan Methodists, the Free Church and the United Presbyterians had all established church bodies separate from those of the parent society. Of perhaps greater importance, the 1840's witnessed the first great wave of college building. The

Methodists built Victoria and Mount Allison; the Presbyterians, Knox, Queen's, and Presbyterian College, Halifax. The evangelical churches hoped to use these institutions to train a new generation of leaders and thereby lessen their dependence upon British and Scottish missionary societies.

Significantly, Protestantism as a whole followed the example of the evangelical churches. By 1867, even those churches most loyal to the connection between church and state (Anglican and Church of Scotland) had accommodated themselves to the environment in ways similar to their evangelical opponents. A churchman such as John Strachan, ostensibly so committed to the connection between the colonial church and the imperial state had, as early as 1839, experimented with a "voluntary" method of church finance. As well, he created diocesan institutions such as a newspaper and seminary to lessen reliance upon British support. In the wake of the secularization of the Clergy Reserves, Strachan, in 1857, successfully established the machinery for the independent election of local bishops; they would no longer be nominated by the British Crown. By 1867, the Lambeth Synod officially recognized the "Canadian" nature of the Anglican church by allowing it full powers to decide its own internal affairs. "Canadianization," though a gradual process, was one in which evangelicalism decisively etched the character of colonial Protestantism. A "middle way" between British and American examples was defined. Evangelicalism was the major impulse in creating what both John Webster Grant and William Westfall have defined as an "omnibus" Protestant denomination and culture.

Between Awakening and Enlightenment: Creed and College in British North America

If the evangelical impulse powerfully impressed itself upon the religious demography of early nineteenth century British North America, it also affected the contours of intellectual life in English Canada between 1815 and 1870. It has been generally recognized that Protestant Christianity provided the basis for a variety of early nineteenth century Anglo-Canadian beliefs. However, it is harder for the historian to define the relationship of the colonial societies to the late eighteenth century world of enlightenment, revolution, and religious awakening. To examine the life of the Rev. Thomas McCulloch, who arrived in Nova Scotia in the first decade of the nineteenth century as a Secessionist Presbyterian ministry, founded the Pictou Academy in 1817, and was chosen as the first Principal of Dalhousie University in 1838, is to enter the ambiguous borderland between the surging passion of Evangelicalism and the cultured intellectual pursuits of the Enlightenment.

Speaking at the dedication of the new college building at Pictou in 1819, McCulloch stated his views concerning the goals of education. In the first place, he reminded his students, man had been designed by the divine power for intellectual and moral improvement. But, the Principal cautioned, the inspiration and end of education lay removed from the realm of human reason and attainment. "I do not pretend," he declared, "that any system of education will change the heart, or conform the actions of man to the standard of divine law. This is the prerogative of the gospel impressed upon the mind by the Holy Spirit." Christian faith and devotion, in McCulloch's estimation, must guide, inform, and validate any system of sound education. Thus a spirit far removed from the eighteenth century Scottish spirit of inquiry prevailed at Pictou. Scottish education glorified scientific and moral improvement through the independent use of human reason and critical faculties, especially through the discipline of moral philosophy. For thinkers of the calibre of Thomas Reid, Dugald Stewart, and Sir William Hamilton, moral philosophy was the key link between the human intellect and moral convictions, and it enabled them to posit, through rational inquiry, laws of the human mind and society. Cosmopolitan, reasonable, and optimistic, this "Common Sense" philosophy promoted a spirit of inquiry detached from the doctrinal constraints of the national church. In the sphere of religion, it sought to replace the old Calvinism with a religion resolved into a benevolent code of duty and obligation.

Such independent philosophical inquiries failed to take root in the evangelical church colleges established in British North America. These institutions were the creatures not of the late eighteenth century spirit of cosmopolitanism and the application of Newtonian science to human society, but of the attempt of evangelical leaders like McCulloch, Egerton Ryerson, and John Mockett Cramp to digest and Christianize this cultural legacy. McCulloch's conclusion that the truths of divine revelation must discipline human reason marked the resolution of a creative but bitter contest not only in his Scottish homeland, but in the wider Anglo-American culture. Although "Evangelicalism" and the "Enlightenment" intersected at many points, men like McCulloch realized that the terms encompass a basic disagreement concerning the character of the Christian tradition. Was Christianity a religion which exalted the revealed truths of Scripture over the achievements of the human intellect? Did it insist on the sinfulness of the unredeemed soul and the perverted nature of reason divorced from divine revelation? Or, was it a faith anchored on human benevolence, an optimistic creed preaching a rational epistemology, and a moral philosophy which set forth a precise calculus of duties and obligations?

It is difficult to resist the temptation to moor English Canada more firmly within the cultural world of the Anglo-American Enlightenment, which held as an article of faith the sufficiency of reason to illuminate the essential order in man and nature. In England, Scotland, and America, however, the Enlightenment was a product of an urban culture, dependent for its propagation upon a network of clubs, literary societies, coffee houses, taverns, and universities, where the canons of polite learning were discussed and codified by an educated "literati." Such an Enlightenment was not present in the newly- settled Canadian colonies whose towns simply lacked the institutions and amenities offered by urban centres like Edinburgh, Boston, New York, and Philadelphia. Perhaps even more importantly, in the critical period between 1815 and 1840, when the social life of British North America began to take on a firmer shape, the Enlightenment had already been subsumed and redefined by a more powerful and popular current of ideas: evangelicalism.

The impact of evangelicalism on the eighteenth century intellectual inheritance can be discerned most clearly in the church colleges. Men like the Methodists Egerton Ryerson and Samuel Nelles of Victoria; and the Presbyterians Thomas McCulloch of Pictou; James George of Queen's; William Lyall of Presbyterian College, Halifax; and J.M. Cramp of Acadia sought a balance of Christian piety and reason. Although they relied upon the moral philosophy texts of Thomas Reid and Dugald Stewart, they were simply not interested in original inquiry or contributions to the complex philosophical tradition of Common Sense. This stood in marked contrast to the experience of evangelical denominations in the United States. By the early nineteenth century, in the American Protestant churches, the teaching of biblical studies and theology was cast largely in terms of Common Sense Philosophy, a term which included three distinct emphases. First, the epistemological, derived from the writings of Thomas Reid, which asserted that human perceptions reveal the world as it actually is; second, the moral, which posited that just as humans know intuitively some basic realities of the physical world, so they know by the nature of their own being certain foundational principles of morality; and finally, the "methodological" or the scientific, closely connected with the exaltation of Francis Bacon, which stated that truths about consciousness, the world, or religion must be built by a strict induction from irreducible facts of experience.

Although the evangelical creed in English Canada was certainly influenced by the Common Sense philosophy, the connection between the two was far less intimate. For inspiration and intellectual sustenance, preacher-professors in the fledgling church colleges turned to the great figures of the awakening, such as the Presbyterian Thomas Chalmers or the Methodist John Wesley, rather than to the philosophers. Of the three emphases outlined above, only "methodological" Common Sense (Baconianism) became a staple of teaching in the British North American colleges. It was the one element of the Common Sense programme ultimately compatible with the evangelical insistence on the supremacy of the Bible in education and culture. However, the overshadowing of the culture of the Enlightenment by the evangelical impulse did not imply religious obscurantism. In an address to a group of college students in 1857, Principal Samuel Nelles of Victoria College reminded them that piety and intellect could not be divorced. Without education, religion degenerated into superstition, while learning, if deprived of the Christian faith, was apt "to grow proud, shallow, and unprofitable." Ministers like Nelles extolled the blessings of a reasonable faith and a faithful reason. The pairing of these concepts reveals not only the tension between revelation and the inquiring reason, but also the little appreciated flexibility and tolerance possessed by the evangelical creed in its age of expansion.

The difference between the ideals of Evangelicalism and those of the polite culture of the eighteenth century can be more fully appreciated by contrasting the rival views of college education set forth by the Anglican leader John Strachan and those promoted by the Presbyterian Thomas McCulloch and the Methodist Egerton Ryerson. Born in 1778 into a Scottish Presbyterian family, Strachan had attended the University of Aberdeen, graduating with an M.A. in 1796. There he had revealed an aptitude for both moral and natural philosophy, the two disciplines at the heart of the Scottish Enlightenment programme. After being ordained into the Church of England in 1803, Strachan founded the Cornwall Grammar School. The school emphasized the classics and natural philosophy. Strachan advocated what the historian Sheldon Rothblatt has described as the "Georgian ideal" of a liberal education distinctively associated with superior social standing. The classics furnished the ideal models for promoting the "lubrication of interpersonal relations" and a concern for public affairs in an outgoing, social age. Strachan's address to the students in 1807, as has already been pointed out, stressed the cultivation of taste and manners. In particular, he called for the regulation of the "passions" through observation and emulation of models provided by classical literature, history, and biography. "[T]he civility of manners which I would recommend," stated the Anglican leader, "flows from the heart, and is intimately connected with all the finer affections that can adorn human nature."

Evangelicalism was one of the most powerful cultural forces contributing to the unsettling of liberal education. The whole civilizing ideal of the Enlightenment was, by the early nineteenth century, undergoing a time of trial and reassessment in the light of the experience of revolution and social change. The improvement in manners, the delicate adjustments in personal conduct, and values of sociability and liberality so forcefully pressed upon the grammar school students by John Strachan did not go out of fashion, but they began to lose their moral urgency and educational supremacy. The approach to education advocated by evangelical leaders in their new academies and colleges broke sharply with eighteenth century ideals, while at the same time modifying certain elements of the Enlightenment legacy.

In the first place, for evangelicals, college education had to be, first and foremost, explicitly Christian in character and outlook. Barry Moody, in a recent study of the origins and outlook of the Baptist Acadia College, has noted that although there were no explicit religious tests for students and faculty, Baptist congregations placed their reliance upon the Christian character of the professors and the institution itself. As President John Mockett Cramp stated in his 1851 inaugural address,

> The second point . . . is the importance of religious influence, pervading the whole course of study, and sanctifying, so to speak, all the arrangements. This College is open to all denominations, no religious tests being imposed either on students or Professors; nevertheless we must claim the right of aiming to imbue literature with the spirit of religion, and of inculcating, from time to time, those principles of our common Christianity, and those moral lessons which are admitted by all who wish to shun the reproach of infidelity. Habitual recognition of God, should distinguish every seat of learning, so that while the din of controversy is never heard, and party contentions are unknown, all may be taught that 'the fear of the Lord is the beginning of wisdom.'

Such sentiments would have elicited ready approval from Cramp's Methodist and Presbyterian counterparts. Although they were as insistent as John Strachan on the goal of education being formation of character, they were far more emphatic concerning the primacy of biblical study and Christian evidences in the curriculum over the imitation of "pagan" classical models. In his 1842 inaugural address at the opening of Victoria College, President Egerton Ryerson forcefully refused to "make the House of God a philosophical Lecture-Room, or the Christian Minister a literary teacher or metaphysical disputant, or divert his chief meditations from the great truths of the Sacred Scriptures."

Evangelicalism also transformed the inherited ideals of liberal education in a second, and perhaps equally fundamental, way. Men like McCulloch, Ryerson, and the Baptist founders of Acadia realized that they lived in a new society that lacked the amenities and cultured social elites of Britain. Therefore, they maintained, "liberal education" must be both broadened and made more practical than the Oxford and Cambridge system of educating young gentlemen for a life of polite conversation and good manners. In a letter to his friend Charles Archibald, Thomas McCulloch, who had recently been appointed Principal of Dalhousie University in Halifax, explicitly rejected the supremacy of the classics in the curriculum:

> That he who teaches these languages [Greek and Latin] in Dalhousie College should know his business will or respectability requires but that boys should in Halifax or elsewhere spend six or seven years on Latin and Greek and then four more in College partially occupied with the same languages is a waste of human life adapted neither to the circumstances nor the prosperity of Nova Scotia . . . If Dalhousie College acquire usefulness and eminence it will be not by an imitation of Oxford but as an institution of science and practical intelligence.

Similar ideas were advanced by Egerton Ryerson at Victoria College. His inaugural address, significantly entitled The Advantages of an English and Liberal Education, promoted not the training of a polite elite, but a broad exposure to English culture aimed at developing the powers of the mind. The graduates were to become thorough, practical men. Ryerson's original design envisioned an English curriculum in the preparatory course, with a Classical and Scientific education in the collegiate section. The older idea of liberal education was thus modified by considerations not only of religion but of utility: the true "gentlemen," for the evangelical, was a pious Christian and a practical man, bent on applying his talents to the improvement of self and society.

The definition of a new ideal of "liberal education" in the

evangelical colleges possessed broader cultural significance in the early nineteenth century. Although the Methodist, Baptist, and Presbyterian colleges were, by today's standards, tiny institutions, their importance to the formulation and defence of the evangelical creed was out of proportion to their small size. By virtue of their positions as professors, men like Egerton Ryerson, J.M. Cramp, Michael Willis, and Thomas McCulloch attained positions of prominence and power in their respective churches. Their task was not simply the training of preachers and a rising group of "Christian gentlemen;" rather, they all combined the activities of professor and preacher in such a way that their theology could never become simply an academic tradition. Through their own sermons and those of their students, their teaching on the inspiration and authority of the Bible, the relations of religion and science, and the connections between church and society penetrated the local congregations. Their leadership not only directed the intellectual response of many Protestant Christians in their encounter with secular interpretations of human nature and society, but it placed value upon a distinctive spirit of harmony and accommodation between evangelical religion and newer currents of thought.

For the clergyman-professor, the vital task was that definition of a proper relationship between revelation, the Bible, and the products of the human intellect. Fundamental to the culture of evangelicalism was the belief that the books of the Old and New Testament contained the absolutely certain record of God's dealing with the human race. It consistently revealed to the believer the doctrines of sin, salvation, and judgment; principles for which evangelicals claimed universal validity. Although the Bible was regarded primarily as the source of doctrine and belief, it also functioned as a source of authority on a second level. Scripture, evangelicals maintained, was history, for it contained an account of the origins of the universe and man, an explanation of human sin, and a revelation of the miracle of salvation. Also important to the evangelical vision was the way in which the Bible looked to the future. Through study of its prophecies, Presbyterian, Methodist, and Baptist preachers believed that they could discern the future of their society and the entire human race. They maintained that history and theology could not be separated without irreparable damage to the authority of the Bible. Thus, students were constantly reminded that the religious value of the Bible depended on its accuracy and reliability as an account of human history.

For evangelical educators in British North America, the Bible was either true on the level of history, or it was not. Given the bond linking history and theology, any impairment of the historical reliability of Scripture would shake the foundations of theological and moral certainty. As the young Methodist preacher Henry Flesher Bland reminded his congregation, Christian belief could not be a half-way house. Only two possible attitudes regarding the Bible existed for the evangelical Christian. It had to be accepted either as "a Divine Revelation," or dismissed as "a consummate forgery." Yet this left unresolved a serious question. How could one determine whether or not Scripture was, indeed, a revelation of the divine will and purpose?

This conundrum was the most fundamental problem facing the evangelical mind during its formative decades. Between 1820 and 1860 Protestant Christians faced, in the words of the great English historian Owen Chadwick, "the question whether historians, by probing the moments of time associated with religion, could affect its meaning." Evangelicals in the British North American colonies founded their colleges against a background of intellectual and cultural change in the Atlantic world of which their revival was only one element. Their theology and the position of the Bible in their mental universe was thus defined in relation to rival beliefs concerning the proper relationship between Scripture and historical knowledge. One of these rivals was "historicism," represented by German historians and biblical critics who stressed process and change in the world. Although most of the German "idealists" were deeply religious men convinced of the presence of the divine spirit in the world, evangelicals were troubled by their denial of normative value to the biblical text and to the doctrines it contained. Indeed, German critics and historians maintained that while Scripture and human history manifested the divine spirit, the biblical record must be interpreted through reason and intuition, not from the standpoint of faith or theology. "Historicism" thus reversed the evangelical Christian subordination of reason to faith, and located the meaning of human history not in revelation or miracle, but in the historical process itself. German idealist thought affirmed the power of the human mind, acting without reference to belief or tradition, to discern the mind of God.

As a solution to the difficulty of constructing a proper relationship between the Bible and historical enquiry, aspiring preachers and other students were directed by the founders of the church colleges to turn their attention to the internal evidence of the text itself. Interpretation of the Bible, they held, was a function of the prior possession of Christian faith. To assist their study, professors and students relied upon two eighteenth century works, Joseph Butler's *The Analogy of Religion* and Archdeacon William

Paley's *The Evidences of Christianity*. The writings of these English clergymen were not designed, however, to meet the intellectual problems raised by the "historicist" outlook of the German biblical critics. The works of Paley and Butler dated from an earlier period of religious controversy and were honed in response to the English Deist assault on miracles and the reliability of the biblical text. Butler and Paley adopted a double line of defence. First, they pointed to the Old Testament prophecies and their fulfillment in the words and actions of Christ as evidence for the internal consistency and integrity of the biblical text. Second, they used a more rational line of argument, based upon the reliability of the "testimony" of the biblical authors, whose narratives, they assumed, were written contemporaneously with the event they purported to describe.

The use of the Anglican apologists Butler and Paley merely buttressed, however, a more fundamental and widespread attitude which, for evangelical leaders, must govern the claims of faith and the pursuit of knowledge. Evangelical educators in all Atlantic societies specifically cautioned against the potential of the human intellect to be the disturbing factor in the delicate balance of reason and faith. In a lecture to the students of Pictou Academy, Principal McCulloch reminded them that "[p]reconceived opinions, and vicious modes of reasoning, and especially inaccurate methods of enquiry" had contributed to retarding the progress of knowledge. "Men evidently came to the Book of Nature, just as they came to the Book of Revelation," he cautioned them, "not to learn but merely to seek confirmation of their own preconceived opinions." McCulloch's assumptions were twofold. His juxtaposing of nature and revelation maintained, implicitly, that a similar mode of inquiry could discover laws or principles underlying each. By this he hoped to preserve a relationship in which revelation would guide both scientific and historical research. Second, the Principal drew a sharp distinction between "sound" and "unsound" modes of inquiry. "Unsound" inquiry, he admonished, would imperil the religious foundations of human civilization itself.

Avoidance of this perilous abyss dictated a particular strategy of education and inquiry. Professor-preachers devoted a great deal of energy to the proper definition of "sound" inquiry. In his 1817 lecture on the subject of liberal education, McCulloch looked to "the improvement of man in intelligence and moral principle." The acquisition of knowledge was, however, a rigorous process, and could not be attained by mere dabbling or speculation. It must begin with detailed study of individual phenomena and proceed, through comparison, to knowledge of abstract truths or principles. According to McCulloch, these principles, the fruit of inductive reasoning, acted as "the primary objects of science, which, in its various parts, constitutes the materials of a learned education." McCulloch's advocacy of the inductive method situates him within a powerful early nineteenth century intellectual movement. "Baconianism" was a current of thought which legitimated the scientific enterprise by insisting that it be carried on in a framework defined by the needs of Christian doctrine. In no sense, however, can Baconianism be described as a philosophical system. Coterminous with the beginnings of the evangelical rejection of the primacy of reason, it shared a number of attitudes with evangelicalism. First, the Baconian ideal based itself on the inductive methodology of current science, in which the general laws of nature were derived from a meticulous survey of particulars. Second, exponents of the inductive method propagated an emphatically empiricist approach to all forms of knowledge, declaring a marked preference for objective fact over hypotheses. Finally, clergymen and scientists who subscribed to these beliefs indicated a distrust of reason itself.

In the context of the ambiguous relationship between evangelicals and the culture of the eighteenth century, Baconianism assumed particular importance. In contrast to both Britain and the United States, where both "epistemological" and "moral" versions of the Common Sense tradition acted on the evangelical mind, what the historian Mark Noll has termed "methodological Common Sense" operated as the sole strand of the Scottish philosophical tradition in British North America. Though grounded on certain assumptions of eighteenth century Scottish inquiry, the Baconian ideal allowed clergymen to establish the limits of reason, particularly in the disputed borderland between religion and scientific inquiries. It was in this cultural use of "Baconianism" that evangelical clergymen diverged from the scholarly communities. Scientists and philosophers sought the unity of the moral and the scientific in the inductive method. Such a goal could only be secondary to clergymen concerned with discerning a biblical and theological foundation to human conduct and social organization. For them, Baconian induction was the intellectual matrix of Christian revelation and theology. Far from establishing science as the idiom of culture, Baconianism offered the much-sought guarantee against "unsound" or impious research.

Following the Baconian ideal, criticism of the Bible, like human reason itself, was barred from an independent function in matters of religion. This move arose not only from the evangelical elevation of faith and theology, but from the intellectual difficulties of post-Enlightenment Protestantism. Evangelicals sought, like many of their early Victorian contemporaries, to use the study of history as a source of stability and authority. For colonial clergymen, the task was even more compelling. Far more was at stake than maxims of political behaviour or the moral character of nations. They had to locate, in an age of competing philosophical and scientific currents, the permanent, immutable elements of Christian belief. These elements alone could provide intellectual and moral certainty. The denial of permanence represented by the German biblical criticism forced Methodist, Presbyterian, and Baptist clergymen to subordinate historical study to the literal, unerring inspiration and authority of the biblical text. In case of conflict between historical reason and Christian doctrine, students were reminded by no less a figure than Principal Thomas McCulloch that

> Christianity demands absolute submission to the veracity of God in his word; and, respecting those particulars which he has not been pleased to explain, man must walk by faith... Besides, man, by weakness of intellectual capacity, tendencies of constitution, and acquired prejudices, is destitute of that accuracy and enlargement of view, which constitutes the perfection of reason . . . It becomes not reason, so defective in all . . . to accommodate revelation to its own standard.

Assuming the complete inspiration and accuracy of the Scriptures and the validity of Christian doctrine, biblical theology formed the central endeavour of the evangelical colleges. Their outlook claimed the alliance of faith and reason but was in fact founded upon a relationship of inequality. Any suggestion of greater independence in the application of biblical criticism carried the taint of rationalism or infidelity.

Another, perhaps equally powerful, factor made evangelicals so intent on defining a proper relationship between their faith and historical inquiry. Colonial evangelicalism was, in fact, a culture deeply shaped by a particular view of past, present, and future. Through the sermons of men like the Methodist preacher Henry Flesher Bland, congregations were reminded that even in a new land, their communal efforts were linked to the great events and heroic acts which marked the history of Christianity. All these occurrences, preachers declared, presented a clear and unequivocal message to the Christian believer. God's hand was evident in all history, both national and individual, and the facts of history could not fail to indicate the activity of an overruling Providence. Thus the confidence expressed by these men concerning the possibility of moral reform and improvement was linked to a wider historical struggle. This struggle displayed the triumph of political liberty and social progress, which the preachers particularly associated with the expansion of the Anglo-Saxon peoples. The significance of this linking of a self-conscious sense of Anglo-Saxon superiority to the evangelical creed extended beyond the expression of an aggressively Protestant outlook in the culture of British North America. The nineteenth century ideas of liberty, individualism, and progress were derived from an explicit theology of history which held that the past was infused with a divine purpose, and that present and future events testified to the unfolding of God's design.

For evangelicals, the power to interpret the past was derived from the Bible, but their creed depended for its authority upon the ability of professors and preachers to predict the future course of events, to link the occurrences of the past to a meaningful sequence of trends and portents. The bond between past, present, and future, they declared, was provided by the prophetic elements of Scripture. Did not the Bible contain the mysterious Book of Daniel and the Revelations of Saint John? These oracles offered to the believer the power to foretell the exact fate of nations and empires and their role in the divine plan. In the rising evangelical culture of British North America, history was nothing less than the fulfillment of prophecy.

Protestant clergymen thus forcefully maintained that history had explicitly religious overtones. It not only emphatically articulated the doctrine of salvation, the dominant element in the evangelical creed, but implicitly subordinated knowledge of the past to a specific set of theological assumptions. Writing in 1850, Rev. Samuel Nelles, Professor of Moral Philosophy and President of Victoria College, stated that there was "no right study of history except along the line of Redemption." He sharply criticized those students of history who mistakenly undertook "to find order or end in the march of time without reference to the great economy and its destined consummation." For colonial evangelicals, history possessed a sacred character. Not only did the record of the past provide certain evidence of the workings of providence, but more importantly, as faithful Christians, they believed that God had actually entered history to redeem mankind from sin. The evangelical view of the right relationship between their theology and the writing of history was most fully articulated in the addresses and writings of Rev. Robert Burns, Professor of Church History at Knox College between his arrival in Upper Canada in 1844 and his death in 1869. History, he informed his classes in 1848, assumed a central place in Christian experience and thought because it provided the only sure record of the divinely ordained scheme of salvation. It was, he declared :

the history of God's arrangements with our world, for displaying his own glory, and securing the salvation of his people: the history of successive dispensations of grace in behalf of guilty man: the history of the doctrines, the worship, the institutions of the visible Church: the history of the effects of true religion on the literature, the arts, the civilization of the species: the history of the relations established betwixt truth and error for the mastery. On such a history much precious instruction may be grafted, and the historian and herald of the Churches, may become also the minister of God for the salvation of his people.

History, Burns concluded, was concerned first and foremost with the problem of salvation. The study of the human past was thus larger than the academic horizons of the colleges. The belief that history fulfilled God's design elevated historical study to the level of prophecy.

The final sentence of Burn's address was perhaps the most crucial. He clearly regarded the historian, the preacher, and the prophet in synonymous roles. By equating them, he attempted to resolve the tensions which existed in the early Victorian world between the evangelical theology of history and history as practiced by more secularly-minded British and American writers. The difference, Burns believed, lay not so much in method as in outlook. The study of history informed by Christian doctrine was, he reminded his students, "a solemn and spiritual exercise." Because it attempted to "follow out the agency of the Redeemer . . . on the scale of the world's history," the Christian vision of history was superior to "the temperament of the mere civil historian." The latter was animated by "a low and dwarfish aim," namely, the gathering of facts and "the chronicling of them for curiosity."

The vision of history expounded in British North America by Burns and his Methodist and Baptist counterparts, and preached in so many congregations, had already become deeply rooted in the popular traditions and scholarly discussion of Protestant Europe. Central to this theology of history was the belief that the Bible displayed God's providence actively exercised for human salvation. The doctrine of divine providence thus served as a philosophy of history which enabled clergymen to assert that all events were meaningful. The Christian theology of history thus rejected chance or contingency as a feature of historical reality. In churches resting upon the central doctrines of sin and salvation, this interpretation of history maintained God's active role in history. The power of the human will was denied except insofar as it was an instrument of the divine purpose. Finally and most importantly for the promoters of Christian culture, it guaranteed that history had an overriding purpose and shape: the divine order revealed in Scripture was ultimately reflected in human affairs.

"Scripture history," preached Samuel Nelles in 1848, "is God teaching by Providence. Scripture history is an unfolding to some extent of the divine administration toward a part of the human race. And from a part we learn the whole." Contained within this brief statement were several important assumptions which underlay study and preaching. Nelles assumed that the history as recorded in the Bible was, because of its sacred origins in divine revelation, superior to all other forms of historical writing. Indeed, this was a position little different from that articulated by Egerton Ryerson, Nelles's mentor, in a series of addresses to the students of Victoria College delivered in 1843. Sacred history, Ryerson declared, was accurate down to the smallest detail. Further, it explained to the believer "what all profane historians were ignorant of." These elements were crucial to the understanding of human behaviour, and included "the origins of nations . . . an account of the peopling of the earth after the deluge, as no other book in the world ever did give; and the truth of which all other books in the world, which contain anything on the subject, confirm."

Although these views affirmed the separation of "sacred" and "profane" history, they clearly assumed the existence of a link between the biblical history and what they termed "universal history." For clergymen whose creed was premised on God's activity in the world, no final separation was possible. Although the Bible was more reliable and superior because of its divine origin, Presbyterians, Methodists, and Baptists maintained that the entry of Christ into history had widened the sphere of redemption, and united all humanity, to some extent, in a common salvation. In an address delivered before the Fredericton Athenaeum in 1857, Rev. John Brooke, a New Brunswick Presbyterian, informed his audience that "Secular and Sacred History are like two rivers that run parallel, and that may sometimes even meet in the same channel; or, at least, some portion of the stream may occasionally pass from one to the other."

By suggesting the influence of the sacred upon the secular, however, colonial clergymen like Brooke faced nagging problems associated with attempts to relate religion and intellect. A recent account of early Victorian social thought has argued that the vitality of the evangelical impulse was responsible for a reassertion of biblical views of human origins and behaviour in the four decades between 1820 and 1860. According to this scheme, all human beings were presumed to be descended from one original pair formed by God as the final act of creation. Further, God has revealed the one true religion and certain other fundamental institutions of civilization to these human ancestors. Central to the biblical paradigm was the degeneration, rather than the progress, of non-Christian peoples, both past and present. As well, as sharp distinction was made between humans and other animal forms. History was conceived as a single grand system of grace, divided into dispensations. Preacher-professors like Egerton Ryerson and Robert Burns maintained that although each of these periods differed from the preceding one, all were governed by the same immutable and eternal principles: the conflict between sin and salvation, the persecution of the true church by the enemies of the faith, and the decline and revival of religion.

Such an organization of time accorded well with the central tenets of the theology of history taught in the colonial colleges. Because each period flowed from God, this scheme of history preserved the vital belief in divine transcendence. Further, it provided evangelicals with an explanation for the degeneration and decay of human societies: in all ages, sin and defection from the true faith was the cause of decline. Here was a concept of history that made no pretension of objectivity or impartiality; evangelicals were certain both of the meaning of truth and salvation and the source of error and sin. Professors and preachers read into past, present, and future the doctrines of Protestantism, and equated these with liberty and progress. They were equally specific concerning the source and persistence of evil in human societies. This they located in the "heathenism" of pre-Christian times, an element which predominated in the Roman Chuch with its papalism, ritual, and cult of the saints. Such Roman distinctives implacably opposed to the "true" or biblical faith believed and taught by patriarchs, prophets, Christ, his apostles, and evangelicals. Actually, "evangelicals" were seen, throughout the Christian centuries, to constitute a "true" church in opposition to "Antichrist," a term used interchangeably with "Rome."

In their equation of Romanism and sin, clergymen-professors could draw upon a rich body of popular tradition dating back to the Reformation. Works like John Foxe's *Book of Martyrs* stressed in lurid detail the threat of Roman Catholicism to civil and religious liberty and dwelt lovingly on the sufferings of Protestant martyrs as the defenders of true religion. Beneath the monotonous and often repellent catalogue of the persecution of the "true" faith by the Roman agents of "Antichrist," there lurked a question of vital significance for evangelicals. Because the dispensational structure of time was cyclical, there was a danger that such a view of past and future might lead to inertia and despair among ordinary Protestants who might otherwise assume that the struggle would go on eternally without resolution or progress. Thus the attempt to prove the superiority of Protestantism was no mere academic exercise: it involved nothing less than impressing upon students the fact that, with the Reformation, the universal struggle between truth and error had been at least resolved. As John Mockett Cramp noted in a letter to the eminent American Baptist educator Francis Wayland:

> We only see now the beginning of the end. A great conflict is at hand. Church tyrants are maturing their plans, and marshalling their forces for the fight, sternly resolved to gain the ascendancy over the human mind, for which the dark ages were distinguished, and to trample their opponents in the dust. But the eyes of men are opened. Knowledge is everywhere diffused. Education is all but universal. We have the Bible, the Press, and, above all, a noble army of intelligent Christians in both hemispheres, who are prepared to make a bold stand for truth and primitive godliness, and to use vigorously those weapons of warfare which are not carnal, but mighty through God, to the pulling down of strongholds. The battle will be sharp, probably long, and some painful reverses may be experienced by the advocates of New Testament piety. Nevertheless, let no man's heart fail him. The cause is God's, and victory is sure.

Cramp's views left no doubt that Romanism was at long last in decline, and that the long cycle of persecution had ended. The last centuries of the Christian dispensation, they earnestly believed, would be characterized by the "restoration" or "revival" of the spiritual life characteristic of the primitive, apostolic church. A cyclical return to origins would ensure a linear and final unfolding of the true faith, the only possible source of social progress.

Thus, in spite of the cyclical character of the dispensational structure of history, colonial evangelicals, for the most part, did not draw from it pessimistic or catastrophic implications. Each dispensation, they believed, was more inclusive and universal than the last. By the nineteenth century, evangelical leaders like John Mockett Cramp could confidently inform their students that "the age is remarkably progressive." They looked forward to the salvation of the entire world, not through some catastrophic divine intervention, but through the missionary, and reformist efforts of churches. Eventually there would be a "Christianization" of individuals, governments, and voluntary associations. In his lectures on biblical topics, Robert Burns stressed the "gradual manner" in which the divine providence had unfolded. Such a vision, which might be termed "postmillennial," equated liberty and progress with the power of the evangelical impulse. Such an equation enabled the professors and preachers of the mainline churches to counter the "premillennial," catastrophic prophecies of groups such as the Millerites. These premillennialists saw no hope in a sinful world, and predicted the end of the world in a fiery consummation in 1844.

As the historian William Westfall has explained, both pre- and post-millennialists shared the same insistence on the literal, interpretation of the Bible and the links between history and prophecy. The "Protestant" version of history, however, enabled post-millennialists to offer a convincing, optimistic vision of the gradual mingling of providence and the human world so that an earthly kingdom would be realized in time. By 1860, many prominent evangelicals believed in the final absorption of the secular by the sacred as the "Christian" dispensation ended and Christ's rule was gradually established over all in a millennial kingdom. In contrast to the premillennialists, however, Henry Flesher Bland reminded his congregation in 1864 that this kingdom need not await the personal coming of Christ in order to be realized. Rather, he declared, it would be achieved gradually as the "full development of the kingdom of grace in its present form."

Providence, prophecy, and the Protestant millennium — here were the fundamental pillars of the evangelical concept of history, through which preachers and professors sought to assert their control over the emerging colonial mind and ensure the triumph of the sacred over the secular. One serious difficulty, however, existed. The very relationship between history and prophecy depended upon maintaining inviolate a body of theological truth premised upon the belief in the reliability of Scripture. The Bible had to be universally valid and unchanging at the level of both history and theology. Yet, the perplexing question of the relationship between the biblical text and the results of historical inquiry would not disappear.

By the 1840's and 1850's, the old assurances that faith and reason could not conflict were confronted by a welter of historical and archaeological research. Such research was not easily accommodated into the biblical picture of human origins. For example, uniformitarian geology of Sir Charles Lyell greatly extended the age of the earth and cast doubt upon the story of creation contained in the Book of Genesis. Educated Protestants would have observed from a cursory reading of the periodical literature of the 1850's that the new study of man was not simply a quest of agnostics or enemies of Christianity. Figures as respectable as the pious German diplomat Baron Christian Bunsen, and "Liberal Anglican" clerics such as Thomas Arnold, revised the traditional biblical chronology by arguing that there were human societies of greater antiquity than accounted for in Scripture. Given the close relations between religion, geology, and the emerging "human sciences" characteristic of Victorian intellectual life, it was not surprising that the logic of scientific law was increasingly applied to human societies. The progress of diverse cultures, men like Sir Henry Maine argued, could be discerned not by the dialectic of sin and salvation or by the interposition of divine miracle. Rather, human progress followed natural and social laws of development accessible to human reason. Furthermore, these laws were operative in Christian and non-Christian societies alike.

By calling into question the inductive certainty of events which undergirded the evangelical theology of history, the new "human sciences" and social thought placed at risk the factual basis of biblical preaching. It was no wonder, then, that even in British North America, evangelicals scanned with trepidation the newspaper reports of expeditions to distant biblical lands and reviews of the latest literature on the subject of universal history. In 1854, the Halifax *Presbyterian Witness* optimistically reported on the research of the British traveller Austen Henry Layard at Nineveh, the ancient capital of Assyria: "Among the more modern sources of evidence confirmatory of the historic facts narrated in the Bible are those subterranean discoveries which have recently been made."

The impact of these discoveries held forth the threat of a divorce between theology and history, and the subordination of the inspired record of the Bible to secular dynamics of time and social change. Here, for evangelical clergymen, was the crux of the problem: How does one convincingly relate a presumably static body of truth to a culture already thinking in terms of intellectual and social progress? How does one relate the Bible to culture for those who now turn to secular modes of causation to explain societal changes? It was the relationship of the evangelical creed to the "human sciences" rather than to the "natural sciences" which perplexed the evangelical mind. For evangelicals in British North America, the great Victorian battleground between faith and doubt which dominated transatlantic intellectual life in the decades after 1860 was waged less over the impact of biology, geology, and Darwinism and more over the problem of history, the new German biblical criticism, and its impact on theology.

Church and State: Evangelicals and the Reshaping
of Colonial Politics

In a memoir concerning John Strachan, his successor as Bishop of Toronto, A.N. Bethune, explained that the "preeminence of England amongst the nations of the world, in material power as well as in moral influence," was due largely to "the diffusion of that sober moral tone and healthful spirit of subordination, which a wide-spread religious teaching, provided by her established Church, has steadily maintained." Social utility, however, provided only one argument in defence of the principle of religious establishment, for Bethune left no doubt in the minds of his readers that in his estimation, the duty of the state to support a church was "divinely derived." To bolster his argument, the bishop drew explicitly upon the Bible, directing the attention of his readers to the injunctions contained in the Mosaic legislation which commanded the ancient Israelites to render support to the "priestly tribe," a "Divine arrangement" which he considered "as equitable as it was wise."

By the time Bethune penned the memoir of this eminent predecessor in 1870, the British North American colonies had, some sixteen years before, emphatically severed the overt vestiges of the connection between Church and State. This turn of events, both Bethune and Strachan believed, was "a public misfortune." These Anglican High Churchmen had based their religious beliefs and public philosophies around the notion of active government support for religion, and held as an article of faith that:

> the fixed and permanent establishment in every township of
> the Province, of one or more clergymen of the Church of
> England, — of men who would combine with a piety and zeal
> a liberal education and some social refinement, and who,
> bound by the wholesome restraint of Scriptural articles of
> faith and a Scriptural form of worship, would present an
> unvarying front of opposition to erroneous doctrines and the
> capricious desire of change, — would have proved a large and
> lasting blessing to the land.

Here, in a nutshell, was the ideology of the ancien regime, where, far from being a mere client of the state, the church would play an active part in defining and reinforcing political loyalty and obligation. This would be accomplished, first, through the inculcation of "restraint" and "social refinement." Second, and perhaps more importantly, a cult or mystique of allegiance to the person of the King would be fostered. Indeed, the view of "loyalty" advanced by High Tories like Strachan and John Beverley Robinson assumed an implicit connection between devotion to the

Anglican Church and enjoyment of the full privileges of colonial citizenship.

At the conclusion of the Napoleonic Wars, the ideology of the old society appeared, at least on the surface, to be strongly entrenched in the British North American colonies. Anglican supremacy was officially enshrined through a variety of legal enactments in both the Maritimes and Upper Canada. These legalities included monopolies over the performance of baptism and marriages, clerical control of public education, and the system of Clergy Reserves by which a portion of the public lands were specifically set aside for the financial support of the clergy of the established church. The Church of England could rely upon the support of powerful home missionary societies such as the Society for the Propagation of the Gospel and, more importantly, the political support of the official community in each colony. Anglican leaders like John Strachan, conscious of the need to shape their developing societies in opposition to the republican experiment to the south, played an active role in the colonial governing councils, thus publicly testifying to the alliance of church and state.

Between 1815 and 1840, however, the privileges of the Church of England became one of the most divisive issues in colonial politics, both in Upper Canada and the Maritimes. The story of the great public debates over the relationship between church and state is a familiar one to Canadian historians. The debates revolved around three major questions: First, should the Clergy Reserves be the exclusive property of the Church of England, or should the funds be distributed according to some formula between all religious denominations, or, more daringly, should the Reserves be completely secularized, the funds devoted to the assistance of public education? Second, should the state have sole responsibility for financing and managing a system of common schools, or should this be left to "separate" schools run by each of the major religious denominations? And, third, should the various denominational colleges be merged into a single, secular state-supported provincial university, or should public funds be committed to supporting a much looser structure of church colleges?

By the late 1850's, there was no doubt that the British North American colonies had emphatically rejected the notion that a stable, harmonious social order should be based upon an overt alliance between church and state. In 1841, Lord Sydenham, governor of the new Province of Canada induced the imperial government to enact a scheme which ended the exclusive Anglican control of the Clergy Reserves, creating, in essence, a "plural establishment." Now Anglicans, Presbyterians, Methodists, and

Roman Catholics divided the income generated by land sales. Only the Baptists, who explicitly eschewed any connection between church and state, did not draw upon the fund in the period between 1841 and 1854. Far from settling the question, however, Sydenham's action proved to be a renewed point of contention. In the early 1850's after the Great Disruption of the Church of Scotland in 1843-44, and the rising tide of anti-Catholicism which coincided with the triumph of the Reform Party in 1848 a new Protestant consensus had emerged on the subject of the Clergy Reserves. By 1854, when the new Liberal-Conservative government finally produced a plan to completely secularize the Reserves, only High Anglicans like John Strachan stood in opposition to a tide of "voluntaryism" that permeated even the "evangelical" wing of his own church.

Given the evangelical Protestant nature of British North America in 1861, it might be easily assumed that the High Anglican social vision was doomed to almost certain defeat. Yet, it must be stressed that even in 1840 a vast majority of Protestants would have accepted Strachan's political theology, believing that no organized society could exist without an explicit connection between church and state. Church of Scotland Presbyterians themselves belonged to a church legally established in their homeland. Even more surprisingly, a large section of Canadian Methodism, influenced by British Wesleyanism, was prepared to accept with equanimity the superior status of the Church of England as the legitimate "establishment." Only the Baptists, who resisted any connection with the state, were prepared to dissent from the ideology of the ancien regime.

What occurred between 1841 and 1854 was less a revolt against the idea of church establishment itself than a growing realization that the old High Church rationale for the alliance of church and state did not work in the peculiar religious environment of British North America. Men like Egerton Ryerson, whose reading included the eighteenth century classic High Church defences of Church establishment by Archdeacon Paley, Bishop Burnet, and Sir William Blackstone, was quite prepared to accept the validity of this principle as applied to the British Isles, but not to British North America. Indeed, the effectiveness of Ryerson's criticisms were largely due to his acceptance of much of the Tory Anglican rationale: like them, he couched his political thought in terms of reverence for the balanced English constitution and the imperial connection. Such "conservative" elements had also appeared in John Wesley's own political thinking. However, as David Mills has argued in a recent study of the issue of loyalty in Upper Canada, Ryerson and other evangelical leaders were troubled by the "exclusive" nature of the Tory definition. Instead, they drew upon a more "liberal" strand of the eighteenth century Whig-Tory outlook that they had inherited from Wesley. Writing in response to John Strachan's Ecclesiastical Chart of 1827, Ryerson declared that:

> I aver that the term [dissenter] is not at all applicable to the religious denominations in this country. From what Church have they dissented? Indeed, most of the first inhabitants of this country never belonged to the Church of England at all. They were from the first attached to the denominations . . . Nor had they any apprehensions, while supporting the rights of the Crown, that an ecclesiastical establishment of ministers of whom they have never heard, was to be imposed, upon them, as a reward for their loyalty! Indeed, they had the faith of the Government pledged, that they should enjoy the rights of conscience. And in view of this was the charter of the Province formed, to secure liberty of conscience and freedom of thought.

Ryerson reminded his readers that the underlying spiritual principle of the British constitution was not the alliance of church and state, which even Anglican apologists after the 1790's had defended in terms of social utility, but, rather, "liberty of conscience" and "freedom of thought." He used his Wesleyan inheritance to argue that the exclusive High Tory definition of political loyalty was, in fact, subversive of the harmony and social order which they were trying to create in a new society.

Ryerson's appeal to the Wesleyan inheritance reveals much concerning the impact of evangelicalism on colonial political thought and practice. English Canadian historians have long observed that political ideologies in this country have a strong propensity to gravitate to the middle, with political power generally being wielded by "conservative liberals" or "liberal conservatives." A recent study by Gordon Stewart has suggested that unlike the United States, where a decentralized, "country" ideology of opposition inherited from eighteenth century English thought defined the shape of politics, English Canada had adopted by 1867, an extreme "court" version of English politics. Great stress was placed upon administration and patronage, thus reducing ideological polarization in the name of stability. Crucial questions, however, remain unanswered. Was there any positive impetus, other than fear of social breakdown and desire for the "spoils of office," to the emerging "politics of accommodation?" Did the redefinition of the relationship between church and state in the 1840's have some bearing upon the new shape of Canadian politics?

Historians, it may be argued, should look again at the rising power of evangelicalism in British North American society, which coincided with the forging of the "politics of accommodation." Professor Goldwin French once wrote that Egerton Ryerson and the Methodists displayed a peculiar ambiguity of "liberal" and "conservative" strands in their views of politics and society, an ambiguity which can be traced to John Wesley's own reworking of his High Church inheritance. Indeed, as the British historian J.C.D. Clark has suggested, "evangelicals" in both the Methodist and Anglican churches shared a common intellectual origin in the culture of the eighteenth century High Church "Whig-Tories": William Law, Bishop Burnet, and Sir William Blackstone. Theirs was a "political theology" which could not be categorized according to the modern polarizations of "conservative" and "liberal." In fact, a majority of Upper Canadians in the 1830's and 1840's shared this strand of eighteenth century thought with the Methodists and the emerging "evangelical" wing of the Anglican Church. Many factors contributed to political developments at this time, including the drift to rebellion in 1837, radical republican "Reformers" like William Lyon Mackenzie, and the Baldwinite "Reform" concept of "responsible government." Still, it may be that the most creative development in colonial political ideology was represented by the convergence of "moderate Whig" Egerton Ryerson (Methodist), the "moderate Reformer" Robert Baldwin (Anglican Low-Church), and the "moderate Tories" Ogle Gowan and William Draper (both Anglican Low-Church). These religious leaders represented the "conservative-liberal" outlook that stood between the High Toryism of Strachan and Beverley Robinson and the radical republicanism of Mackenzie. These Methodists and Low-Church Anglicans shared a common commitment to maintaining the British connection with its balanced constitution. Except for Baldwin, they also deplored the emergence of "parties" and organized oppositions.

More importantly, their common evangelicalism endowed them with a social vision which, to a large extent, was realized in the decade of the 1840's. In the first place, although they were committed to social harmony and balance, they understood that "liberty of conscience" dictated resistance to any exclusive Anglican claims to alliance of church and state. This, however, raised a concern. The eighteenth century roots of their thought expressly held that there must be some vital, spiritual principle at the root of each stable society that was needed to resist corruption and decay. They found an alternative to a state church in the evangelical creed's emphasis upon "conscience." By the mysterious faculty of the conscience, the individual will encounter that of God. In the converted believer, the conscience would serve as a moral rudder, ensuring that the individual would act "responsibly" in both personal and social conduct.

It might be asked by critics like Strachan, what definition of individual responsibility would prevail in the absence of an established church? Further, how could one ensure that "conscience" was animated by Christian principles of conduct? It was here that the second great point of contention in the relations between church and state, the creation of a system of common schools, became an important issue. It was no coincidence that the final "secularization" of the Clergy Reserves in 1854 occurred only after a viable, state-controlled system of public education had been established. Now, the key figure was the "conservative-liberal" Egerton Ryerson, who resigned from the presidency of Victoria College in 1844 to become Chief Superintendent of Education for the Province of Canada. Public education would not mean the creation of a school system devoid of religious influences. Ryerson explicitly described his policy for making state and society religious "a liberal system of common school education, free from the denomination of every church, and aiding colleges which may have been established by any church, we may rationally and confidently anticipate the arrival of a long-looked for era of civil government and civil liberty, social harmony, and public prosperity." Ryerson's vision of "non-sectarian" education did not mean "secular" education. He was an emphatic believer in the need for the common schools to teach "the essential elements and truths and morals of Christianity," and thus he consistently defended the reading of Scripture and "religious instruction." Indeed, Ryerson envisioned the public school system as a more effective substitute for formally established churches. Evangelicals might well claim that the school system could teach more people than could Strachan's vision of an exclusive establishment, therefore more effectively guarding the spiritual character of state and society.

In the Maritime provinces, the relationship between the evangelical impulse and the shaping of political identities was similarly forged. For several decades conflicts arose over the legal establishment of the Anglican Church and the unwillingness of Tory elites to grant charters to Presbyterian and Baptist institutions of higher learning. Like their counterparts in Upper Canada, Maritime evangelicals could be found on both sides of the divide between "conservative" and "liberal," but with a strong tendency to converge towards the moderate centre of the political spectrum. During the 1840's, the prominent Baptist layman J.W. Johnston, the "moderate Tory" leader of Nova Scotia, presided over a coalition executive council which included his "reform" adversary Joseph Howe. The politics of moderation made Nova Scotia in 1848 the first British colony in which the principles of "responsible government" were actually applied. Of equal importance in shaping the culture of the Maritime provinces, however, was the influence of evangelicalism in the sphere of education. While Methodists, Baptists, and Presbyterians strongly supported the establishment of a public system of non-sectarian common schools, they were equally insistent upon the maintenance of denominational colleges for the purpose of furthering "Christian education." Baptists and Methodists played a leading role in blocking the establishment of a secular university for the Maritimes. In doing so, the churches secured a leading role in training the professional leadership of Maritime communities. For the remainder of the nineteenth century, the cultural power of evangelical religion in the wider society was buttressed.

Public schools and colleges were, however, only the most prominent of a myriad of new social institutions. Temperance societies, public libraries, missionary agencies, public charities, local improvement societies, and municipal institutions such as town councils and police increased in the Province of Canada and the Maritimes between 1840 and 1867. While it would be too much to claim that all of these were created by the evangelical impulse, it is significant that all rested upon the wide acceptance of the principle of individual responsibility that lay at the root of the evangelical anthropology. Differences of wealth and status had always existed in British North America, but, by 1850, these were no longer considered merely "natural." Somehow they were to be located in the individual. Poverty, most evangelicals fervently believed, was the penalty for immoral or "irresponsible" conduct. Even government, by 1849, was now considered "responsible." This word was pregnant with significance and its religious implications have yet to be explored by intellectual historians.

SUGGESTIONS FOR FURTHER READING

By comparison with the United States, the study of evangelicalism in early nineteenth century English Canada is still in its infancy. English-Canadian historians have yet to produce a synthesis of the calibre of Sydney Ahlstrom's *A Religious History of the American People* (New Haven: Yale University Press, 1972), or Owen Chadwick's magisterial *The Victorian Church*, Vols. I and II

(London: A. and C. Black, 1966, 1969). There are few specialized studies of such culturally central processes as the revivalist impulse. Nonetheless, developments during the last decade have suggested a revival of interest in religious history in academic circles. The publication in 1988 of John Webster Grant's *A Profusion of Spires: Religion in Nineteenth Century Ontario* (Toronto: University of Toronto Press, 1988) augurs well for the future of the historical study of religion by providing a splendid overview and synthetic treatment of the religious experience. Further, it explains the convergence of Anglican and evangelical perspectives during the years 1840-1867.

General studies of the meaning of evangelicalism in the Canadian context owe much to the seminal study of Goldwin French, whose important article, "The Evangelical Creed in Canada," in W.L. Morton, ed., *The Shield of Achilles* (Toronto: McClelland and Stewart, 1968) is still essential reading. Boyd Hilton's splendid *The Age of Atonement* (Oxford: Oxford University Press, 1988), though set in Britain, restores the centrality of the evangelical perspective to the intellectual life of the early Victorian age. Because British North America remained a colonial society during this period, the importance of this study, and the social history of A.D. Gilbert, *Religion and Society in Industrial England: Church, Chapel, and Social Change,* 1740-1914 (London: Longman, 1976) cannot be too often stressed.

On religious revivalism, and in particular the evangelical atmosphere of the Second Great Awakening, historians of religion owe a great debt to the insights and concepts honed in the United States. See the seminal study by William McLoughlin, *Revivals, Awakenings, and Reform: An Essay on Religion and Social Change in America, 1607-1977* (Chicago: University of Chicago Press, 1978). A particularly good treatment of the relationship between the revivalist impulse and the evangelical creation of institutions after 1830 is provided in Donald G. Mathews, *Religion in the Old South* (Chicago: University of Chicago Press, 1977). Nathan O. Hatch's *The Democratization of American Christianity* (New Haven: Yale University Press, 1989) treats the entire cultural experience of the United States during the period 1800-1860, but the work appeared too late to be consulted in this study.

The problem of revivalism and its relationship to the Protestant culture of English Canada has begun to draw the interest of English-Canadian religious historians during the last decade. For the Maritimes, see the influential study by George Rawlyk, *Ravished by the Spirit: Religious Revivals, Baptists, and Henry Alline* (Kingston and Montreal: McGill-Queen's University Press, 1984). This study,

while devoted to the evangelistic activities of Henry Alline during
the 1780's, is particularly suggestive because it explores the reasons
for the emergence of the Baptists as the leading Protestant
denomination in the Maritime provinces. A second study by the
same author, *Wrapped Up in God: A Study of Several Canadian
Revivals and Revivalists* (Burlington: Welch Publishing Company,
1988), treats the persistence of revivalism as a centrepiece of
evangelical culture during the nineteenth and twentieth centuries.
Two additional studies, both published by McGill-Queen's Press in
1989, offer important and sensitive insights into the culture of the
nineteenth century Protestant revival. William Westfall's *Two
Worlds: The Protestant Culture of Nineteenth Century Ontario*
(Kingston and Montreal: McGill-Queen's University Press, 1989)
Chapters 2 and 3, describe the conflict between the revivalist mood
of evangelicalism and the eighteenth century "religion of order,"
and the "tempering of revivalism" as evangelicals sought social
responsibility after 1830. Marguerite Van Die's *An Evangelical Mind*
(Kingston and Montreal: McGill-Queen's University Press, 1989),
presents the importance of evangelical views of home, family, and
womanhood in rooting the revivalist impulse in the more structured
institutional world of mid- Victorian English Canada.

The evangelical "mind," and in particular its relationship to the
eighteenth century world of "Common Sense" philosophy and
natural theology, has also begun to attract some attention in
scholarly circles. Again, American studies have led the way. See the
important work by George Marsden, *Fundamentalism and American
Culture* (New York: Oxford University Press, 1980). On the
"Baconian" outlook, see Timothy Dwight Bozeman, *Protestants in
an Age of Science: The Baconian Ideal and Antebellum American
Religious Thought* (Chapel Hill: University of North Carolina Press,
1977). Compare, however, the seminal article by Mark Noll,
"Common Sense Traditions and American Evangelical Thought,"
American Quarterly, 1987.

For the Canadian scene, the basic study remains D.C. Masters,
Protestant Church Colleges in Canada (Toronto: University of
Toronto Press, 1966). This should be supplemented by Brian
McKillop, *A Disciplined Intelligence: Critical Inquiry and Canadian
Thought in the Victorian Era* (Montreal: McGill- Queen's University
Press, 1979), which argues for the importance of philosophical study
in the evangelical colleges. Carl Berger's *Science, God, and Nature in
Victorian Canada* (Toronto: University of Toronto Press, 1983), also
testified to the importance of science and natural history in shaping
colonial cultural life. Evangelicalism, however, rested upon a very
ambiguous relationship to both science and philosophy. This

ambiguity is explored by Michael Gauvreau in *The Evangelical Century: College and Creed in English Canada from the Great Revival to the Great Depression* (Kingston and Montreal: McGill-Queen's University Press, 1991), especially chapters 1-3. This study suggests the central importance of history, and particularly the study of the Bible, to understanding the attitudes displayed by evangelicals who sought to chart a course between the claims of faith and inquiry.

On the subject of Christian education and college life, see, for a provocative study of the transformation of "liberal" education in the early nineteenth century, Sheldon Rothblatt, *Tradition and Change in English Liberal Education* (Cambridge: Cambridge University Press, 1976). For the evangelical churches, consult the recent specialized studies by Barry Moody on Acadia University, in G.A. Rawlyk, ed., *Canadian Baptists and Christian Higher Education* (Kingston and Montreal: McGill-Queen's University Press, 1988) and Marguerite Van Die, *An Evangelical Mind,* which studies the Methodist Nathanael Burwash and Victoria University. On the millennialist impulse, which spurred not only the evangelical "mind," but also much of evangelical social thought, see Westfall, *Two Worlds*, especially Chapter 6; and Gauvreau, *The Evangelical Century,* Chapter 3.

The relationship of evangelical religion to the problem of church-state relations is the subject of considerable literature. On Canadian politics in the early nineteenth century, see the brief but stimulating work by Gordon Stewart, *The Origins of Canadian Politics* (Vancouver: University of British Columbia Press, 1987). Specialized studies include the classic work by J.S. Moir, *Church and State in Canada West: Three Studies in the Relation of Denominationalism and Nationalism, 1841-1867* (Toronto: University of Toronto Press, 1959); and Goldwin French, *Parsons and Politics: The Role of the Wesleyan Methodists in Upper Canada and the Maritimes from 1780 to 1855* (Toronto: Ryerson Press, 1962). Professor French's work is particularly suggestive as it seeks to explore the complex question of a Methodist "political ethos" which had wider implications for English-Canadian political attitudes in the later nineteenth century. Although no comparable monograph exists for Presbyterians, see J.S. Moir, *Enduring Witness: The Presbyterian Church in Canada* (Toronto: Presbyterian Press, 1976), and, more recently, Richard W. Vaudry, "Peter Brown, the Toronto Banner and the Evangelical Mind in Victorian Canada," *Ontario History*, 77, 1985. William Westfall's *Two Worlds,* Chapter 4, provides a stimulating reassessment of the breakdown of the alliance of church and state which eighteenth century churchmen viewed as so vital to social and political order.

TABLE 1:
THE DEMOGRAPHY OF BRITISH NORTH AMERICAN PROTESTANTISM

The census data recorded in this table refer exclusively to the *Protestant* population of the British North American colonies. This, in my opinion, gives a more accurate sense of the impact of evangelicalism on colonial Protestantism in the nineteenth century.

UPPER CANADA 1842
Total Population: 487,053
Total Protestants: 421,850

Denomination	Total Number	% of Protestant Population
Church of England	107,791	25.5
Methodists	82,923	19.7
Presbyterian	96,149	22.8
Baptists	16,411	3.9

UPPER CANADA 1861
Total Population: 1,396,091
Total Protestants: 1,177,940

Denomination	Total Number	% of Protestant Population
Church of England	311,559	26.4
Methodists	350,323	29.7
Presbyterian	303,374	25.7
Baptists	61,559	5.2

LOWER CANADA 1844
Total Population: 697,084
Total Protestants: 124,645

Denomination	Total Number	% of Protestant Population
Church of England	43,527	34.9
Methodists	15,824	12.7
Presbyterian	38,722	31.0
Baptists	4,063	3.3

LOWER CANADA 1861
Total Population: 1,111,566
Total Protestants: 168,313

Church of England	63,487	37.6
Methodists	30,844	18.3
Presbyterian	43,735	25.9
Baptists	7,751	4.6

NOVA SCOTIA 1861
Total Population: 330,857
Total Protestants: 244,576

Church of England	47,744	19.5
Methodists	34,167	14.0
Presbyterians	88,755	36.2
Baptists	62,040	25.3

NEW BRUNSWICK 1861
Total Population: 252,047
Total Protestant: 166,809

Church of England	42,776	25.6
Methodists	25,637	15.4
Presbyterians	36,632	22.0
Baptists	57,730	34.6

PRINCE EDWARD ISLAND 1848
Total Population: 62,678
Total Protestant: 35,531

Church of England	6,530	18.3
Methodists	4,934	13.8
Presbyterians	20,402	57.4
Baptists	2,900	8.2

ORDERING A NEW NATION AND REORDERING PROTESTANTISM 1867-1914

Phyllis D. Airhart

Apathy is a word chosen often to describe the attitude of the Protestant churches to the proposal that the British North American provinces form the nation of Canada. Church leaders were not alone in lacking enthusiasm in the days leading up to Confederation, for not all prospects for the new nation were promising. The new country was spread across a vast geographical area, much of it an unsettled frontier. Its disparate regions were to be linked by a national transportation system that was still only a dream. It was peopled by the descendants of two races whose linguistic and religious differences had contributed to a long history of animosity. There were no doubt some who feared that Joseph Howe might have been right when he described Confederation as being only a little more ambitious than building the tower of Babel — and church- goers knew how that story had ended.

Protestant leaders did little to bring the new nation of Canada into being, and the churches provided no fanfare to accompany Confederation. Except for an ecumenical Thanksgiving service in Toronto organized by the Evangelical Alliance, the event was not marked by special church services. Confederation, it has rightly been said, was the brain-child of politicians and railroad promoters. Indirectly it was they who also set the agenda for the churches in the years between Confederation and the First World War. It was a politician, Methodist Leonard Tilley of Fredericton, N.B., who

recalled the words of a psalm, "He shall have dominion fr(
sea," to speak of the new Dominion of Canada, and it was the ,
for building a railroad that offered new opportunities for expansion
and evangelism. The twin challenges of creating "His Dominion"
and winning the entire western frontier for Christ were taken on by
churches as they became accustomed to the new realities presented
by disestablishment and the secularization of the clergy reserves.
The new nation thus became an arena where denominational
pluralism was tested.

Quick to see the possibilities of their new situation, Protestant
leaders in many communities led the search for a national identity
in the decades following Confederation. With the majority of the
mid-nineteenth century population affiliated with a church, the
influence of these leaders was considerable. Christians in British
North America had demonstrated even more public religiosity in
the first half of the nineteenth century than their American
neighbours. One sociologist, S.D. Clark, has suggested that there are
few countries in the western world in which religion exerted as great
an influence on the development of the community as in Canada.
Pulpit and religious press combined to galvanize public support for
the nation which Protestants believed would become "His
Dominion." The idea of Canada as "His Dominion" sparked the
Protestant imagination and provided symbolic coherence for a
broadly-based consensus. It expressed a determination to establish
the Kingdom of God in the new country and became a way of
articulating a mission for the nation. In more concrete terms, "His
Dominion" found practical expression in a variety of ways —
among them missionary activities, reform movements, and
voluntary societies.

Undergirding the "home mission" work in the west, the idea of a
Christian Canada became a means of connecting congregations in
the Maritimes and Central Canada to the western region and, in
some cases, encouraged denominations to think in national terms.
Many Protestant church leaders viewed the aftermath of
Confederation as an opportunity for greater consolidation within
denominational families. Buttressed by arguments emphasizing the
practicalities of such unions, several branches of Protestantism
united — a reflection of their interest in dealing with the immediate
situation in Canada rather than with memories of divisive
controversies in Europe and the United States. Four groups of
Presbyterians were united in the Presbyterian Church in Canada by
1875. The Methodists completed a similar process by 1884. Two
Baptist conventions, Ontario and Quebec, merged in 1888. In the
Maritimes the Free Christian Baptists and the Regular Baptists

joined to form the United Baptist Convention during the first decade of the twentieth century. However, more ambitious proposals for a national Baptist federation were rejected. By the turn of the century all of the major Protestant denominations except the Baptists and the Lutherans had developed national organizational structures.

There were soon those who dared to think beyond these denominational mergers, proposing greater cooperation among denominations. The Presbyterian principal of Queen's University, George Munro Grant, had actively supported both Confederation and Presbyterian union. Once those consolidations were achieved his attention quickly turned to presenting his vision for transconfessional "organic union" — a consolidation on a grander scale than what any of the denominations in Canada had accomplished. However, it was the Anglicans who actually forwarded the first official proposal for union across denominational lines, spurred on by the discussion of the issue at their 1888 Lambeth Conference. They made important overtures at a Conference on Christian Union held in Toronto in 1889. However, discussions foundered on the issue of apostolic succession, acceptance of which the Lambeth Conference had insisted.

The Congregationalists, Presbyterians, and Methodists pursued church union most vigorously in the 1890s. Serious negotiations followed an invitation from William Patrick, principal of Manitoba College, when he was sent as the Presbyterian representative to the Methodist General Conference in 1902. N.K. Clifford has observed that supporters of church union in these denominations soon developed a tendency to present their arguments for union with an air of inevitability: denominational union was simply mirroring the political achievement of Confederation. Their optimism was expressed well in the title of one of Congregationalist William T. Gunn's pamphlets: the unionists were "Uniting Three United Churches." He linked this new church to evangelical Protestantism's vision of a Christian Canada, proposing "beyond — other unions still, until we have one great National Church of all that love God, working together to make our Dominion His Dominion from sea to sea and all the kingdoms of this world the kingdoms of our Lord and His Christ." By 1908, representatives of the three uniting denominations had agreed on a Basis of Union for what became in 1925 The United Church of Canada. In the meantime many local churches across Canada (particularly in newly-settled areas of Saskatchewan) formed union congregations.

Church union was made possible in part by the downplaying of creeds that was characteristic of many Protestant groups in this period. Groups as theologically diverse as the Disciples of Christ and the Plymouth Brethren emphasized the importance of Christian unity and proposed solutions that they hoped would diminish creedal differences. In some cases, though, disagreement over proposals for unity served only to create new divisions in local congregations. Creeds remained critically important for some. It was a creed, the Westminster Confession, that became the symbol of the "continuing Presbyterian" resistance to union.

Missionary zeal and interdenominational cooperation (though some denominational competition still persisted) also gave practical expression to "His Dominion" in personal religiosity, organizational structures, and social engagement. Historian John Webster Grant has suggested that this missionary spirit "was probably never decisive in making Canadians what they were, but it went a long way toward determining what they thought they ought to be and accordingly toward shaping their view of the significance of Canada's existence as a nation." The nation of Canada had been formed, but the task of making Canadians of its citizens remained. For many Protestants, cultivating Canadian "character" was linked to legitimating the existence of Canada as a nation. The prospect of creating a distinctively Canadian character was a unifying idea which fostered a sense of destiny. A pervasive sense of national righteousness provided inspiration for the moral and spiritual crusades of evangelical Protestantism. The vision of "His Dominion" provided an ideological and theological framework for a wide variety of voluntary organizations — temperance societies, the Lord's Day Alliance, missionary societies, to name only a few. There was little resistance in Protestant circles to the evangelical moralism that undergirded this vision, although those with high-church Anglican sympathies and some Lutherans were skeptical or showed little interest in it.

CENSUS FIGURES, 1871-1911

YEAR	TOTAL POP.	METHODIST	PRESBY.	ANGLICAN	BAPTIST	ROMAN CATHOLIC
PRINCE EDWARD ISLAND						
1871	94,021					
1881	108,891	13,485 (12.4%)	33,835 (31.1%)	7,192 (6.6%)	6,236 (5.7%)	47,115 (43.2%)
1891	109,078	13,596 (12.4%)	33,072 (30.3%)	6,646 (6.1%)	6,265 (5.7%)	47,837 (43.9%)
1901	103,259	13,402 (13.0%)	30,750 (29.8%)	5,976 (5.8%)	5,905 (5.7%)	45,796 (44.4%)
1911	93,728	12,209 (13.0%)	27,509 (29.3%)	4,939 (5.3%)	5,372 (5.7%)	41,994 (44.4%)
NOVA SCOTIA						
1871	387,800	40,871 (10.5%)	103,539 (26.4%)	55,124 (14.2%)	73,558 (19.0%)	102,001 (26.3%)
1881	440,572	50,811 (11.5%)	112,488 (25.5%)	60,255 (13.7%)	83,761 (19.0%)	117,487 (26.6%)
1891	450,396	54,195 (12.0%)	108,952 (24.2%)	64,410 (14.3%)	83,122 (18.4%)	122,452 (27.1%)
1901	459,574	57,490 (12.5%)	106,381 (23.1%)	66,107 (14.9%)	83,241 (18.1%)	129,578 (28.2%)
1911	492,338	57,606 (11.7%)	109,560 (22.2%)	75,315 (15.3%)	83,854 (17.0%)	144,991 (29.4%)
NEW BRUNSWICK						
1871	285,594	29,856 (10.5%)	38,852 (13.6%)	45,481 (15.9%)	70,598 (24.7%)	96,016 (33.6%)
1881	321,233	34,514 (10.7%)	42,888 (13.4%)	46,768 (14.6)	81,092 (25.2%)	109,091 (34.0%)

Year						
1891	321,263	35,504 (11.1%)	40,639 (12.6%)	43,095 (13.4%)	79,649 (24.8%)	115,961 (36.1%)
1901	331,120	35,963 (10.9%)	39,496 (11.9%)	42,005 (12.7%)	80,874 (24.4%)	125,698 (37.9%)
1911	351,889	34,558 (9.8%)	39,207 (11.1%)	42,864 (12.2%)	82,106 (23.3%)	144,889 (41.1%)

QUEBEC

Year						
1871	1,191,516	34,100 (2.9%)	46,165 (3.9%)	62,449 (5.2%)	8,690 (0.7%)	1,019,850 (85.6%)
1881	1,359,027	39,161 (2.9%)	50,287 (3.7%)	68,797 (5.1%)	8,853 (0.6%)	1,170,718 (86.1%)
1891	1,488,535	39,544 (2.6%)	52,673 (3.5%)	75,472 (5.1%)	7,991 (0.5%)	1,291,709 (86.8%)
1901	1,648,898	42,014 (2.5%)	58,013 (3.5%)	81,630 (4.9%)	8,483 (0.5%)	1,429,260 (86.7%)
1911	2,002,712	42,646 (2.1%)	64,132 (3.2%)	103,812 (5.2%)	9,258 (0.5%)	1,724,693 (86.1%)

ONTARIO

Year						
1871	1,620,851	462,264 (28.5%)	356,442 (22.0%)	330,995 (20.4%)	86,723 (5.3%)	274,162 (16.9%)
1881	1,923,228	591,503 (30.7%)	417,749 (21.7%)	366,539 (19.0%)	106,680 (5.5%)	320,839 (16.7%)
1891	2,114,321	654,033 (30.9%)	453,147 (21.4%)	385,999 (18.3%)	106,047 (5.0%)	358,300 (16.9%)
1901	2,182,947	666,388 (30.5%)	477,386 (21.9%)	368,191 (16.9%)	117,819 (5.3%)	390,304 (17.9%)
1911	2,523,274	671,755 (26.7%)	524,605 (20.7%)	492,435 (19.9%)	132,809 (5.3%)	486,157 (19.2%)

MANITOBA

Year						
1881	65,954	9,470 (14.4%)	14,292 (21.7%)	14,297 (21.7%)	9,449 (14.3%)	12,246 (18.6%)
1891	152,506	28,437 (18.6%)	39,001 (25.6%)	30,852 (20.2%)	16,112 (10.6%)	20,571 (13.5%)
1901	255,211	49,936 (19.6%)	65,348 (25.6%)	44,923 (17.6%)	9,168 (3.6%)	35,672 (14.0%)
1911	455,614	68,412 (15.0%)	103,661 (22.8%)	88,807 (19.5%)	14,003 (3.1%)	74,480 (16.3%)

	TOTAL	METHODIST	PRESBY.	ANGLICAN	BAPTIST	ROMAN CATHOLIC
SASKATCHEWAN						
1901	91,279	12,028 (13.1%)	16,232 (17.8%)	15,996 (17.5%)	2,416 (2.6%)	17,651 (19.3%)
1911	492,432	78,325 (15.9%)	96,564 (19.6%)	75,342 (15.3%)	18,371 (3.7%)	90,092 (18.3%)
ALBERTA						
1901	73,022	10,125 (13.9%)	11,597 (15.9%)	9,634 (13.2%)	3,010 (4.1%)	15,464 (21.2%)
1911	374,663	61,844 (16.5%)	66,344 (17.7%)	55,602 (14.9%)	19,491 (5.2%)	61,902 (16.5%)
BRITISH COLUMBIA						
1871	36,247					
1881	49,459	3,516 (7.1%)	4,095 (8.3%)	7,804 (15.8%)	434 (0.9%)	10,043 (20.3%)
1891	98,173	14,298 (14.6%)	15,284 (15.6%)	23,619 (24.1%)	3,098 (3.2%)	20,843 (21.2%)
1901	178,657	25,047 (14.0%)	34,081 (19.1%)	40,996 (22.9%)	6,506 (3.6%)	33,639 (18.8%)
1911	392,480	52,132 (13.3%)	82,125 (20.9%)	100,952 (25.7%)	17,228 (4.4%)	58,397 (14.9%)
CANADA						
1871	3,689,257	567,091 (15.4%)	544,998 (14.8%)	494,049 (13.4%)	245,805 (6.7%)	1,492,029 (40.4%)
1881	4,324,810	742,981 (17.2%)	676,165 (15.6%)	574,818 (13.3%)	296,525 (6.9%)	1,791,982 (41.4%)
1891	4,833,239	847,765 (17.5%)	755,326 (15.6%)	646,059 (13.4%)	303,839 (6.2%)	1,992,017 (41.2%)
1901	5,371,315	916,886 (17.1%)	842,442 (15.7%)	681,494 (12.7%)	318,005 (5.9%)	2,229,600 (41.5%)
1911	7,206,643	1,079,892 (15.0%)	1,115,324 (15.5%)	1,043,017 (14.8%)	382,666 (5.3%)	2,833,041 (39.3%)

In the four decades after Confederation denominational patterns and relationships in the regions of Canada changed significantly (See census charts). This was only partly the result of the evangelistic zeal that was characteristic of the times. The growth of particular denominations was also a reflection of immigration patterns. The social and economic realities of Canadian life in the first few decades after Confederation, combined with the arrival of immigrants who did not seem to match the picture of the citizen of "His Dominion," at first dashed the hopes of those who expected great things of the new nation. Canada had been created out of only four provinces, there was little interaction between the Maritimes and Central Canada, and the vast unsettled western frontier had yet to be incorporated. In 1891 Goldwin Smith, a historian and prominent political commentator, spoke for continentalists who saw little sense of national purpose and no future apart from joining the United States when he described a country that was merely "a number of fishing rods tied together by the ends." Business historian Michael Bliss has suggested that there was scarcely more to hold together Canada's *ad hoc*, confused, and partly contradictory developmental policies than a vague desire to imitate the economic progress of the United States. By that standard, Canada's economic growth after 1867 did not measure up, despite the railroad, free homesteads on the prairies, an open door to immigrants, and the tariff protection of the National Policy.

Dreams and disappointment transformed late-nineteenth century Canada into a nation of people on the move — from rural communities to cities, from east to west, and from all regions of Canada to the United States. Women who left rural communities usually remained in Canada; men more often went west or south. Many Protestants, uprooted from both their social class and local backgrounds, fit the description of those the American historian Oscar Handlin has called "internal immigrants": persons who could neither identify completely with older elites nor the foreign immigrants. For these "immigrants," their particular type of Protestantism helped to establish an identity that ethnicity did not provide.

Some were well served in their new environs by the ascetic, self-disciplined lifestyle and the social networks of their denominations. One successful wholesaler, Methodist John Macdonald, provided another enterprising Methodist, Timothy Eaton, with a line of credit to launch his retail business. Many successful businessmen became very active in their new church homes and their local congregations were recipients of both their talents and their money. In "Hogtown," bacon made a millionaire out of Joseph Flavelle, a member of

Toronto's Sherbourne Street Methodist Church. The Methodist church was a major beneficiary of the fortune which Hart Massey's farm implements made. In Winnipeg, Methodist James Ashdown became a highly successful hardware wholesaler whose wealth made him a force to be reckoned with in his congregation and at the fledgling Wesley College. In Toronto Baptist circles, the family of William McMaster, president of the Bank of Commerce, helped to set the agenda for both Jarvis Street Baptist and the university named after its major benefactor. The cost of the auditorium of Walmer Road Baptist in the same city was shared by Joseph Shenstone and the farm machine-making family of its first pastor, Elmore Harris.

But not all found the cities so hospitable. Many who hoped to find new opportunities discovered that the late nineteenth century was a time of uneven growth and uncertainty in Canada's future. Ironically, consolidation may have been helped by the challenging social and economic circumstances which at first defied the national ideals and mission rhetoric of "His Dominion." Though church leaders in the various denominations spoke of the Kingdom in national terms, they met with increasingly diverse regions with very different needs. The economic recession characteristic of the first three decades after Confederation profoundly affected religious life. The pages of denominational publications made frequent reference to the difficulties of ministering to communities whose growth was either stagnant or even in decline. For all the hopes of settling the West, the number of persons who moved there did not match expectations. Many in the Maritimes and Central Canada who sought greener pastures were more inclined to look south to the United States rather than west to the Canadian prairies. Hopes were raised with the completion of the Canadian Pacific Railroad in 1885 and the discovery of Klondike gold. But in general, the economic realities of life in late nineteenth-century Canada fell far short of the predictions of politicians and railway promoters. Even in the west, the mood of optimism that had accompanied the construction of the CPR turned to pessimism after its completion. Newcomers, discouraged with prairie farming, deserted their farms and land values collapsed. Hopes for Canada's future were clouded as several hundred thousand moved to the United States between 1880 and the end of the century. As one observer noted, if the Canadian-born population were counted, Boston, not Winnipeg, was the third-largest Canadian city.

The major Protestant denominations met the challenge of the west with proposals that often entailed greater cooperation between regions. Robert Machray, the Anglican bishop of Rupert's Land who arrived from England in 1865 to take up his appointment, persuasively connected the needs of the home mission work in the west to the creation of a national synod. Anglican delegates met in 1890 at Winnipeg to draw up a plan forming the organizational basis for the General Synod of the Church of England in Canada. Its first meeting was held in Toronto three years later. The Presbyterians took up winning the west with new vigour in 1881 after the appointment of James Robertson as a superintendent of missions. They enjoyed success in attracting members in the west that was unsurpassed by other Protestant denominations. James Woodsworth helped to pioneer the westward expansion of Methodism after his arrival at Portage la Prairie, Manitoba in 1882. Here he was still under the jurisdiction of Toronto Conference, which at that time stretched from Belleville to the Pacific. The Methodists formed a separate conference for the northwest in 1883 and named Woodsworth superintendent of Methodist Missions for Manitoba and the Canadian Northwest in 1889. That same year Alexander Grant accepted a call to First Baptist in Winnipeg, opening a new chapter in the story of Baptist work in western Canada that had begun in 1873. British Columbia's first Baptists arrived from the state of Washington and were at first associated with American Baptist organizations. The Convention of Baptist Churches of British Columbia, set up in 1897, oversaw the province's church extension. The region became part of the Baptist Convention (later Union) of Western Canada in 1907. The Lutherans set up a congregation in Manitoba for Icelanders in 1876 and a congregation for German-speaking settlers was organized in 1879. However, Lutheranism showed no significant growth until the arrival of large numbers of German and Scandinavian immigrants at the turn of the century.

The advantage in a situation of shrinking resources and keen competition often went to denominations with an efficient organizational structure. Some historians who have examined the mergers of these decades have suggested it is more than coincidence that the groundwork for several significant denominational mergers was laid in the years during which the Canadian "frontier" was, in practical terms, closed. Another trend was evident in the churches as well: not all regions were affected by national expansion in the same way. In the case of the Presbyterians, for example, Toronto replaced Montreal after 1875 as the newly united denomination's administrative centre. Typical of Maritime regional fortunes at this time, Halifax's institutional role declined as Winnipeg's significance rose.

Added to these organizational complexities were challenges from new religious movements and intellectual currents. The churches were not always quick to realize how profoundly they were being affected by these changes, and certainly few anticipated them. Responding to the stir created by the publication of Henry Drummond's *Natural Law in the Spiritual World* in 1886, an editorial in Methodism's official denominational paper confidently assured readers that "there is no sign of a probability that the Methodist Church will have any occasion to change its ground respecting free will, human responsibility, and the universal redemption" on account of the teaching of Drummond's book "or any other book that is ever likely to be written." Churches experienced the new challenges in a number of ways. Methodism, for example, appeared to come through the controversies over evolution and higher criticism relatively unscathed. Particularly at the popular level, the challenges presented by the Plymouth Brethren and the holiness movement were more troublesome because these movements presented approaches to conversion and sanctification that were at odds with traditional Methodist piety. The impact of these movements, both important strands in what came to be known in the twentieth century as fundamentalism, was much greater than their small number of formal adherents suggests. Denominations which had no organizational links with them were nonetheless influenced by them in a variety of ways. Their popular appeal was enhanced and extended when some of the major urban revivalists propagated their distinctive doctrines.

Canadians were introduced to the ideas of the Plymouth Brethren in the 1860s and 1870s. The movement drew its inspiration from the millennarianism of John Nelson Darby who visited North America seven times in that period. He spent most of his time in Chicago, Detroit, and St. Louis, travelling from the American mid-west to New York by way of Canada. Darby's division of history into "dispensations" and his expectation of the "premillennial" return of Christ to establish an earthly kingdom were distinguishing marks of "Plymouthism." But these were not the only features that created dissension among evangelical Protestants. Methodists found assumptions in Plymouthism's presentation of conversion that were at odds with Methodist revivalism. The group's emphasis on the declarations of Scripture regarding belief in forgiveness through the blood of Christ's atonement differed from Methodism's emphasis on repentance, the witness of the Holy Spirit, and the fruits of regeneration as evidence of conversion. Plymouthism's approach to conversion, also held by the most prominent Calvinist evangelists, signalled a way of becoming, being, and remaining Christian that was inherently at odds with Methodist theology. The prominent

Methodist theologian Nathanael Burwash of Victoria College credited it with having worked a subtle and dangerous change in religious life in the 1860s. Popularized through evangelism, it had reduced the work of the Spirit in the religious life to an intellectual process. What Burwash called "believe the Gospel" evangelism did not lead to assurance of faith through the witness of the Spirit, as taught by John Wesley.

Concern extended beyond the Methodist denominations as many communities found themselves divided over evangelism. In Sarnia, the Free Church Presbyterian minister James Duncan was among the harshest critics of the evangelistic methods of the Plymouth Brethren. But criticism did not run just one way: Plymouth Brethren evangelists reportedly disparaged revivals that required a long sorrowing period that led to self-righteousness and made a virtue of feeling. They criticized the prominence which groups such as the Methodists gave to testimonies of the conversion experience, attacking in particular the testimonies of women. The propositional piety of Plymouthism threatened to undercut the influence of the revival tradition associated with (but not restricted to) Methodism by challenging its more experiential piety. For those influenced by the Plymouth Brethren, salvation was grounded in intellectual assent to biblically-derived propositions that enabled a convert to answer the question "Are you saved?" with a confidence that Methodism's "witness of the Spirit" could not give.

Problems within evangelical Protestantism came from other quarters as the interest in holiness grew. As it had in the 1850s, preoccupation with holiness surged again in the 1880s and 1890s to the point that it became an interdenominational concern. As may be expected, there was no agreement on how holiness was attained or what it entailed. The result was the emergence of a number of distinct movements which in some cases gave rise to new denominations. The Free Methodists, organized in the United States and introduced in Canada in 1876, began to draw more interest. Other movements appeared first in Canada, among them the Holiness Movement Church organized by a former Methodist minister, Ralph Cecil Horner. Horner was convinced that he was called to be an evangelist. After his ordination, he was appointed as a Conference evangelist, which he understood to be a recognition of his special call. Horner soon found that not all accepted this interpretation of his ordination. The emotional displays that often accompanied his evangelistic work contributed to his difficulties with denominational leaders, but his unwillingness to submit to ecclesiastical authority was deemed at least as much a factor. Horner felt betrayed when, instead of reappointment as Conference evangelist in 1890, he was given a pastoral charge. He refused to accept the position and resisted all attempts to regulate his evangelistic activities. Eventually he was officially "deposed."

Meanwhile other holiness movements developed independently in other parts of Canada. Nelson Burns organized the Canada Holiness Association in 1879 after learning about holiness through the writings of Phoebe Palmer, an American who earlier had led holiness camp meetings in Canada. The radical perfectionism implicit in his idea of Divine guidance drew sharp criticism from many who generally supported the holiness movement, Methodism's General Superintendent Albert Carman being a case in point. Particularly troublesome were the views Burns presented in 1885 in his paper, the *Expositor of Holiness*: when God was accepted as absolute Guide, no regrettable mistakes could occur in that person's life.

The Keswick movement was less contentious than the methods and beliefs of holiness teachers such as Horner and Burns. Yet evangelicalism was divided over whether sanctification suppressed the sinful nature, as Calvinists generally believed, or whether sinful nature was eradicated, as Wesleyan Arminiansim generally believed. In the Maritimes, Baptists experienced a holiness split in 1888 when a number of Free Christian Baptists ministers left their denomination to form the Reformed Baptists. The Reformed Baptists would eventually, in the twentieth century, become part of the American-based Wesleyan Church.

These new movements made little headway numerically but the interest in them signalled dissatisfaction with prevailing approaches to the religious life. These movements evidenced some of the fissures along which evangelicalism would later divide. Some who were coping with economic and geographical dislocation found the newer movements better able to meet their particular needs. Whereas at the time of the first census taken after Confederation 80% of Canadians lived in rural areas (that is, outside an incorporated city or town), by the 1911 census the country was 45% urban. Newcomers arriving in the city from rural areas sometimes found that a denomination with a new name offered a simpler and more familiar type of worship service than the sophisticated settings which appealed to the urban middle and upper classes of their own denomination. S.D. Clark has linked the premium which an affluent new business class placed on an educated clergy and beautiful buildings to the growth of new denominations around the turn of the century. Some of the new movements that would make a considerable impact on the religious pattern of Canada in the twentieth century were barely visible at the beginning of that century. The Pentecostal movement, for example, claimed only 515 adherents in the 1911 census. While voluntary societies provided opportunities for friendship as well as purposeful activity to ease the difficulties of transition for many, not all churches proved able to meet the demands of this new situation.

At that same time that different approaches to evangelism and holiness were troubling Christians in some circles, others were grappling with the challenges posed by evolution and higher criticism. Evolution was a pervasive idea with implications extending far beyond the natural sciences. It changed the outlook of the general populace from a static to a more dynamic world view. Although Darwinianism is sometimes posited as having had a devastating effect on traditional orthodoxy, there was considerable optimism that a reconciliation between religion and science might be reached. While this optimism may have been premature and even unfounded, there is every indication that it was genuine and widespread. The concept of theistic evolution popularized specialized ideas into widely held social attitudes. While the popularizers failed to convince many in the scientific community, they won out with the public. Those who calmly insisted that evolution and theology were compatible outmatched in numbers and influence those who argued the reverse. By the 1890s evolution had become almost a fashionable creed, equated with progress, advance, and improvement. Even when evolution was questioned, it was often because of its use as a concept of development, not as a theory of origins. Believing that evolution was the way that change happened in the realm of the mind and morals, as well as in creation, seemed to throw shadows over belief in a personal God. By encompassing a theory of progressive moral development, evolution appeared to restrict the freedom of God to act in history. It made God's action unnecesary by substituting the rise of humanity for the Fall of Genesis. This gave to the direction of history an optimism which Darwin himself had not guaranteed.

The extension of scientific methods into new areas of inquiry also had a considerable impact on biblical studies. Advanced for many years in Europe, the methods of "higher criticism" made headway in North American circles in the last quarter of the nineteenth century. Before this time, biblical scholarship had been concerned with studying the original language — in other words, a linguistic rather than historical study of the Bible. With the historical approach of higher criticism came the presupposition that the Bible was like any other historical document. Transmission of new ideas about the Bible was aided by the publication of the Revised Version of the New Testament in 1881. The fanfare accompanying its distribution publicized information about discrepancies in the documents used for the translation. It was clear that the "originals" were no longer available. It was in this decade that Canadian scholars trained in the methods of historical criticism found positions in Canadian universities.

In some circles the spread of biblical criticism moved slowly. Nathanael Burwash did not present it to the theological students at Victoria College until the mid-1880s and was careful to distinguish his "reverent criticism" from the destructive type associated with the rationalistic German critics. Acceptance of the new approach to the Bible was by no means automatic. Salem Bland, who in the twentieth century became one of Canada's leading advocates of the social gospel, at first denounced those who introduced him to higher criticism at a Queen's Alumni Conference in 1893. He protested that if there were scholars determined to pursue such unprofitable studies, they ought either to keep their findings to themselves or at least publish them in highly professional publications that no ordinary Christian would be tempted to read!

Biblical scholars did not, of course, heed Bland's advice and they introduced Canadian theological students to these new methods, much to the consternation of those holding more traditional views. At Victoria University George Workman, an Old Testament professor, was eventually dismissed from the theological faculty when he presented his controversial views in the 1890s. He was also asked to leave Wesleyan College in Montreal in 1907 for holding doctrinal positions that were deemed to be unorthodox. In 1909 another Methodist, George Jackson, came under scrutiny for a lecture he gave at the Y.M.C.A. shortly before taking up a position as professor of English Bible at Victoria University. The General Conference held the following year supported Jackson by refusing to condemn the teaching of higher criticism at Canadian Methodist colleges.

Other institutions saw similar developments. McMaster University allowed I.G. Matthews to present his interpretation of the Old Testament despite criticism in many Baptist circles. Accusations of doctrinal heterodoxy followed theological innovators in other denominations. Presbyterians debated over what to do with persons who had doubts about the doctrines of the Westminster Confession, in particular its presentation of eternal punishment. Theological professors and ministers, among them John Campbell of Montreal's Presbyterian College and D.J. Macdonnell, were questioned but compromises were reached in order to accommodate a variety of theological viewpoints.

In spite of these social and intellectual changes, many old

attitudes remained entrenched. Most notably, divisions between Protestantism and Catholicism remained. At the time of Confederation Quebec was overwhelmingly Roman Catholic. Protestant groups were unsuccessful in attempts to change this situation. Baptists organized the Union des Eglises Baptistes de langue francais in 1868 and the Presbyterians set up a Board of French Evangelism in 1875. The colourful Father Charles Chiniquy worked with a number of Protestant groups after he was "defrocked" by the Catholic church. His evangelistic missions to French Catholics, begun in 1875, became associated with the distribution of anti-Catholic literature, such as an allegedly true account of the "Awful Disclosures of Maria Monk" about life in a Quebec convent, first published in 1836. Several denominations made efforts to capitalize on some dissatisfaction within Roman Catholicism in the aftermath of the First Vatican Council, but none was able to make significant permanent inroads. On the other hand, Roman Catholicism won few converts from Protestantism in Quebec. Like non-English groups outside Quebec, the English minority in Quebec linked their cultural preservation to their religion. The descendants of the New Englanders who settled the Eastern Townships of Quebec remained Protestant, and pockets of Protestantism could be found in the Gaspe Peninsula and the Ottawa Valley as well. In Montreal, Protestants, especially the Anglicans and Presbyterians, exerted commercial and political influence that far outweighed their numbers.

Quebec was by no means the only locus for Catholic- Protestant tensions. Efforts at evangelization in places that had long been Catholic strongholds, such as areas of New Brunswick, were not uncommon. Settlers to the west were often preceded by both the RCMP and the churches, but this was more by accident than design — Protestants were able to keep up with change initially because of the slower than anticipated growth. This enabled them to make their mark in important ways as communities were established. For many years the native peoples of frontier areas were the main recipients of these efforts but attempts were made to make Protestants of as many newcomers as possible. Nevertheless Manitoba entered Confederation in 1870 with the Roman Catholic church in the majority.

The unpredictability of the religious make-up of areas of western settlement created by the massive influx of immigrants who brought their religion with them soon added to the complexity of dealing with pluralism. As the religious pattern in Manitoba changed over the next two decades, a religious controversy began to brew. The protest of the Metis in the North-West led by Louis Riel was quelled in 1869 and the Manitoba Act passed the next year, but not before the execution of Thomas Scott, an Orangeman and former Ontarian. The memory of Scott's execution was kept alive in both Ontario and Manitoba and used to fan anti-Catholic agitation. In English-speaking Canada there was little sympathy for Louis Riel when, after returning from exile to lead another unsuccessful rebellion in 1885, he was hanged. Longstanding linguistic and religious differences were heightened by the incident. In this climate the schools became arenas for testing the limits and power of the churches. Setting the tone for the debate were religious leaders such as the Roman Catholic archbishop A.A. Tache and Presbyterian George Bryce.

Educational rights of minorities had become a contentious issue in several areas of Canada. The British North America Act had given the provinces jurisdiction over education, so each one was legislatively free to deal with religion and language in the schools as they saw fit. In New Brunswick, for example, legislation in 1871 forbade the teaching of religion and French- language instruction in tax-supported schools, although some modifications were eventually made. Schools for English-speaking Protestants in Quebec were protected by provision of an autonomous school system. Separate schools for Catholic children were constitutionally guaranteed in Ontario, but subsequent legislation in 1892 and 1901 restricted them. In Manitoba the dual-school system was replaced in 1890 and a non-denominational system that no longer provided rights for instruction in minority languages. When French-speaking Manitobans protested, the federal Conservative party promised to remedy the situation.

The Manitoba Schools Controversy consequently became an issue in the 1896 federal election. Fearing that federal intervention in this matter would set a dangerous precedent for interference in Quebec, Wilfrid Laurier and his Liberal party fought and won the election by taking the side of Manitoba's right to provincial autonomy in educational matters. A compromise was worked out the following year providing for religious instruction outside class hours and provision of French schools in some cases. Minority education again arose as a contentious issue when Saskatchewan and Alberta became provinces in 1905.

Laurier's election victory seemed to augur well for Canada and the turn of a new century coincided with a remarkable turnabout in the nation's fortunes. Whereas business had come of age in the United States by the late nineteenth century; the scale, structure, and organization of economic activity in Canada had remained small, owner-operated, and competitive. It was not until after 1900 that market forces, capital, new technologies, and mergers in various sectors of the economy combined to produce a Canadian version of the "big business" that we associate with the nineteenth century in other industrialized nations. The "Laurier boom," fuelled by Canada's resource industry, brought almost uninterrupted economic growth between 1900 and 1913. The long-awaited immigrants finally arrived to fill the prairies. The availability of jobs in Canada stemmed the tide of emigration to the south. The flow of capital northward indicated that even Americans were convinced of Canada's future. News of large profits was commonplace and there seemed to be no end to prosperity. Laurier's boast that this would be "Canada's century" suddenly seemed to have more substance than most election promises.

With economic prosperity a pattern emerged in Canada that was well underway in the United States. Aided by a range of technological innovations, business underwent an organizational revolution that signalled the passage of capitalism from a competitive to corporate stage. Mergers, acquisitions, and trusts became more commonplace. Multifunctional and multilocational corporations gradually subsumed small businesses. The wealthy and even the middle class poured their money into new investment strategies, disregarding warnings from the churches about "speculation." The repercussions of this revolution were felt in the political, intellectual, and cultural spheres. By propagating new educational and scientific ways of looking at the world and modelling new life-styles, corporate capitalism began to reshape everyday life. The principles of "scientific management" and assembly line production transformed the workplace. The growth of the service sector created new career opportunities for women. The middle class mushroomed with the addition of "white collar" workers to its previous complement of skilled workers, shop owners, small manufacturers, farmers, and members of the professions. Technology revolutionized the home as well. Increased productivity brought the price of such new consumer items as washing machines, and eventually even automobiles, within sight. By the turn of the century advertising had developed into a sophisticated art of persuasion designed to create a desire to consume rather than simply to inform the public about goods and services. Timothy Eaton's mailorder catalogue evolved from a simple flyer in 1884 to compete with the Bible as the most widely distributed publication in Canada (Michael Bliss guesses that it was probably better read!). Railroads transported many from the country to the city. Newspapers, mass marketing, and motion pictures standardized urban culture and carried it to the country.

Though accomplished remarkably peacefully, such extensive reconstruction was not without cost. Rural depopulation remained a problem. The profits of prosperous times were not shared equally. For example, in the first two decades of the twentieth century, real wages for the working class in Toronto did not keep pace with price increases. Though working conditions in factories slowly improved, this may have been for greater efficiency rather than for humanitarian reasons. Technological advances in transportation made it possible for people to live further away from their place of employment. Now new suburbs such as Toronto's Parkdale or High Park appealed to many, leaving the inner city to the less affluent. Newspaper accounts apprised readers of the horrible living conditions, but cleaning up the slums only exacerbated the shortage of affordable housing for the poor. Even prosperity was not without its perils. Noting the increase in suicide rates that often accompanies good economic conditions, sociologist Emil Durkheim has suggested that such a period may contribute to instability in moral ideals that govern behaviour, making it difficult to articulate collective goals. This seems to have been the case in Canada. Many both loved and hated the changes which they were experiencing — attracted by the promises and opportunities offered, but apprehensive about the sweeping changes that were everywhere apparent.

Over this reconstruction of economic organization hung the spectre of wasteful duplication and needless competition. Farmers, bankers, workers, manufacturers, politicians, and reformers shared (for different reasons) a disenchantment with competition. Under the banner of "progressivism," they made plans to meet the challenges of this new world. They shared a growing sense of the corporative nature and connectedness of life. What J.S. Woodsworth observed about the city aptly expresses how progressives viewed everyday experience in general: "City life is like a spider's web — pull one thread and you pull every thread." Progressives combined with this a willingness to intervene in the economy — and in the lives of other people if necessary. With what one historian describes as a mix of the ethos and nineteenth-century Protestant evangelicalism, the new methods of science, and large-scale organization, they attempted to restore community purpose.

In the last decades of the nineteenth century the Canadian churches' discussion of social problems seems, in retrospect, to have been a bit like people waiting for a storm to arrive. Social problems were, of course, not new to Canada. Rural areas had long been affected by the exodus to new frontiers. Newspaper reports informed readers of the evils of British and American cities, and Canadians could find enough evidence in their own cities to believe them. Yet in a sense Canadians first experienced religious progressivism later in their own economic development than did the British or the Americans. Other countries' proposals for reform were modified to suit the Canadian situation even before the full brunt of social change was felt.

From this side of the cultural shift that took place in the early twentieth century, it appears that what happened to Protestantism was part of a broader cultural "organizing process" which affected virtually every social institution. The turn-of- the-century changes spelled the beginning of the end of the old evangelical Protestant consensus. The new "organizing process" set in motion the formation of new alliances along lines of fissure that had been developing for decades. A movement within Protestantism congealed around the idea of loyalty to the traditions of the Protestantism of the past; another gathered under the banner of a forward-looking progressive approach to the Christian life. One movement claimed to spurn the "modernism" that the other embraced; but it is clear in retrospect that neither resisted modernism's charms. The extent of the reorganization was at first obscured by a variety of overlapping concerns that made possible a more or less peaceful coexistence. Even progressives at first retained a lingering confidence in the evangelical consensus that had elsewhere been eroded, since old evangelistic methods were not put to the test in Canada as quickly. Many denominations developed new approaches to evangelism such as mass evangelism, city missions, and social reform, but older assumptions about evangelism were entwined with them.

Among the proposals to save the city and win the west, none were more prominent than evangelistic campaigns. Richard Allen estimates that the appearance of evangelists and revival teams became more common in Canada after 1884. In hindsight it is tempting to read the enthusiasm for winning not only Canada but the world for Christ as a desperate effort to shore up a dying way of religious life. To do so overlooks how the initial success of these campaigns in the late nineteenth century bolstered confidence that older approaches to evangelism were still effective. An intermingling of old and new was apparent in the work of the professional evangelists. While in one sense they merely conducted the old protracted meetings on a grander scale, they also introduced new ideas and practices.

A number of Canadian evangelists, including the most celebrated team of H.T. Crossley and John E. Hunter, visited the major population centres. Women held revival meetings in smaller churches. Even large Gothic churches were the scenes of revivals. William Howland, who eventually became mayor of Toronto, attended evangelistic meetings at St. James Cathedral conducted by American evangelist W.S. Rainsford in 1877. According to one of Howland's biographers, Rainsford found Howland a conventionally devout Anglican and left him a fervent evangelical Christian. D.L. Moody was another of the prominent American revivalists invited to Canada. At the nine services he held in Toronto's Metropolitan Church in 1885, the "Methodist Cathedral" was filled to capacity. It was estimated that at least 25,000 persons, half the adult population of the city, heard him. Among them were nearly 300 ministers from various denominations who gathered for a special ministerial conference, an event that Moody reportedly said would have been impossible even twenty years previous. In Winnipeg a group of Presbyterians led by Principal John Mark King of Manitoba College succeeded in bringing Moody to the city in 1897. Crowds estimated at over two thousand at some of the meetings received Moody and other evangelists enthusiastically. For nearly thirty years Crossley and Hunter travelled across Canada, visiting every major town and city in the country. The more than 100,000 converts who walked down the aisle to the penitent bench during this time included, according to a newspaper account of one of their Ottawa meetings, the Anglican Prime Minister John A. Macdonald.

The spirit of cooperation displayed by many Protestants during such evangelistic campaigns grew, at times, into missionary and reform activities. Evangelicals of many denominations supported the hospitals, schools, and industries set up by Wilfred Grenfell, a medical missionary inspired by D.L. Moody to go to Labrador in 1892. Yet, alongside these notable demonstrations of interdenominational cooperation, there were signs of some of the problems which would later divide Protestantism. Recalling the work of his father and Crossley, Ernest Crossley Hunter maintained that they were the only evangelists on the continent who did not preach about the "second coming." More specifically, premillennialism became a striking feature of evangelistic preaching. Since it was associated with the dispensationalism of the Plymouth Brethren, those who had difficulty with that approach to piety found themselves torn between their support for evangelistic preaching and their opposition to some ideas propagated by it. At biblical and prophetic conferences held at Niagara-on-the-Lake, Ontario, dispensational premillennialism and an approach to the Bible that insisted on the inerrancy of the "original autographs" were popularized during the same decades that higher criticism was introduced to Canadian theological students. A growing interest in the movement was exhibited by persons of diverse social and denominational backgrounds. The closely-knit group in Toronto which supported ventures such as the Toronto Bible Training School (later Ontario Bible College), the Bible League of Canada, the Willard Tract Depository, and missionary enterprises included the president of the Toronto Board of Trade and mayor of Toronto William Howland, as well as some of the most successful leaders in civic and business affairs. In these ventures they demonstrated a strong sense of commitment to Christian unity; yet there was no lasting consensus about what that unity entailed. Many were pessimistic about the prospects of achieving union before the time of the return of Christ; and yet their expectation of that event was a bond that held them together.

Professional revivalism was not the only attempt made to deal with the new challenges facing the churches. New associations and organizations emerged which showed an intermingling of old and new. These, however, eventually demonstrated as well the growing tensions within Protestantism. The most visible of these was the Salvation Army, a group which had grown out of the holiness movement. The Army found a promising situation in Canada when it was introduced by English immigrants in 1882. It began its work at a time when some of the larger denominations, notably the Methodists, were experiencing the difficulties of their recent mergers. The growth of the Salvation Army in its early years was impressive. By the end of 1884, the Army boasted an army of seventy-three corps, thirty- five outposts divided into five divisions, under the command of 142 officers. The Army captured attention in a variety of ways — initially with its noisy parades complete with bands, banners, and quickly growing ranks, but perhaps most effectively in the long run with its social work among the poor. The publication of founder William Booth's book *In Darkest England and the Way Out* generated good public relations and heightened interest in the work of city missions. Although these Christian soldiers were ridiculed and even jailed for disturbing the peace, their work inspired other groups to work with the religiously and socially neglected.

Some of the wealthier churches responded to this challenge by funding downtown missions. In Winnipeg, a Methodist Sunday school teacher named Dolly Maguire asked to give up her regular class to organize one especially for immigrant children. The class quickly outgrew the space provided inside the church. A large lean-to outside the church and a rented tent soon proved to be too small and so the mission moved to a building near the C.P.R. station. Outside the building a large sign in eight languages welcomed people with the words: "A House of Prayer for all People." The mission soon picked up the name "All Peoples' Mission." Like many of the others established in this period, the mission provided religious teaching and, after staff additions in 1893, a broad range of social services. Besides Sunday school classes, there were prayer meetings held three nights a week, house-to-house visitation, relief aid to the sick and the poor, and employment bureau, mothers' meetings, and night schools. Methodists expanded their city mission activity in Toronto after a hall was built in 1894 by H.A. Massey in memory of his son Fred Victor. The work initiated there by Mary Sheffield was supported with workers and funds from five nearby churches.

Many other denominations undertook ambitious mission work projects. After supporting several small ventures in Toronto, Walmer Road Baptist launched what was to become the largest outreach program in Canadian Baptist history. Building on the work begun at Walmer Road by Nellie MacFarland, Memorial Institute started its work in 1912 in an ethnically mixed area of the city with a staff of six workers, including MacFarland. By the end of its first year, the staff of the Institute, aided by 145 volunteers, was working with over 7,000 persons a month. The program offered educational, recreational, employment, and medical services for all ages in addition to religious services. There were even separate meetings for some of the more numerous ethnic groups. The Presbyterians established similar programs, notably St. Christopher House in Toronto and Robertson Memorial Institute in Winnipeg, both organized in 1912. The parish halls of some Anglican churches became centres for work with the poor and the movement for free pews was a recognition of the plight of the poor. In addition to providing social services, Anglo-Catholics sought to emphasize ceremony and colour in worship as a way of providing important elements of what they believed was missing in the everyday life of the poor. Along with social services, evangelical Anglicans organized Bible classes, evangelistic services, Sunday schools, and clubs.

City mission work provided unique opportunities for women, as they were still excluded from the ordained ministry. Some became workers in university settlement houses such as the one established by Sara Libby Carson in Toronto. For others the denominational deaconess order was a route to recognition of service to Christ that in some (though not all) cases even involved a salary, albeit a small one. In 1893 the Church of England made the first move to involve women in the work of the church in this way when evangelicals in that denomination opened the Deaconess and Missionary Training Home.

The deaconess orders became an important auxiliary to the work of the city missions. The Fred Victor Mission was the largest single employer of members of the largest and most influential of the orders: the Methodist order of deaconesses founded 1894. That same year the Methodist church formally opened the Toronto Deaconess Home and Training School funded, like the Fred Victor Mission, by generous gifts from the Massey family. Other denominations made similar arrangements. In 1908 the Presbyterian Church in Canada officially instituted an order of deaconesses which was to consist of "women trained for the service and devoting their whole time thereto, and of godly women of mature years, soberminded, thoroughly tested in the school of experience." The Ewart Training Home, which had been established in 1897 to train women who intended to work in foreign missions, was directed to offer a program for deaconess training. The Congregationalist Union of Canada did not formally approve an order, but a number of local churches employed women workers who were given this title. Some Congregationalist churches had "Boards of Deaconesses" whose duties were similar to the Boards of Deacons.

While the deaconess orders offered new opportunities for women, they were not without controversy. The deaconesses were sometimes nicknamed "Protestant nuns," but denominational leaders vigorously tried to discourage further comparisons to Roman Catholic orders for women. They prohibited the taking of vows, and only reluctantly approved uniform dress and the establishment of homes where deaconesses could live together. The relationship of diaconal ministry to ordained ministry also became a difficult issue. The formation of deaconess orders seems to have become for some denominations a way of recognising the work of women in "home missions" while deferring the troublesome question of their ordination. The Presbyterian General Assembly, for example, expressly declared that recognition of the deaconess order was not to be regarded as endorsement for the ordination of women.

Old assumptions of "separate spheres" for men and women persisted in the duties thought appropriate for the deaconess: nursing, teaching, and visiting the infirm and imprisoned. Women who married were required to resign from their order. Deaconesses were denied some of the most visible activities of ordained ministry such as administering the sacraments and performing marriages. They were reimbursed at a fraction of what men, and even women outside the church, were paid for similar work. Some were, like the Anglican deaconesses, initially paid nothing at all, the explanation being so that "this work may remain wholly a service of love and mercy." Not surprising many women eventually chose employment elsewhere. Some went into social work, an expanding field in the early twentieth century, while others used their teaching and nursing abilities in secular settings. Still others continued to work for their church but left diaconal work in Canada to become missionaries abroad.

The evangelical activism of the vision of "His Dominion" was channelled into voluntary societies in order to bring Christian faith to bear on the problems of the day. Many Protestant men and women linked societal problems to alcoholic beverages and consequently became active in the temperance movement. Temperance had been promoted in some Protestant circles for many years; in fact a small Nova Scotia community in Pictou County established in 1827 what was claimed to be the first temperance society in North America. However, the cause was advanced with renewed vigour in the late Victorian period in both rural and urban areas of Canada. In some denominations even the sacramental use of wine was questioned and discontinued. After much discussion the Methodists took this step in 1883. The decision initiated a search for recipes for unfermented wine and created a market for American Methodist T.B. Welch's grape juice, developed in 1869. The Woman's Christian Temperance Movement became the largest and most effective of the newly formed societies. The Canadian branch of the W.C.T.U. (which some men claimed stood for "Women Constantly Tormenting Us") was organized in 1874 by Letitia Youmans of Picton, Ontario. Horrified by the harm she saw done to the children in her Methodist Sunday school class because of their families' use of alcohol, she became active in the movement at both the local and the national levels.

The temperance movement gained momentum from the connection made between alcohol use and poor conditions at home and at work. In their writings and speeches, women like Letitia Youmans and Nellie McClung painted graphic pictures of the evils of alcohol on families. They at first hoped that women would be able to change these dreadful conditions by the force of moral suasion. They visited saloons singing hymns and carrying Bibles, hoping to persuade owners and patrons of the rightness of their cause. In churches, schools, and even door-to-door campaigns, they appealed to men, women and children to pledge "by the help of God to abstain from the use of all intoxicating drinks as a beverage." One social gospeller, Samuel Dwight Chown, recalled that he had consented to his signature on the pledge even before he could write his own name! Many expanded the traditional role of protectors of the home assigned to women by Victorian culture to move into the public sphere where their activity was thought to be inappropriate. They began to agitate for legislation to prohibit the selling and consumption of alcoholic beverages. Even speaking at public gatherings on their own behalf was for many women a new and empowering experience that had implications beyond the temperance movement itself. In the face of intransigent political leaders, some were emboldened to support the radical idea that women be allowed to vote. The women believed that many of these politicians were supported by the "liquor interests."

Far more than an issue that concerned only women, temperance reform became one of the leading items of the social gospel agenda. Because alcohol was thought to be a contributor to poverty, disease, family problems, and accidents at the workplace, temperance reform was included with proposals for curbing the spread of moral and social evils. Sabbath observance was another issue which drew the attention of early social gospellers. Shocked by the ravages of industrialization in an urban setting, many Protestants joined the Lord's Day Alliance headed by Presbyterian J.G. Shearer. The supporters of the Lord's Day Act legislation passed in 1906 argued that uninterrupted work was brutalizing. To cultivate the spiritual life, leisure was necessary. There was growing concern about labour conditions, although suspicions of labour unions persisted in most church circles.

Involvement in reform movements was often connected to traditional concerns and attracted many who were convinced that evangelism and social reform were inseparable. That assumption was challenged, however, when even successful city revivals seemed to show little evidence of improving social conditions. In many denominations there was talk of a "new evangelism" which combined evangelistic work with social reform to create a "scientific evangelism." For many this new evangelism was a way of consolidating enthusiasm for evangelistic work, social reform, and progressive theology. George Jackson, who is now remembered for his role in Methodism's controversy over higher criticism in the first decade of the twentieth century, had previously worked in an Edinburgh city mission and was regarded there as an "evangelist." Actually, Canadian Methodists were first introduced to Jackson as this kind of evangelist, and not as a higher critic.

Not only were methods of evangelism changing. The model of the religious life that was presented by the new progressivist evangelists sounded to many like a new gospel. Just as important as the impact of the natural sciences on the understanding of what the religious life entailed was that of the new social sciences, especially psychology and sociology. There was less emphasis on the importance of a dramatic conversion experience, particularly after the popularization of the ideas of psychologists of religion William James and George Coe linked it to an abnormal mental state. Replacing an emotional conversion was a commitment to service and a more "natural" understanding of how God worked in the world. Accompanying this "natural" understanding of religious experience was an approach to cultivating the religious life which saw it as part of everyday life. Repeated calls for Christians to engage in acts of "sacrificial service" created an ethos sympathetic to the concerns of the social gospel.

Divisions about religious ideas and experience were accompanied by differences in matters of religious practice. In the Anglican church much attention focused on parish worship. Around the time of Confederation most parishes had begun to offer communion monthly rather than quarterly. From that point, the influence of Anglo-Catholicism grew, particularly in some of the Toronto churches, so that weekly communion in the morning service was celebrated. The evening service, originally advocated by Anglo-Catholics, eventually was opposed by them. The sometimes less formal evening service was, on the other hand, welcomed by evangelical Anglicans. It became very popular after the 1880s, its attendance in many places surpassing the morning service.

As part of the truce that accompanied the election of their candidate as bishop of Toronto in 1879, evangelicals agreed to disband the Church Association. However, in 1893 the Anglo-Catholic wing of the denomination organized the Canadian Church Union to promote practices such as private confession, remembrance of the faithful dead in public prayers, and weekly communion — practices regarded by evangelicals as "too Roman." Concerned by the growing emphasis on sacramental piety, evangelicals responded by forming the Protestant Churchman's Union to influence opinion by meetings and literature distribution. Discussion of the use of vestments for choirs, gifts of candles and crosses, and selection of hymnbooks became occasions for expressing disagreement over alternative approaches to piety.

As the evangelical consensus dissolved, one party coalesced around the ideals of religious and social progressivism: voluntarism, professionalism, cultural abundance, a scientific world view, and interventionism. In voluntarism, the old ethic of self-reliance was given new expression that fit the associative temper of the times. Old voluntary societies provided an outlet for enhanced individualism associated with the emphasis on sacrificial service. A high profile to the laity developed. At the same time, specialization made its impact in many aspects of religious work, notably in religious education and social service. This was accompanied by a professionalization of the ordained ministry. The ethics and values of "self-denial" that had characterized nineteenth-century Protestantism seemed less compatible with the new gospel of abundance that promised to make the world a heaven on earth. Caught up in a technological revolution, progressives were persuaded that science offered unlimited possibilities for the future. Understandably, then, Christian progressives exuded a confidence that the Kingdom of God was at hand and might be brought nearer still by the intervention of Christian reformers at home and missionaries abroad.

The old evangelical consensus which had been showing signs of strains for years was unable to survive the impact of a new cultural world view. Since many non-religious institutions experienced related changes, this was more than simply a "secularization" process. Protestantism underwent a metamorphosis that divided denominations within as much as against each other. The broader understanding of evangelism as a "social gospel" was not acceptable to all of evangelical Protestantism and there were those who resisted cultural change in the name of preserving tradition. While many Christians engaged modernity by becoming actively involved in the progressive movement, others responded to the organizational revolution with a renewed and even aggressive affirmation of their faithfulness to tradition. However, even traditionalists were not immune to change. In fact, developments among those who claimed to be loyal to the traditional "fundamentals" bear a striking resemblance to what was happening with progressivists who claimed the past in a different way. Despite the growing popularity of "premillennialism" with its pessimistic social outlook, activism remained characteristic of significant numbers of Protestants uneasy about social gospel evangelism. New approaches to spreading the "old gospel" were striking. New organizational patterns developed and new leaders came to the fore, channelling the energy of the two wings of the old consensus in parallel yet different directions.

The development of new educational institutions is a case in point. New links between denominational colleges and state-supported higher education were forged in the period after Confederation. A pattern was set by the University of Manitoba in 1877 when a number of small denominational colleges federated in a plan that devised common standards for granting of degrees. In the 1880s several denominational schools in Toronto achieved a federation that had long been under discussion. There were exceptions to this pattern of church-related schools. Queen's University and the University of Western Ontario, for example, decided to drop their religious affiliation. Others such as Acadia University, Bishop's University, McMaster University, and Mount Allison University remained independent. Where preparation for ministry was conducted at the university-related schools it was affected by the North American trend towards professionalization near the end of the nineteenth century. Along with new theology, higher criticism, and evolution this new professionalism of the ministry alienated some supporters of the older theological schools. This is not to say that education was unimportant for those who resisted professionalism; on the contrary, they set up new schools to train Christian workers and placed great emphasis on teaching the laity.

Tensions had for a number of years been running high between clergy and laity in several denominations. Alan Hayes has suggested that many of the theological divisions associated with the so-called Oxford Movement within Anglicanism developed because of the resistance of the clergy to largely evangelical lay leadership. Anglo-Catholics reiterated the understanding of the clergy authority coming from Jesus Christ through the historic episcopate. Compare this with the strong lay leadership of the early fundamentalist movement where laity often outnumbered clergy in many of the committees and organizations. The importance of a theologically-educated laity, coupled with the belief in the imminent return of Christ gave rise to evangelical training schools that would quickly prepare men and women to do evangelistic and missionary work both at home and abroad.

Evangelicals hoped that these Bible schools would provide an alternative to what seemed to be the too heavily academic and less practical program of the university-based denominational colleges. The development of the Bible college/training school movement was at first slower in Canada than in the United States, perhaps in part because the advantages of the uniquely Canadian pattern of federation were difficult to counter. The Mission Training School was organized in Niagara Falls, Ontario in 1885, three years after the first such school was started in the United States. Soon the Canadian school relocated in Philadelphia. Plans were soon in the making for another school. After some abortive efforts, the aims of this group were realized with the establishment of the Toronto Bible Training School in 1894. At first under the auspices of the Walmer

Road Baptist Church, the school was supported by some of Toronto's most prominent business leaders. Explicitly interdenominational, T.B.T.S., later renamed Ontario Bible College, became the model for similar schools that sprang up across Canada in the 1920s, 1930s, and 1940s.

New organizations also provided alternative networks and literature to the progressivist organizations. For example, progressives were likely to choose Sunday school literature based on the International Uniform Sunday School Lessons available after 1872; conservatives turned to publications such as the *Sunday School Times,* which by the end of the First World War was alarming some religious educators with its premillennarianism. Conservatives denounced modernism in some of its forms while adapting a few of its most central tenets and techniques to preserve and propagate the faith. New techniques in communication made possible the wider dissemination of conservative ideas. Evangelists made extensive use of advertising and methods of business efficiency in planning campaigns. Both progressives and conservatives developed distinctive ways of articulating their beliefs. Both manifested a high degree of aggressiveness in promoting their agenda, and yet each could find ways to temporarily retreat: whether at a prophetic bible conference; by a visit to a Chatauqua-like outdoor setting; or in the beauty of a liturgical service. Reading the Scofield Bible with its dispensational notes was as illuminating for some as the tools of higher criticism were for others. Both sides believed that their new knowledge would unlock the meaning of the biblical texts so as to make them intelligible to the ordinary person in the churches.

Both groups were also profoundly affected by the missionary movement that swept the continent in the late nineteenth and early twentieth century. Missionary activities of various student organizations were consolidated internationally in 1888 by the Student Volunteer Movement for Foreign Missions (SVM) which was in large part an outgrowth of the evangelistic work of D.L. Moody. Over the next thirty years the SVM sent out over 8,000 missionaries, among them many Canadians. The organization was active on college campuses and became the major recruiting agency, inspiring students by its motto: "The Evangelization of the World in This Generation." Canadian Methodists concentrated their activities in Japan and China; Presbyterians worked in China, India, Korea, and Taiwan; Congregationalists went primarily to Angola. Anglican missionaries were supported by denominational agencies, notably the women's missionary societies, others reflected the interdenominational cooperation that characterized other

Protestant crusades. Canada was represented by delegates to the 1910 World Missionary Conference in Edinburgh, the forerunner of the World Council of Churches. Others joined the China Inland Mission, the model for the later "faith missions" of conservative evangelicals. The missionary movement soon reflected the growing divergence within Protestantism. In the work of some missionaries, progressivism's social understanding of evangelism and its emphasis on sacrificial service, were evident. Others shared an expectation of the premillennial return of Christ that significantly altered the view of what "the evangelization of the world in this generation" entailed.

Interest in missions was evident even among those who did not leave Canada for foreign fields. By the end of the century missionary societies for women were among the most successful of the various denominational agencies. Baptist women in Ontario and Quebec formed a missionary board in 1876; Maritimes women followed suit in 1884. The Presbyterian Woman's Foreign Missionary Society was formed in 1876, while the Woman's Missionary Society of the Methodist Church was organized in 1881. Anglican women formed an auxiliary to the Domestic and Foreign Missionary Society in 1885 but did not set up an independent organization until 1911. Women not only raised remarkable sums of money; they also controlled it to support female missionaries. With this support, missionary women found professional opportunities in medicine, administration, and teaching that were denied them in Canada. Women found that the autonomy of gender-based missionary societies provided opportunities and denominational influence seldom if ever afforded before.

While an optimistic activism continued to characterize Protestantism in this period, it was tempered by a number of developments at home. The missionary movement had captured the imagination of many men and women who volunteered to evangelize overseas. Yet now, in the early twentieth century, persons from these faraway lands were at their doorstep in Canada. What to do with the large numbers of immigrants was one of the major challenges for both traditionalists and progressives. "Christianizing" the immigrants was barely distinguishable from "Canadianizing" a culture which, outside Quebec, was primarily Anglo-Saxon in its mores. Brown, Ralph Connor's fictional missionary pastor in *The Foreigner*, expressed these assumptions aptly when he asked what he was doing in Saskatchewan. He admitted that he couldn't preach much, but his "main line" was "the kiddies." He explained, "I can teach them English, and then I am going to doctor them, and, if they'll let me, teach them some of the elements of domestic science; in short, do anything to make them good Christians and good Canadians, which is the same thing."

The work of "home missions," most of which had been directed initially to the native peoples of Canada, expanded to include work with newcomers to Canada. The situation was particularly acute in the newest provinces of Manitoba, Saskatchewan, and Alberta, where between 1901 and 1911 a million people settled; the massive movement of people was halted only temporarily by the First World War. Strategies of the Protestant denominations varied to a degree. For example, the Church of England made few official overtures to non-English-speaking immigrants since its work with the large influx of British immigrants had severely taxed financial resources. Anglicans were also reluctant to set up missions that might interfere with the religious work of another denomination with whom they were in communion. Because evangelization among those who were members of other churches was considered improper, Anglican missionary work took place among the "heathen," in particular the native peoples.

Others did not share this reluctance. A publication prepared by C.J. Cameron for the Baptist Home Mission Board of Ontario and Quebec in 1913 expressed sentiments widely held among other Protestant denominations. In *Foreigners or Canadians?* he proposed that the church "Canadianize the foreigner by Christianizing him." This, he continued, was the greatest opportunity and the gravest responsibility, "for if we do not Christianize him he will paganize us, and if we do not instill in him the highest ideals the saloon-keeper and the ward politician will fill him with the lower levels." The strategies of the other major Protestant denominations which saw themselves as "national churches" were similar to those described by Cameron.

Chaplains from the major denominations were assigned to the various points of entry into Canada where they could gather the names of the new immigrants and provide them to the nearest church. The greatest success was expected among the English-speaking newcomers. The only exception to this rule were the Mormons, who, according to Cameron, carried "a Bluebeardish horror" and were regarded as "a deadly menace." For immigrants from southern and eastern Europe additional strategies were proposed: mission halls, night schools, street meetings, medical dispensaries, household science classes, literature in various languages, and employment bureaus in mission halls and churches.

Protestants were frustrated to find that, as had been the case earlier with French Canadian and Irish Catholics, religion became intertwined with resistance to assimilation. While many of the newcomers were suspect because of their Catholicism, others were targeted for home mission work because of their distinctive type of Protestantism. This was the case with the Russian Mennonites who began arriving in the west in great numbers during the 1870s. The Baptists tried to evangelize the Mennonites in Manitoba, regarding them as "fallen-away or gone-astray Baptists." The Methodist General Superintendent S.D. Chown wondered why this denomination's best missionaries were sent to the Chinese when there were so few ministers and missionaries to work with the Saskatchewan Mennonites. Chown conceded that the Mennonites had "a species of religion," but this would not by itself make them good Canadian citizens. Noting that only one third of the population was British born, Chown concluded that it was this group that had "the unprecedented burden thrust upon them of converting two-thirds of the population to high ideals of Christian citizenship." He urged his denomination to put its best and most committed workers "into the solving of this moral tragedy."

The religious concerns expressed by the various denominations were closely tied to broader cultural fears. Chown raised the most basic of these in the title to an article calling the Methodist church to action: "How Shall the Foreigners Govern Us?" The fear of becoming a political minority was echoed in other denominations. Religious assumptions reinforced political insecurities since so many of the immigrants were Catholic and thus members of a church characterized by Protestants as autocratic, hierarchical, and undemocratic. Although such attitudes are often linked with conservative forces, progressives were among the chief proponents of assimilation. Much of their work was, after all, tied to work in the cities. Since so many of the immigrants found their way to the cities, evangelizing them often became linked to the "new evangelism" of the social gospellers and their efforts to save society.

There was strong support for the establishment of hospitals and schools that formed the basis of missionary work among the immigrants. In the Pakan area of Alberta northeast of Edmonton, heavily populated by Ukrainians, the Methodists opened the George McDougall Memorial Hospital in 1907. Five years later a second Methodist hospital was opened at Lamont with both the medical and educational work in the area sponsored by the Woman's Missionary Society. The Presbyterian WMS also supported hospitals and schools in parts of the prairies settled primarily by Ukrainian immigrants. Special boarding schools were set up to educate children in the customs of the "Canadian" home. By 1914 the Woman's Home Missionary Society of the Presbyterian Church was financially supporting seven hospitals, seven school-

homes and eleven mission fields. It was taking care of eight
deaconesses, workers at the Robertson Memorial Institute in
Winnipeg, and others who worked in various ways with new
immigrants.

Religious leaders were dismayed and surprised to discover that
people's religious choices were often guided as much by familiarity
with traditions and trappings as by theological inquiry into the
choices presented to them. This was true of English-speaking no
less than non-English-speaking immigrants: the Church of
England and even the relatively new Salvation Army enjoyed the
benefits of their familiarity to recent arrivals from England.

This was the Protestant tradition as it appeared in September of
1914 when Canada found itself on the brink of war. Protestants were
searching for unity yet they were divided not only by theology, but
by region, class, and ethnicity from within. They were also
challenged on various fronts from without. A glance at the census
figures at the national level might suggest that little had changed,
for the relative balance between the major denominations had
hardly changed over the half century since Confederation.
However, a closer look at developments reveals a very different
Canada. Alongside the continuing enthusiasm of three
denominations for consolidation was a new recognition, and even
widening, of significant differences. Already there were signs of a
growing reluctance to tolerate these differences, such as an interest
in new sectarian movements and, more commonly, involvement in
extra-denominational associations. The tensions were eased,
though only temporarily, by the Great War.

SUGGESTIONS FOR FURTHER READING

The themes of nation-building and national identity have been
central to the historical analysis of the Protestant experience in
Canada between Confederation and the First World War. The
importance of the idea of creating a Christian Canada is
characteristic of many of the major interpretations of developments
in this period. The significance of this vision of Canada is analysed
by John Webster Grant in a number of his books and articles,
among them *The Church in the Canadian Era* (Toronto: McGraw-
Hill Ryerson, 1972); "Canadian Confederation and the Protestant
Churches," *Church History* 38/3 (1969): 327-337; and "The Church
and Canada's Self-Awareness," *Canadian Journal of Theology* 13/3
(1967): 155-164. Other interpretations that discuss the impact of the

new nation on Protestantism include Neil Gregor Smith, "Nationalism in the Canadian Churches," *Canadian Journal of Theology* (1963):112-125 and Robert T. Handy, *A History of the Churches in the United States and Canada* (New York: Oxford University Press, 1976). The denominational response to Confederation is examined by the contributors to John Webster Grant ed., *The Churches and the Canadian Experience* (Toronto: Ryerson Press, 1963).

The persistence of regional and ethnic loyalties in the period after Confederation proved to be a powerful challenge to the nationalist assumptions of proponents of a Christian Canada. This is discussed in N.K. Clifford, "His Dominion: A Vision in Crisis," *Studies in Religion* 2/4 (1973):315-326. The interplay of tendencies towards unity and disunity is central to the thesis which sociologist S.D. Clark develops in *Church and Sect in Canada* (Toronto: University of Toronto Press, 1948) which remains a thought-provoking interpretation of religion in Canada. Several studies have featured aspects of religionism and/or ethnicity. As is evident in Terence Murphy's review of the literature in "The Religious History of Atlantic Canada: The State of the Art," *Acadiensis* 15/1 (1985):152-174, there is a paucity of information on Maritime Protestantism in this particular period, especially as compared with the fine recent studies of pre-Confederation Christianity. The exception is the Baptists, who receive attention in several essays in Robert S. Wilson ed., *An Abiding Conviction: Maritime Baptists and Their World* (Hantsport, N.S.: Lancelot Press, 1988). One of the recent works to examine the cultural impact of Methodism in the Maritimes is John Reid's *Mount Allison University: A History* (Toronto: University of Toronto Press, 1984). Central Canada has fared much better with the publication of John Webster Grant's masterful *A Profusion of Spires: Religion in Nineteenth-Century Ontario* (Toronto: University of Toronto Press, 1988). An excellent collection of essays on western Canada can be found in Dennis L. Butcher et al., *Prairie Spirit: Perspectives on the Heritage of the United Church of Canada in the West* (Winnipeg: University of Manitoba Press, 1985). On the disunity created by language and Protestant-Catholic tensions see Robert Choquette, *Language and Religion: A History of English-French Conflict in Ontario* (Ottawa: University of Ottawa Press, 1975); J.R. Miller, "Bigotry in the North Atlantic Triangle: Irish, British and American Influences on Canadian Anti-Catholicism, 1850-1900," *Studies in Religion* 16/3:289-302 and Paul Crunican, *Priests and Politicians: Manitoba Schools and the Election of 1896* (Toronto: University of Toronto Press, 1974).

Many of the developments towards greater consolidation of

Canadian Protestantism that resulted in church union in 1925 took place in this period. For a discussion of events leading up to the formation of the United Church of Canada, see Burkhard Keisekamp, "Presbyterian and Methodist Divines: Their Case for a National Church in Canada, 1875-1900," *Studies in Religion* 2/4 (1973):289-302 and John Webster Grant, *The Canadian Experience of Church Union* (Richmond: John Knox Press, 1967). For the story of those who countered this consolidation, see N. Keith Clifford, *The Resistance to Church Union in Canada,* 1904-1939 (Vancouver: University of British Columbia Press, 1985). New religious movements provided other alternatives to the tendencies toward consolidation. Notable among these were the numerous groups which had connections to what is referred to as the "holiness movement." R.G. Moyles, *The Blood and Fire in Canada: A History of the Salvation Army in the Dominion, 1882-1976* (Toronto: Peter Martin Associates, 1977) presents the story of one of the best known, while S.D. Clark's *Church and Sect in Canada* is a mine of information on some of the lesser-known groups.

One of the most important characteristics of the period following Confederation was the attraction of innovative approaches to theology. These developments are the subject of a number of important studies, among them Carl Berger, *Science, God, and Nature in Victorian Canada* (Toronto: University of Toronto Press, 1983); Michael Gauvreau, "The Taming of History: Reflections on the Canadian Methodist Encounter with Biblical Criticism, 1830-1900," *Canadian Historical Review* 65/3 (1984):315-346; H. Gordon Harland, "John Mark King: First Principal of Manitoba College," in *Prairie Spirit*; A.B. McKillop, *A Disciplined Intelligence: Critical Inquiry and Canadian Thought in the Victorian Era* (Montreal and Kingston: McGill-Queen's University Press, 1979); John S. Moir, *A History of Biblical Studies in Canada: A Sense of Proportion* (Chico, CA: Scholars Press, 1982); Tom Sinclair-Faulkner, "Theory Divided from Practice: The Introduction of the Higher Criticism into Canadian Protestant Seminaries," *Studies in Religion* 10 (1981):321-43 and Marguerite Van Die, *An Evangelical Mind: Nathanael Burwash and the Methodist Tradition in Canada* (Montreal and Kingston: McGill- Queen's University Press, 1989).

Innovation became a hallmark of progressivism, a movement whose impact on twentieth-century Protestantism was profound and far-reaching. My own work on progressivism owes much to such studies of turn-of-the-century American culture as T.J. Jackson Lears, "From Salvation to Self-Realization: Advertising and the Therapeutic Roots of the Consumer Culture," in *The Culture of Consumption: Critical Essays in American History, 1880- 1980,* ed.

Richard Wightman Fox and T.J. Jackson Lears (New York: Pantheon Books, 1983), 3-38 and Martin Sklar, *The Corporate Reconstruction of American Capitalism, 1890-1916* (New York: Cambridge University Press, 1988). The impact of economic change on Canadian life is presented by business historian Michael Bliss in *Northern Enterprise: Five Centuries of Canadian Business* (Toronto: McClelland and Stewart, 1987). Insight into the implications of cultural change on Protestantism can also be gleaned in recent biographies of prominent Canadian business leaders and politicians who were important denominational leaders, for example Methodists N.W. Rowell (Margaret Prang), Joseph Flavelle (Michael Bliss) and Timothy Eaton (Joy L. Santink).

The period with which this chapter deals also saw the beginnings of the type of evangelicalism referred to in the twentieth century as fundamentalism. Historians of religion in Canada have learned much from the studies of the movement in the United States by Ernest R. Sandeen, *The Roots of Fundamentalism: British and American Millenarianism, 1800- 1930* (Chicago: University of Chicago Press, 1970) and George M. Marsden, *Fundamentalism and American Culture: The Shaping of Twentieth-Century Evangelicalism, 1870-1925* (New York: Oxford University Press, 1980). The early stages of the movement's development in Canada is examined in Ronald G. Sawatsky, "'Looking for That Blessed Hope': The Roots of Fundamentalism in Canada, 1878-1914," (Ph.D. dissertation, University of Toronto, 1985). Tensions within evangelicalism were not simply theological, as Alan L. Hayes indicates in "The Struggle for the Rights of the Laity in the Diocese of Toronto, 1850-1879," *Journal of the Canadian Church Historical Society* 26/1 (1984):5-17; also see Richard E. Ruggle, "The Saints in the Land 1867-1939," in *By Grace Co-Workers: Building the Anglican Diocese of Toronto 1780-1989,* ed. Alan L. Hayes (Toronto: Anglican Book Centre, 1989): 187-216 and D.C. Masters, "The Anglican Evangelicals in Toronto, 1870-1900," *Journal of the Canadian Church Historical Society* 20/3-4 (1978):51-66.

Related in part to the developing tensions within evangelical Protestantism, but due to the acceptance in many denominations of a professional model of ministry, were changes in theological education. Among the studies which shed light on these developments are D.C. Masters, *Protestant Church Colleges in Canada: A History* (Toronto: University of Toronto Press, 1966); Ben Harder, "The Bible Institute/College Movement," *Journal of the Canadian Church Historical Society,* 22 (1980):29-45; and G.A. Rawlyk ed., *Canadian Baptists and Christian Higher Education* (Montreal and Kingston: McGill-Queen's University Press, 1988).

The research projects on the history of Knox College (Brian Fraser) and Trinity College (C.T. McIntire and William Westfall) will add considerably to our understanding of theological education in the university context, as well Michael Gauvreau's forthcoming book *The Evangelical Century: College and Creed in English Canada from the Great Revival to the Great Depression* (Kingston and Montreal: McGill-Queen's University Press).

Analysis of the development of movements of social reform within Protestantism in Canada has resulted in a number of interesting studies. A second edition of Richard Allen's seminal *The Social Passion: Religion and Social Reform in Canada, 1914-1928* (Toronto: University of Toronto Press, 1971) has recently been issued. A useful summary of some of Allen's main ideas can be found in "The Social Gospel and the Reform Tradition in Canada, 1890-1928," *Canadian Historial Review* 49/4 (1968):381-399. Ramsay Cook's provocative thesis developed in *The Regenerators: Social Criticism in Late Victorian English Canada* (Toronto: University of Toronto Press, 1985) links religious social reform to secularization. The impact of social Christianity within particular denominations has been examined in a number of studies; see W.H. Magney, "The Methodist Church and the National Gospel," *The Bulletin*, No. 20 (1968); Brian J. Fraser, *The Social Uplifters: Presbyterian Progressives and the Social Gospel in Canada, 1875-1915* (Waterloo: Canadian Corporation for Studies in Religion, 1988); Alan L. Hayes, "Repairing the Walls: Church Reform and Social Reform 1867-1939," in *By Grace Co-Workers: Building the Anglican Diocese of Toronto 1780-1989*, ed. Alan L. Hayes (Toronto: Anglican Book Centre, 1989): 43-96; Edward Pulker, *We Stand on Their Shoulders: The Growth of Social Concern in Canadian Anglicanism* (Toronto: Anglican Book Centre, 1986); Donald Goertz, *A Century for the City: Walmer Road Baptist Church, 1889-1989* (Toronto: Walmer Road Baptist Church, 1989); and John S. Moir, "*The Canadian Baptist* and the Social Gospel Movement, 1879-1914" in *Baptists in Canada: Search for Identity Amidst Diversity*, ed. Jarold K. Zeman (Burlington: G.R. Welch, 1980). Social gospel novels by authors Alberta A. Carman, Agnes Machar, Nellie McClung, and Ralph Connor provide another perspective from which to view reform. To illustrate these insights see Mary Vipond, "Blessed Are the Peacemakers: The Labor Question in Canadian Social Gospel Fiction," *Journal of Canadian Studies* 10/3 (1975): 32-43 and R.R. Warne, "Literature as Pulpit: Narrative as a Vehicle for the Transmission and Transformation of Values in the Christian Social Activism of Nellie L. McClung," (Ph.D. dissertation, University of Toronto, 1988).

Some of these novelists also hint at the relationship between the social gospel and concerns about the influx of immigrants to the cities and the prairies; in particular, see Ralph Connor's *The Foreigner*. Home mission work, much of it among the immigrants, was important to all the major Protestant denominations and has received attention in several studies. Missions to the Indians is the subject of John Webster Grant's *Moon of Wintertime* (Toronto: University of Toronto Press, 1984). Frank A. Peake has done a good deal of work on Anglican missions, for example, "From the Red River to the Arctic" in a special issue of the *Journal of the Canadian Church Historical Society* 31/2 (October 1989) and *The Anglican Church in British Columbia* (Vancouver: Mitchell Press, 1959). For an early study of the Baptists see C.C. McLaurin, *Pioneering in Western Canada: A Story of the Baptists* (Calgary: [by the author], 1939); for more recent interpretations, see Donald Goertz, "Alexander Grant: Pastor, Evangelist, Visionary" and Gordon H. Pousett, "Baptist Home Missions and Church Extension in British Columbia," in *Costly Vision: The Baptist Pilgrimage in Canada,* ed. Jarold K. Zeman (Burlington: Welch, 1988). Methodist missionary work on the prairies is described by J.H. Riddell in *Methodism in the Middle West* (Toronto: Ryerson Press, 1946). For a study of the extension of the Presbyterian denomination to Manitoba (which also includes an analysis of Presbyterian involvement in the province's schools question) see Ian M. Manson, "Serving God and Country: Evangelical Piety and the Presbyterian Church in Manitoba, 1880-1900," (M.A. thesis, University of Manitoba, 1986). Accounts of this work by those involved in it can be found in J.S. Woodworth, *Strangers within Our Gates, or Coming Canadians* (Toronto: Missionary Society of the Methodist Church, Canada, 1909) and *My Neighbor: A Study of City Conditions, A Plea for Social Service* (Toronto: Missionary Society of the Methodist Church, Canada, 1911); and C.J. Cameron, *Foreigners or Canadians?* (Toronto: Standard Publishing, 1913). For analysis of religious social work among the immigrants, see J.E. Rae, "'My Main Line is the Kiddies ... Make Them Good Christians and Good Canadians, Which Is the Same Thing'," in *Identities: The Impact of Ethnicity on Canadian Society* (Toronto: P. Martin Associates, 1977); Marilyn Barber, "Nationalism, Nativism and the Social Gospel: The Protestant Church Response to Foreign Immigrants in Western Canada," in Richard Allen ed. *The Social Gospel in Canada* (Ottawa: National Museums in Canada, 1975); John Webster Grant, "The Reaction of WASP Churches to non-WASP Immigrants," (Papers of the Canadian Society of Church History Papers, 1968); Michael Owen, "'Keeping Canada God's Country': Presbyterian School-

Homes for Ruthenian Children," in *Prairie Spirit*; and Marilyn Fardig Whiteley, "Women Learning to Work for Women," (Papers of the Canadian Methodist Historical Society, 1988).

Members of voluntary societies were important catalysts in movements of social reform. The most popular of these in the period prior to the First World War were the temperance societies and missionary societies. On the temperance movement see Ruth Spence [Arndt], *Prohibition in Canada* (Toronto: Ontario Branch of the Dominion Alliance, 1919); Ernest Forbes, "Prohibition and the Social Gospel in Nova Scotia," *Acadiensis* 1/1 (1971):11-36; Gerald Hallowell, *Prohibition in Ontario* (Toronto: Ontario Historical Society, 1972); Wendy Mitchinson, "The Women's Christian Temperance Union: A Study in Organization," *International Journal of Women's Studies* 4/2 (1981):143-56, and John H. Thompson, "The Prohibition Question in Manitoba, 1892-1928 (M.A. thesis, University of Manitoba, 1969). The overseas missionary movement has recently begun to receive the attention it deserves; see Alvyn J. Austin's *Saving China: Canadian Missionaries in the Middle Kingdom, 1888-1959* (Toronto: University of Tornto Press, 1986) and forthcoming studies by Ruth Compton Brouwer, *New Women for God: Canadian Presbyterian Women and India Missions, 1876-1914* (Toronto: University of Toronto Press, 1990) and Rosemary Gagan, *A Sensitive Independence: Canadian Methodist Women Missionaries in Canada and the Orient* (Montreal and Kingston: McGill-Queen's University Press, 1991).

Other studies of voluntary societies include Paul Laverdure, "Sunday Secularism? The Lord's Day Debate of 1906," (Papers of the Canadian Church History Society, 1986) and A.M.C. Waterman, "The Lord's Day in a Secular Society," *Canadian Journal of Theology* 11 (1965):108-23 on the Lord's Day Alliance. For Sunday Schools see Neil Semple,"'The Nurture and Admonition of the Lord': Nineteenth-Century Canadian Methodism's Response to 'Childhood' " *Social History* 14 (1981):157-75 and Patricia Dirks, "Finding the 'Canadian' Way: Origins of the Religious Education Council of Canada," *Studies in Religion* 16/3 (1987):303-316.

Voluntary associations and involvement in religious reform movements became important avenues of Christian service for many women. For their general history, see Alison Prentice et al., *Canadian Women: A History* (Toronto: Harcourt Brace Jovanovich, 1988). For an autobiographical account of one woman's experience as a reformer, see Beatrice Brigden, "One Woman's Campaign for Social Purity and Social Reform," in Richard Allen ed., *The Social Gospel in Canada* (Ottawa: National Museums in Canada, 1975); on Brigden see Joan Sangster, "The Making of a Socio-Feminist: The

Early Career of Beatrice Brigden, 1888-1941," *Atlantis* 13 (1987):13-28. On the deaconess movement see Alison Kemper, "Deaconess as Urban Missionary and Ideal Woman: Church of England Initiatives in Toronto, 1890-1895," in *Canadian Protestant and Catholic Missions, 1820s to 1960s,* ed. John S. Moir and C.T. McIntire (New York: Peter Lang, 1988) and John D. Thomas, "Servants of the Church: Methodist Deaconess Work," *Canadian Historical Review* 65/3 (1984):371-95.

THE CANADIAN PROTESTANT
TRADITION 1914-1945

Robert A. Wright

It is said that the generation of 1914-1945 presided over Canada's emergence as a full-fledged nation; that Vimy Ridge and Dieppe no less than the Statute of Westminster propelled Canada into nationhood and onto the world stage. Not only in matters of national and international prestige, however, was Canada transformed in these years. In virtually every walk of life, the Canadian nation that emerged from the Second World War barely resembled that which had entered the first. Various institutions, social patterns, cultural and intellectual precepts, and political ideas were fractured and then recast during this tumultuous period.

Like the nation at large, Canadian Protestantism underwent fundamental changes between 1914 and 1945. The major Protestant denominations — Anglican, Methodist, Presbyterian and Baptist — had been among the 'corporate' institutions that had shaped the nation in the late nineteenth and early twentieth centuries. Accustomed to considerable influence in the intellectual, social, and cultural life of the burgeoning dominion, they had grown large, bureaucratic, and ill-equipped to cope with accelerated change. As a result, Protestant church life in Canada in the years between the wars was marked by considerable stress and fragmentation. The theological consensus of the late nineteenth century was shattered in the interwar period, first by the fundamentalist-modernist controversy and later by the neo-orthodox assault on liberalism. The Great War and the disillusionment that followed undermined the confident optimism of so-called liberal evangelicalism and its social gospel in the 1920s. Both clergy and lay people were divided on the questions of war and social reconstruction right up to World War II. Church union, arguably the greatest achievement in Canadian Protestantism in these years, was consummated with the founding of the United Church of Canada in 1925 but it left Presbyterians divided well into the 1930s. Canadian clergy could take little consolation as they looked beyond their own borders. As one of a host of church reports on the state of worldwide religion noted just after the Armistice in 1918, "the Protestant religion is at least in the trough of a wave, so far as the influence of the church as a formal institution is concerned." Nowhere was this more apparent than in the decline of the vast Anglo-American missionary enterprise, a venture in which Canadians had been well represented and in which they had taken great pride.

In addition to these internal pressures, the leadership of the Protestant churches in Canada observed that Canadians were experiencing spiritual and moral rootlessness in the 1920s and 1930s. Not in generations had clergymen been so adamant against what one of them called "the poisonous breath of atheism, impiety, lawlessness, godlessness and immorality." The turn away from traditional forms of Protestant worship was apparent in the local church membership rolls, which confirmed that congregations in the established churches were aging. Enthusiasm of the rank- and-file for evangelism and foreign missions was declining. Immigration from the British Isles had buoyed the strength of Anglicans and Presbyterians in Canada between the census years 1911 and 1921 but the Methodists and Baptists suffered declines in strength over this decade. In the years 1921-1941, the proportional strength of all of the mainline churches declined. Anglican strength in Canada fell from 16.1 per cent to 15.2 per cent, while Baptist strength fell from 4.8 per cent to 4.2 per cent. Because church union obscured the membership data for the three uniting denominations — Methodist, Congregationalist and Presbyterian — as well as for the continuing Presbyterians, its is possible to compute only a composite figure for these groups in the years 1921-1941. Here too, however, the trend is one of continual decline, the proportion of adherents to the Methodist, Congregationalist, Presbyterian, or United Churches falling from 29.7 per cent in 1921 to 26.4 per cent in 1941. That the decline in the strength of these denominations was uniform is suggested by the census figures for the years after church union. Between 1931 and 1941 the proportional strength of the new United Church of Canada declined from 19.5 per cent to 19.2 per cent, while that of the continuing Presbyterian Church in Canada declined from 8.4 per cent to 7.2 per cent.

Equally troubling, from the vantage point of the mainline Protestant denominations in Canada, were the net gains being made during this period by Roman Catholicism, Lutheranism, Judaism, and many smaller Protestant sects. The turn away from the historic churches was evinced most strikingly in the growth of the Pentecostal churches, whose adherents soared from 515 in 1911 to 57,742 in 1941. Also enjoying constant growth over these years were the Seventh-Day Adventist Church, Christian Science, the Church of Christ (Disciples), the Evangelical Church, the Mormon Church, the Salvation Army and a host of new fundamentalist groups. As the census summary itself stated in 1941, the most noteworthy trend in the seven decades since 1871 was the 945.1 per cent growth of these smaller bodies as compared with the 203.7 per cent growth of the principal denominations.

[handwritten margin note: big ↑ in the Pentecostal movement!]

TABLE I: Percentage Distribution of the
Population by Religious
Denominations, for Canada, 1911–1941

Religious Denomination	1911	1921	1931	1941
All Denominations	100.0	100.0	100.0	100.0
Anglican	14.5	16.1	15.8	15.2
Baptist	5.3	4.8	4.3	4.2
Jewish	1.0	1.4	1.5	1.5
Lutheran	3.2	3.3	3.8	3.5
Roman Catholic	39.4	38.7	41.3	43.4
United Church of Canada	—	0.1	19.5	19.2
Congregationalist	0.5	0.3	—	—
Methodist	15.1	13.2	—	—
Presbyterian	15.6	16.1	8.4	7.2
Adventist	0.2	0.2	0.2	0.2
Buddhist	0.1	0.1	0.2	0.1
Christian Science	0.1	0.2	0.2	0.2
Church of Christ, Disciples	0.2	0.1	0.1	0.2
Confucian	0.2	0.3	0.2	0.2
Doukhobor	0.2	0.1	0.1	0.1
Evangelical Church	0.2	0.2	0.2	0.3
Greek Catholic	*	*	1.8	1.6
Greek Orthodox	1.2	1.9	1.0	1.2
Mennonite, Hutterite	0.6	0.7	0.9	1.0
Mormon	0.2	0.2	0.2	0.2
Pentecostal	—	0.1	0.3	0.5
Salvation Army	0.3	0.3	0.3	0.3
Other	1.9	1.6	1.5	1.3

* Greek Orthodox and Greek Catholic were combined under the term "Greek Church".

Source: *Census of Canada* (Ottawa: Dominion Bureau of Statistics, 1941), pp. 290, 292.

Viewed from another perspective, however, the fragmentation and conflict that beset the conventions of traditional evangelical Protestantism in Canada brought liberation. The so-called sectarian movement was itself an expression of this impulse. So, too, was the coalescence of fundamentalism in the 1920s and the brief resurgence of revivalism in the early 1930s. The politicization of "radical" Protestantism in the 1930s, in "prophetic" movements like William Aberhart's Social Credit party, and in the "social gospel styled" Cooperative Commonwealth Federation, was another manifestation of the willingness of some churchmen (and ex-churchmen) to break with tradition. Even in the seminaries, a change of temper was apparent in these years. Like some prominent European and American theologians, a handful of Canadians brought great passion to their search for theological constructs that would speak to the realities of life in the postwar world and bring Protestantism back to "orthodoxy." The movement to make Protestant Christendom a force for international justice and brotherhood also had its origins in the period between the world wars, as did the drive to turn "foreign missions" into "indigenous churches."

The story of the Protestant in Canada in the three decades after the Great War is that of the churches' efforts to adapt to the pace of life in "modern" Canada, to meet challenges for which they were unprepared, and to accommodate to a world in which religious authority was under rigorous scrutiny. It is also the story of the deterioration of the evangelical consensus that had animated spiritual life in English-Canada since Confederation, of the efforts of some in the churches to uphold tradition, and of the efforts of others to forge ahead with innovation and experimentation.

I

However heavy the heart of Canadian Protestantism may have been in 1914 at the news of war in Europe, the churches almost without exception took the view that the struggle against the Kaiser was both necessary and just. It is commonly said that the Canadian patriotic response to the Great War was led by the Church of England but in truth only the so-called pacifist sects and those denominations with large numbers of recent German immigrants escaped the patriotic tide that swept Protestant Canada in the autumn of 1914. With the significant exception of pacifists like J.S. Woodsworth, Methodist and Presbyterian social gospellers perceived that many of the Anglo-American and "Christian" principles that they were intent upon establishing as the bedrock of Canadian society were at stake. They took the view that the war advanced the cause of social reform by defeating oppression, by extending political democracy, and by inculcating a spirit of sacrifice in the peoples of the allied nations. Conservative evangelicals and fundamentalists alike supported the war effort, believing that German armies represented a threat to civilization and to the progress of the Gospel.

The churches' participation in the war effort was total. Chaplains were recruited for overseas service and pastoral duties were enlarged to cope with the trauma of war at home. Sermons were written to evoke commitment, sacrifice, and honour, and the Gospel assumed a decidedly muscular air. As the war that was supposed to be over within months dragged into carnage-filled years, some clergy endowed it with redemptive and, in some cases, apocalyptic meaning. To an extent that many churchmen later regretted, the pulpit became a centre of recruitment and the Protestant press a vehicle of patriotic propaganda. By and large the leadership of the Protestant churches fell in behind Prime Minister Robert Borden's call for conscription in 1917, and more than one clergyman exacerbated the ensuing political crisis by assailing the Roman Catholic hierarchy in Quebec for its apparent obstruction of the war effort. Spokesmen for the churches gave in to the prevailing view of the "Hun" as the embodiment of evil, the "butcher" and "rapist" of the civilized world. How liberal Protestants were able to take this view of the nation that had given them some of their most important theological ideas is difficult to ascertain. In the minds of conservative evangelicals and fundamentalists, by contrast, the case was clear: Germany's moral failure lay in its abandonment of the God of the Bible and the divinity of Christ in favour of Darwinism and other "speculative fancies."

The Great War tested both the mettle of Canadian pacifists and the capacity of the patriotic majority for toleration of dissent. The right of the Mennonites and other pacifist sects in Canada to exemption from combat duty was for the most part honoured during the Great War, though some Doukhobors and Russellites (renamed the Jehovah's Witnesses in 1931) were jailed by zealous local officials. The Mennonites, who were specifically excluded from the Military Service Act of 1917, made a substantial contribution to the war effort in the areas of relief work and fund-raising. Their efforts did not prevent abuse at the hands of the English-Canadian majority, though, for whom Germany and passive resistance were equally detestable. The Society of Friends (Quakers) did more than any other group to advance the cause of pacifism in Canada, lobbying the Borden government on behalf not only of the historic peace sects but of all "whose conscience forbade them to carry arms regardless of their membership in any particular church or society."

As Thomas P. Scoknat has suggested in his *Witness Against War* the liberal Protestant pacifist witness in Canada has had an emphemeral history, waxing in peacetime and waning in time of war. Though only a handful of clergymen from the mainline churches had been actively involved in the peace movement in the early twentieth century, the principle that war was contrary to the spirit of Christ was elsewhere widely espoused, particularly among Methodists. In contrast to the pacifist sects, however, for whom aversion to war was rooted in the historic traditions of non-resistance and separation from society at large, the liberal Protestant anti-war movement had been bourgeois in its outlook, equating peace with order and stability. Hence, when the Kaiser appeared to threaten the "international order" that had prevailed since the 1870s, self-proclaimed pacifists like *Christian Guardian* editor W.B. Creighton became ardent patriots. Conscientious objection became anathema in the mainline Protestant denominations. J.S. Woodsworth's absolute pacifism, as expressed in his opposition to Methodist support for conscription, compelled him to resign from the ministry in 1918. Hounded and even incarcerated, young men who attempted to claim conscientious objector status received virtually no support from the mainline clergy.

If, as Paul Fussell has suggested in *The Great War and Modern Memory*, the war catalyzed "crucial political, rhetorical and artistic determinants on subsequent life" in the West, so, too, did it challenge many of the assumptions upon which Anglo- American Protestantism had been built. The legacy of the struggle for the social gospel in Canada was mixed. The call for sacrifice at home and abroad reduced vice in Canada, at least for a time. Temperance, the *cause celebre* of a generation of Canadian social activism, became increasingly popular during the war and by 1918 prohibition legislation had rendered the entire nation dry. The same spirit of sacrifice was apparent in the determination of the Protestant social service boards to translate the "moral and spiritual lessons of the war" into vital social Christianity in the subsequent peacetime. In the aftermath of the conflict, all of the major Protestant denominations issued calls for a new economic and social order based upon cooperation rather than the exploitation and competition that had come to be associated with "unfettered capitalism." The most far-reaching of these was the report of the

Methodist Committee on Social Service and Evangelism in 1918, which called for nothing less than a planned economy in Canada. Though this committee offered few hard details, it asserted its dissatisfaction with corporate monopoly and privilege, advocating instead the democratization of industrial organization, the creation of social welfare programs, and the redistribution of wealth.

Schism was apparent in the ranks of the social gospellers, even before the Armistice. Some like Salem Bland, most notably — called for a radical reorientation of the Gospel along explicitly socialist lines. This position would test the limits of Canadian Methodism on the social question and try the patience of moderates like Principal J.H. Riddell of Wesley College. Others, more radical still, left the institutional church altogether to form "labour churches" or to enter politics. At least one Methodist minister, A.E. Smith, joined the Communist Party of Canada, believing with Marx that brotherhood, cooperation, and social and economic justice were possible only after the creation of a classless society.

By the early twenties the apparent meaninglessness and the sheer carnage of the war had cast a long shadow over the ethos of enlightened progress that had animated liberal Protestantism and the social gospel. The conflict had not, as the most optimistic social gospellers had hoped, ushered in the millennium; rather, it seemed to have derailed the once compelling notion that human history was nothing less than the progressive revelation of the Kingdom of God on earth. Most Canadian Protestants of all denominations would have agreed with the *Canadian Churchman* in 1922 that the Great War had been "scientific butchery" for which all civilized nations were responsible. Instead of ushering in a cooperative commonwealth in Canada, moreover, the war had crystallized nascent discontent in the ranks of youth, working people, and farmers.

Given the now familiar horrors of the trenches, it should not be surprising that veterans of the Great War — some of whom were seminarians — returned to Canada as changed men. Like all wars, the Great War represented, for the young men who fought, a confrontation with the world of their parents. Consequently, the 1920s saw an unprecedented spirit of rebelliousness among Canadian youth. Among the casualties of this "generation gap" was traditional religious observance. Many of the 4000 veterans who returned to Canadian colleges and universities in the autumn of 1919 openly rejected what they called "official religion" and they were joined by a good many non-veteran students who had also been affected by the war. The clergy's complicity in the wartime propaganda push was seen by these students to represent the "practical failure of Christianity." The students lashed out, as well, against the churches' apparent acquiescence in an exploitive social system, their refusal to come to grips with modern intellectual and scientific advances, and their seemingly incessant theological squabbling. That the veterans' rebellious disposition had its origins in the mud of the trenches had not escaped the notice of frontline YMCA workers like E.A. Corbett. In 1918 Corbett had reported to the *Canadian Student:*

> I must confess I have seen no evidence of a revival of religion here. The Church Parade with its formalism and its compulsion is an abomination to the Tommy, and in his illogical way he blames the church for it. He sees no reason why he should have to stand "at attention" in a hurricane of wind and rain to listen to what for the most part is a very platitudinous and prosy presentation of religious truth. Frankly, it does not interest him, and of course does not touch his heart.

As Canadian veterans filed home, all of the mainstream denominations took note of their rejection of "the old appeals and the old methods" of religion and of their demands for "the abolition of camouflage, both social and ecclesiastical."

The rebellious attitude of Canadian youth led to a decline in student membership in the YM and YWCAs during the war and the flowering of the Student Christian Movement (SCM) in its aftermath. However horrid their experience of the war, many Canadian university students showed great enthusiasm for social reconstruction and even for the possibility that the Kingdom of God might be built in the postwar world. Launched at the University of Guelph over the Christmas break of 1920-1, the SCM became a rallying point for these impulses. Theologically, it was the most liberal organization in Canadian Protestantism in the 1920s, practically celebrating scientific inquiry and humanizing Jesus unabashedly. Organizationally, the SCM strove for full democracy. Rejecting the strict membership bases of the earlier Christian youth movements, SCM organizers were adamant that the new fellowship be entirely student-run. By 1922 it had absorbed all but two student YMCA groups nationwide, but it continued to maintain a somewhat aloof posture toward the churches. In the mid-1920s the militant postwar generation of SCM leadership would yield to students who had not participated in the war and, as a result, the Movement would become less strident and relations between it and the churches would warm considerably.

Most clergy lamented the rebelliousness that seemed to be sweeping the ranks of Canadian Protestant youth in the 1920s. Here was clear evidence, they thought, of the decline of religious authority in Canada. Some university faculty members, however, whose contact with Canadian veterans was intimate, recognized that their turn away from traditional forms of worship had been inspired in part by a new appreciation of the "inner values of religion." While the experience of the trenches had undoubtedly soured some veterans on religion altogether, it had fostered in others a deepened sympathy for Jesus' sufferings and a new appreciation of the power of the Cross. In Canada as elsewhere, this new awareness of the redemptive message of Christ directly informed the theological debate of the 1920s. As Michael Gauvreau has suggested, some leading Methodist and Presbyterian academicians — Robert Law of Knox College and John Baillie of Emmanuel College, for example — appealed to the "religious" experience of the trenches in their formulation of new theologies. They neither despaired of the waning social gospel nor waffled in the face of challenges to their prewar progressive orthodoxy. Instead they attempted to strip away false concepts of religion and to create "realistic" theological constructs. The result was a movement toward a neo-Kantian or Idealistic synthesis of faith and critical thought. The earlier dependence of liberal theology on culture and historical knowledge was rejected, although the complete separation of history and theology of the Barthian "crisis" theologians was also avoided. Ironically, however, for all of the insight these scholars may have derived from this theological experimentation, dissatisfaction with institutionalized religion among university students continued and enrolment in divinity programs declined in the 1920s.

However much Canadian social gospellers may have anticipated the dawning of a new social and economic order, events in Winnipeg in May 1919 revealed that the gulf between labour and capital in Canada was as great as ever. In what was, in retrospect, an unfortunate coincidence of events, disgruntled workers in that city embarked on a city-wide general strike only six weeks after the convening of the radical, pro-Bolshevik Western Labour Conference in Calgary. The aim of the Conference was the creation of the Marxian One Big Union while the strikers more modestly demanded the right to bargain collectively. The subtle distinction between the two escaped the notice of alarmed government officials. Many in the Protestant clergy were equally ill-disposed to make this distinction. From the first news of Lenin's October Revolution (1917) church officials had been among Canada's most bitter critics of the communist "red menace." Almost without exception they had applauded the Allied intervention in Russia in 1918, which included the Canadian Expeditionary Force. Further, they supported government measures against supposed communist agitators in Canada, particularly those suspected of infiltrating the ranks of organized labour. Notwithstanding the support of J.S. Woodsworth and some local clergy for the Winnipeg strikers, representatives of the churches, like most of the Canadian middle class, were intimidated by the scale of the protest. Some openly condemned the strike; most were ambivalent. Among the major Protestant periodicals, only the Methodist *Christian Guardian* took an unequivocally pro-labour position on the strike.

Canadian farmers, too, emerged from the war in a mood of unrest. Reacting to such threats to "agrarian life" in Canada as rural depopulation, the tariff, corporate capitalism, and government corruption, various farmers' organizations had begun to press for reforms in the closing days of the war. These calls for reform echoed those emanating from the radical wings of the churches. W.C. Good of the United Farmers of Ontario (UFO) and Henry Wise Wood of the United Farmers of Alberta (UFA) borrowed many of their ideas and most of their rhetoric from the social gospel. In 1919 Good called for the creation in Canada of a "Kingdom of Righteousness" based upon a move away from urban values and industrial growth. The American-born and ministry- trained Wood went even further, equating "perfect" political and economic democracy with the Kingdom of Heaven. Ironically though, the churches were among the institutions he accused of accommodation to the "false ideals" inherent in the vision of an urban industrial Canadian society.

The alienation of the English-Canadian agrarian movement from the "old-line" parties culminated in its entry into politics in the guise of Progressivism; it was here that the Protestant social gospel first affected political life in Canada on a grand scale. The surprising provincial victories of the Ontario and Alberta farmers' parties and the remarkable second-place showing of the Progressive party in the federal election of 1921 revealed that Canadians were deeply divided, both by class and by region. What is more, it indicated that a vision of Canada reconstructed on a foundation of economic and social justice had broad appeal. That the election of 1921 also sent J.S. Woodsworth and William Irvine to parliament under the auspices of the Labour party suggests further the mixing of the sacred and the secular in these years. Prime Minister Mackenzie King, whose own debt to social gospel currents in Canadian Presbyterianism was apparent in his pedantic study of industrial relations *Industry and Humanity* (1918), successfully undermined the Progressive party in the 1920s by wooing many of its members into the Liberal party.

The exodus of the radical social gospellers from the Methodist and Presbyterian churches and the absorption of the Progressives into the moderate reform wing of the Liberal party marked the end of a social gospel consensus in Canada. The strike at Winnipeg had revealed the essential moderation of the leadership of Canadian Protestantism on matters of social reform. Demands from within the churches for sweeping changes to Canadian society would not be heard for a decade, and then they would be voiced only by an independent handful of radicals from the United Church. Although the leaders of the Canadian churches were not as reactionary as some radicals believed, they certainly fuelled the fires of the "Red Scare" in 1919-20 and again in 1927-28, applauding the action of the Canadian and American governments in curbing the activities of undesirable aliens, suspected "anarchists," and "Bolsheviks." That T. Albert Moore of the Methodist Board of Evangelism and Social Service cooperated with the RCMP in the surveillance of the labour church movement displays the level of fear and frustration some reformers in the churches had in these years.

Even at the grassroots, Canadians seemed to have grown weary of talk of social reconstruction. The air of urgency that had animated the prewar and wartime social gospel seemed curiously incongruent with the prosperity and levity of life in Canada during the Roaring Twenties. Having made it through the war and reconstruction, Canadians felt that they were due some self-indulgence. Reformers in the churches lamented that interest in social concerns was being displaced by secular forms of recreation such as radio, motion pictures, and automobile travel. This new spirit of personal liberation in the nation brought about the decline of prohibition. In Quebec prohibition had been imposed during the war by the federal government and was quickly abandoned in its aftermath, merely confirming the prejudices of some English-Canadian clergy. British Columbia's decision to end prohibition in 1920 was far more decisive for, as many Canadian Protestant reformers feared, it turned out to be the thin edge of the "wet" wedge in English-Canada. By 1926 all of the provinces except Prince Edward Island had abandoned prohibition. The most enduring and uniting of the social action campaigns in which both liberal and conservative churches had been involved was now dead.

II

Many members of the Canadian Protestant churches were

disheartened at the marginalization of the social gospel in the 1920s but they were not without other triumps to celebrate and other causes to trumpet. Two generations of Protestant ecumenism culminated in the creation of the United Church of Canada in 1925, a milestone not only in the lives of the uniting churches but in the life of the nation. The movement to render Canadian Protestantism a vehicle of international fellowship and peace was also consolidated in the 1920s and the 1930s. Together the ecumenical and the international impulses reoriented the reform tendency in Canadian liberal Protestantism and fostered the global perspective that has distinguished the Canadian churches, particularly the United Church, in the nuclear age.

As John Webster Grant and others have argued, the church union movement was a product of the spirit of consensus that had characterized liberal Protestantism in Canada in the first decade of the twentieth century. The urge to cooperation, if not to full-blown ecumenism, had been a characteristic of Canadian Protestantism practically since Confederation. Divided Methodist and Presbyterian churches in Canada reunited with the strong support of the social gospellers. Even the Baptists and the Disciples of Christ experimented with cooperative ventures. The view that denominationalism was not only inefficient but contrary to the will of God was gaining wide currency at the turn of the century in Canada, as it was elsewhere in the English-speaking world. More pragmatically, church leaders perceived a need for cooperation in social outreach, especially in the acculturation of large numbers of non-Anglo Saxon immigrants in Canada. This was particularly true on the prairies, where communities tended to be small and isolated. An agreed division of labour between the clergy of various denominations had been the norm in the Northwest for some time; it had wide appeal as well in the handful of burgeoning Canadian cities, where the problem of the "new Canadian" was manifested in the crowded slums of the working classes. The Moral and Social Reform Council (later the Social Service Council) was the most important of many cooperative ventures founded in the early twentieth century to orchestrate the social work of the churches. This cooperative effort, or comity, had also proven an effective means of rationalizing foreign mission work since the 1880s. Consequently, many felt that an organic union of the Protestant denominations could only improve the already significant Canadian contribution to the Anglo-American missionary enterprise.

Nationalism, or "nation-building," had been one of the central concerns of Canadian Protestantism since Confederation and this may have provided the driving force behind the union movement. The Protestant churches had preceded the birth of the nation and they identified deeply with Canadians' emergent sense of nationality and community. The leaders of all of the Canadian churches had been swept up in the euphoric nationalism of the Laurier era; there seemed to be little doubt that the twentieth century would be Canada's. Conservative evangelicals may have stressed personal salvation while liberals stressed the redemption of society at large, but all agreed that Canada ought to be fashioned into "God's dominion" — a Christian, democratic, and preferably British nation from sea to sea. In the end, only a minority of English-Canadian Protestants would join the United Church, but those who declined were also compelled by this national vision in the early twentieth century. Even T.T. Shields, the fundamentalist Baptist leader, subscribed to the powerful idea of "His Dominion." The mark of this nationalist upsurge on the church union movement in Canada was unmistakable. As C.E. Silcox wrote in his celebratory *Church Union in Canada* (1933), "Canada is our parish. It is the vision of Dominion-wide service that inspires the new Union. . . There will be not a hamlet or a rural community in the whole land where the United Church will not serve."

Denominational reunions in the late nineteenth century had led Methodists, Presbyterians, Congregationalists, and even Anglicans in Canada to consider the idea of consolidating Canadian Protestantism in some kind of organic union. Little came of these discussions, primarily because they had been spearheaded by the Church of England in Canada and were premised on the demand of the Lambeth Quadrilateral of 1888 that the historic episcopacy be maintained. In 1902, Canadian Methodists, Presbyterians, and Congregationalists reopened the question of union, this time on a non-episcopal basis. Responses were sufficiently warm that a Joint Committee was struck to work out the details of a merger. It took the committee only four years to produce a Basis of Union —
testimony not only to the determination of the representatives of the uniting churches to achieve a workable consensus but also to the relatively relaxed theological environment in which they worked.

There was remarkable agreement as to the essentials of faith and polity in a United Church in Canada. The Basis of Union was a theologically conservative document, blending mild Arminianism and mild Calvinism. It drew heavily upon the Brief Statement of the Reformed Faith that had been prepared in 1902 by the Presbyterian Church in the United States. The advanced age of the eighty-three men who sat on the committee (there were no women included) accounts somewhat for this conservative consensus but so, too, does their refusal to see their great vision of a "national" church dashed on the rocks of theological dissension. It is noteworthy that W.W. Bryden of Knox College remained aloof to the Presbyterian debate over union because he was alarmed by the indifference toward theology displayed by both sides. As for polity, the Basis proposed a pyramidal structure of government moving down from a General Council to regional conferences, presbyteries, and local congregations. A concession, however, was made to the Congregationalists so that individual congregations could name ministers if they so desired.

In spite of the remarkable ease with which the Basis of Union was designed, the road to Church union in Canada was far from smooth. From the beginning the Methodists and Congregationalists voted overwhelmingly in favour of union, the single exception being the traditionally isolated Newfoundland Conference of the Methodist Church. The Presbyterians, by contrast, were divided from the outset. As time passed the hostility Presbyterians were able to generate toward one another over the union question became woefully apparent. Although the General Assembly of the Presbyterian Church approved the Basis in a vote in 1910, twenty of seventy presbyteries decided against union in a popular vote. The great majority of opposition was centred in old and wealthy churches in Ontario and the Maritimes. The reasons for the intransigence of the Presbyterian minority were many: some objected to the Basis on doctrinal grounds, believing that the tenets of the Westminster Confession of Faith and the doctrine of predestination were not adequately represented; condescension toward the "enthusiasms" and the social preoccupations of the Methodists surfaced in the objections of others; still others seem to have been moved by a preference to maintain a distinctly Scottish tradition. Of course, circumstantial pressures and personality conflicts at the local church level played a role. All "resisters" were united, however, as N. Keith Clifford has suggested, by a desire to defend the right of the historic Presbyterian Church in Canada to a continued existence.

The Basis of Union was amended slightly in response to the objections of the Presbyterian resisters and a second vote was held among the church membership in 1915. This time an even larger forty per cent opposed union. In spite of this opposition and with considerable misgiving, the General Assembly voted in 1916 to go ahead with the merger. The indignant opponents of union responded by creating the Presbyterian Church Association to prevent the dismemberment of their historic church. A "truce" between these warring Presbyterian factions during the Great War briefly delayed the inevitable clash. In the West, where the merger had the overwhelming support even of Presbyterians, "union churches" were already forming. Attempts to rectify the schism with federational rather than an organic union, as suggested by the Reverend D.R. Drummond, were not welcomed. In 1921 the Presbyterian General Assembly again resolved to "consummate organic union . . . as expeditiously as possible," resigned itself, finally, to the hopeless deadlock that had beset the church. The Presbyterian Church Association, too, headed by Principal D.J. Fraser of Presbyterian College in Montreal, girded itself for the ensuing conflict.

The critical scenes of battle, as it turned out, were the federal and provincial legislatures and, later, the courts. In 1923 drafts of the bills to legislate church union came before the General Assembly of the Presbyterian Church for the first time. This legislation, which had been approved without controversy a year earlier by the Methodist Church, provided for the entry of the entire Presbyterian Church in Canada into union with the provision that dissenters would subsequently be free to vote themselves out of the merger. This meant that between the time of union and withdrawal the "Presbyterian Church in Canada" would cease to exist. Naturally a heated debate ensued at the General Assembly meeting but, as expected, the pro-union majority ruled the day. The draft legislation was approved by a vote of 427 to 129. Recognizing that church union was now a *fait accompli* as far as the church hierarchy was concerned, Fraser and the Presbyterian Church Association changed tactics. First, they accelerated the "paper war" that was raging in the church press and, second, they tried to block the legislation in the nation's legislatures.

In the propaganda war designed to influence the church membership on the final vote on union both sides proved adept, according to John S. Moir, "in the juggling of figures, the use of innuendo, half-truths and dirty tricks." Because some congregations voted by means other than the ballot, the results of the plebiscite were uncertain and both sides claimed victory. In the end, however, the only true criteria for success or failure was the decision to unite or to separate. When the dust had settled, one-third of Presbyterians in Canada had refused to join the United Church of Canada. As for the legislative struggle, the Association won important concessions. In Ontario and Quebec, where the stakes were the highest, the resisters won the right to a continuing church and the retention of both Knox College in Toronto and Presbyterian College in Montreal. Not until 1939, however, when the United Church of

Canada Act was amended to give them the right to the name "Presbyterian Church in Canada" would the opponents of union consider their struggle to maintain their distinctive spiritual tradition finished.

The United Church of Canada was inaugurated on June 10, 1925. Although the rift in the ranks of Canadian Presbyterians cast its shadow over the consummation of union, representatives of the three amalgamating churches felt themselves to be on the threshold of a new chapter in Canadian religious and national life. The United Church immediately became the largest of the Protestant denominations, with approximately twenty per cent of the Canadian population. The leadership now undertook to make the United Church the "national" church envisioned by its pioneers. Although the social gospel that had done so much to inform the union movement was by this time in retreat, commitment to social action became a hallmark of the new church; the reformist impulse of the United Church was apparent in the high status accorded the Department of Evangelism and Social Service. To an extent that troubled some even within the fold, the United Church emerged as the most theologically open-minded denomination in Canada. It has thus had to contend from the day of its founding with charges of doctrinal looseness and accommodation to secular society; yet it has also earned a reputation, deservedly, for being the most tolerant and socially aware denomination in Canada.

Internationalism was, arguably, the greatest of the liberal reform movements in the Western world in the 1920s. In the English-speaking nations in particular, which not only took credit for victory in the Great War but had been able to return to splendid isolation in its aftermath, the idea of a "new world order" had wide appeal. The rhetoric of 1914 had evoked visions of a postwar world in which peace, justice, and freedom would reign permanently. The horror of the trenches seemed to have illumined, once and for all, the bankruptcy of war as a glorious institution. From curiously incongruent impulses of idealism and revulsion sprang the League of Nations, the cornerstone of liberal internationalism in the 1920s and early 1930s. As well, a plethora of lesser organizations dedicated to international brotherhood and peace arose.

Most Canadian Protestant clergy embraced this new spirit of internationalism wholeheartedly. All of the major church councils and periodicals articulated their support for the objectives of the League of Nations; special days of prayer were designated to coincide with disarmament conferences; and treaties like the Kellogg Pact of 1928, which purported to renounce war as an aspect of diplomacy, were celebrated in church services across the nation.

The most influential figure in the churches' support for internationalism was Newton W. Rowell, a Methodist layman and politician who served as Canada's representative at the League Assembly in Geneva. In the 1920s, Rowell headed the League of Nations Society and lectured three or four times weekly to various citizens groups, university faculties, and church audiences. As Margaret Prang has suggested in her *N.W. Rowell: Ontario Nationalist,* Rowell had an unshakable faith in the capacity of the Christian church to create the necessary atmosphere for international and interracial harmony. To a very large extent it was Rowell's influence that kept the churches in the mainstream of the internationalist movement in Canada in the 1920s and 1930s. His pragmatic approach to foreign affairs, moreover, as exemplified by his insistence that the "reign of law" be substituted for the "rule of force," guided the churches' development of new international roles.

"Pacifism" again came into vogue in liberal Protestant reform circles in the 1920s. Evidence that some businesses had profited enormously from the war raised the suspicion in the minds of some Canadians that war was the logical outgrowth of capitalism and its "international arm," imperialism. The prewar social gospel thus was easily sublimated in the antiwar movement. Few church spokesmen had done more than W.B. Creighton of the *Christian Guardian* to link pacifism and treason during the Great War, yet Creighton himself had by 1924 taken up the antiwar cause. Haunted by postwar disillusionment rather than by thoughtful reconsideration of the ethics of war and peace, Creighton's ambivalence was typical of the inner struggle many Canadians experienced. They faced the dilemma of Christ's pacifist teachings on the one hand and the responsibility of the Christian to oppose evil on the other. Not surprisingly, many members of the Canadian SCM called themselves pacifists in the 1920s but here, too, revulsion seems to have been the motivating factor. The only book-length tract on pacifism to emerge from the ranks of the Canadian Protestant clergy at this time was a collaborative effort of the Protestant Ministerial Association of Montreal entitled *The Christian and War* (1926). This work articulated the somewhat standardized ethic of war among Protestants in Canada: the Christian had a responsibility to become acquainted with the diplomatic and economic roots of war, and the churches had a duty to impress upon governments the necessity of peaceful arbitration in foreign relations. Like most liberal Protestants who fancied themselves pacifists in these years, the authors of *The Christian and War* assumed that the avoidance of war had become an accepted standard of diplomacy among the so-called civilized nations. The foreign policies of Fascist Italy, imperial Japan, and Nazi Germany in the 1930s would reveal the naivete of such assumptions.

The great majority of church leaders were, like N.W. Rowell, "realists" when it came to international affairs. They were revolted by the scale of destruction that accompanied modern warfare but they were not prepared to say that there was no evil greater than war itself. All agreed that Christ alone embodied the ideals of brotherhood, peace, and justice, and the realization of these ideals in the world was impossible without God's special guidance. International Christian fellowship thus assumed a new importance. The leaders of the SCM of Canada undertook to make the World's Student Christian Federation (WSCF) a force for international brotherhood; Canadian Anglicans focused their internationalist energies on the Lambeth (1920) program of ecumenism and participated in the Quaker-dominated World Alliance for International Brotherhood; Baptists in Canada showed a remarkable willingness, given their historic isolation, to provide leadership in the Baptist World Alliance.

Missions became the key agencies of the new Christian internationalism. Canada's Protestant church leaders recognized and promoted the diplomatic value of foreign missions in the 1920s. They believed, as the *Christian Guardian* put it, that "the harmony of the nations shall be maintained, not by the most rigid safeguards of international intercourse, but by the imperative behest of a spiritual agreement." Representatives of the Canadian Foreign Mission Boards were present at the founding of the International Missionary Council (IMC) in 1921, an organization created to orchestrate the liberal wing of the Anglo-American missionary enterprise. Notably, IMC was the first truly ecumenical organization in Protestant Christendom. In the same year, Mission Boards collaborated in the creation of the Canadian School of Missions (CSM) in Toronto. The CSM quickly established itself as one of North America's leading institutions of missionary training, offering missionary candidates courses not given in the church colleges and providing missionaries on furlough with instruction and fellowship. The movement to convert foreign missions into "indigenous, self-governing churches" began in earnest during the 1920s and 1930s. The rise of Asian nationalism was an important catalyst in this process; so, too, was the increasingly broad-minded view Canadian missionaries and church leaders had begun to take toward non-Western civilizations. This reorientation of the missionary enterprise contributed not only to the internationalist impulse in the interwar period but to the spirit of mutual respect that would characterize relations between the Canadian churches and the Third World after World War II.

III

The maintenance of large, pluralistic institutions requires tolerance and a willingness to balance the claims of divergent interests. This principle applies to any organization that aspires to represent a national consensus or to express a national vision. Like the old line political parties in Canada, whose exclusive claims to Canadians' loyalties were tested by the mood of defiance that swept the nation after the Great War, the mainline Protestant denominations learned in the 1920s that even the most "centrist" attitude could not contain dissent in times of social and intellectual ferment.

Notwithstanding occasional clashes, particularly in the Baptist and Presbyterian seminaries of the northern United States, conservative and liberal evangelicals in North America had been able to sit at the same table in the first decade of the twentieth century. Though the theologians had often argued vehemently about evolutionary theory, Biblical literalism, and the relationship of modern thought to Christian faith, the majority of evangelical Protestants, whose day-to-day concerns were less erudite, occupied a middle ground. They did not identify strongly either with the liberal or conservative parties in their churches. Indeed, they continued to cooperate with each other in a variety of ventures, such as Sunday schools, missions, temperance, and evangelism.

By the 1910s, however, "modernist" ideas were taking root in the North American church colleges and they were beginning, albeit slowly, to percolate down to the local churches. Modernism, or liberalism, can best be understood as a movement that sought to reconcile Christianity with the "rationalist" ideas of the Enlightenment. Its roots lay in the thought of Friedrich Schliermacher, Ferdinand Baur, Albrecht Ritschl, and other German theologians of the nineteenth century. The most significant feature of liberal modernism was the willingness of its adherents to embrace "higher criticism" of the Scripture. They taught that the Bible could be scrutinized and interpreted critically, like any historical or literary document. Modernists were best known for their preference for scientific theories of human evolution over a literal reading of the Biblical story of Creation, a debate that reached its historic crescendo in the United States during the Scopes "Monkey trial" of 1925. Three-quarters of Canadian Protestants today belong to churches that are liberal theologically, evidence perhaps of the intellectual attractiveness of modernist ideas. In the 1920s, however, modernism in the Canadian churches and church colleges emerged as a matter of considerable controversy. This was particularly true in Toronto, where the secular press took some pleasure in sensationalizing the issue.

In response to the inroad being made by modernism in the early twentieth century, the right wing of conservative evangelicalism in both Canada and the United States began to close ranks. Conservatives wanted to stop the steady erosion of evangelical orthodoxy. The result was the emergence of a new movement: fundamentalism. This movement took its name from a series of essays written between 1910 and 1915 by American, British, and Canadian conservatives entitled *The Fundamentals*. Here an agenda of the essential elements of evangelical faith was laid out, coalescing with the founding of the World's Christian Fundamentals Association after the Great War. In matters of doctrine, fundamentalism had much in common with conservative evangelicalism, emphasizing Biblical literalism, the vicarious atonement of Christ, His bodily resurrection and return to earth, and the conversion experience. Fundamentalists distinguished themselves, however, by stressing the wrath of God in place of a paternalistic interpretation of His relation to man, by employing premillennial and often dispensational eschatological constructs and, above all, by their militant refusal to compromise with modernism.

Fundamentalism took root in all of the major denominations in Canada and it breathed life into the sectarian movements that had grown up on the nation's geographic and socio-economic periphery. For many ordinary Canadians raised on traditional evangelical orthodoxy, the modernist impulse was deeply disconcerting. From their perspectives, the new theology eroded traditional concepts of sin, individual salvation, Biblical authority and even, apparently, the deity of Christ. In their place, modernism offered few hard truths. Contrary to enduring stereotypes, fundamentalism was not the exclusive domain of immigrants, farmers, and the urban poor. Demographic and class analyses of fundamentalist constituencies in Canada have shown that the movement drew its greatest support from the slightly lower than average socio-economic strata of Canadian society; that is, fundamentalism appealed less to Canadians who were economically impoverished than to those who felt marginalized socially or culturally. Urbanization and industrialization produced the kind of alienation in the lives of the urban lower-middle class that was eased in fundamentalist religion; the precarious state of life on the agricultural frontier made fundamentalism similarly attractive to many pioneering farm families.

In Canada the impact of the fundamentalist movement was felt most dramatically among Baptists. At the centre of the fundamentalist-modernist storm in this historically tolerant denomination was Thomas Todhunter Shields, the controversial pastor of Jarvis Street Church in Toronto between 1910 and his death in 1955. Beginning in the early 1920s,the vigilante Shields embarked on a campaign to protect the Baptist Convention of Ontario and Quebec from the encroachments of modernism. In so doing, he caused an irreparable breach in the Convention, the repercussions of which can be felt down to the present. He also contributed to lesser divisions among Canadian Baptists in the West and in the Maritimes.

Allied with prominent ultra-conservatives in the United States like J. Frank Norris and William B. Riley, Shield fit well within the mainstream of North American fundamentalism. He would accept no compromise on the doctrines of the innate depravity of man and the sovereignty of God. Although he rejected dispensationalism and Scofieldism, his eschatology was decidedly premillennial and pessimistic. Shields is remembered as Canada's foremost fundamentalist because of his scathing, frequently *ad hominem,* attacks upon those he considered to be his modernist "enemies." T.T., as he came to be known, was never far from controversy. In 1921 Shields' leadership of Jarvis Street Church was challenged and he was narrowly sustained. It would appear that his egotism and his "dictatorial" style of leadership were more at issue in this feud than theology, but Shields' accusation that his opponents were modernist, worldly, and heretical had the effect of establishing his reputation for militancy. The following year Shields founded the *Gospel Witness* as a fundamentalist alternative to the "liberal" *Canadian Baptist*.

Like American fundamentalists, Shields was deeply concerned about the intrusion of modernism in Protestant institutions of higher learning. In particular, he was not prepared to see McMaster University, the historic centre of Baptist education in Ontario, succumb to the ravages of modernism without a fight. Elected to the Board of Governors of McMaster in 1920 and again in 1924, Shields assumed as a grave personal responsibility the task of barring liberals from the school. In 1923 he led a successful protest against the decision of the board of governors to present an honourary degree to W.H.P. Faunce, president of Brown University and a renowned liberal missionary statesman.

The inevitable collision between Shields and the leadership of both McMaster and the Baptist Convention of Ontario and Quebec was thunderous. The pretext for the row was the teaching of professor L.H. Marshall, a British theologian appointed to the faculty of McMaster in 1924. In such sermons as "How Professor Pontius Pilate Dealt with the First Fundamentalist," Shields charged Marshall with modernism, claiming that he did not believe in Scriptural inerrancy, the substitutionary atonement of Jesus, and the innate depravity of man. Forced somewhat reluctantly into the public light by mounting publicity, Marshall defended himself on several occasions; he argued that the Bible was inerrant in spiritual matters but not necessarily in matters of science; that the substitutionary theory of the atonement —— in which Christ was somehow "punished" by God —— was contrary to his conception of the perfection of Jesus and of the love of God; and that man could not be "totally" depraved since he had been granted a spiritual faculty by God Himself. At the 1926 meeting of the Convention, where Shields and Marshall exchanged views face to face for the last time, Shields was censured for his abusive allegations. The following year the Convention voted Jarvis Street Church out of its fellowship. Unrepentant, Shields and his fundamentalist followers founded their own denomination, the Union of Regular Baptist Churches of Ontario and Quebec. They also began their own school, the Toronto Baptist Seminary. Seventy-seven Baptist Churches severed ties with the Convention to join the Union, suggesting something of the strength of the fundamentalist movement among Baptists in central Canada and also something of Shields' popularity.

Fundamentalism had a dramatic impact as well among Baptists in British Columbia, the Prairie Provinces, and the Maritime Provinces. In the early 1920s a group of fundamentalists in the Baptist Union of Western Canada, many of whom were dispensationalists, set out to purge the Union of modernist influences. The struggle began in 1920 when Reverend W.A. Bennett of Emmanuel Baptist Church in Vancouver accused Dr. Harris MacNeill of teaching "anti-Scriptural lessons" at Brandon College. After a brief inquiry, the Brandon Board of Governors affirmed their confidence in MacNeill, but this did not appease the conservatives. In 1925 fundamentalists led by Andrew Frieve and F.W. Auvache, anxious about the defection of Baptists to Pentecostalism, founded the British Columbia Baptist Missionary Council and a newspaper, the *British Columbia Baptist*, to function as guardians of the conservative tradition within the Union. Two years later the Council abandoned the Union altogether to form the Regular Baptist Convention of British Columbia, taking 1600 members of a Union total of 5000. With far less disruptive consequences, a Maritime Christian Fundamentalist Association was founded in Nova Scotia in 1925 by J.J. Sidey, a British-born fundamentalist allied loosely with T.T. Shields. A decade later, Sidey and a handful of his followers split with the United Baptist Convention of the Maritime Provinces, creating the Independent Baptist Church. Subsequently the Independents challenged the Nova Scotia Baptist establishment in a sensational civil suit over the ownership of a local parsonage.

In the Church of England in Canada, where relations between "high" and "low" church elements had periodically been acrimonious, the effects of fundamentalism were also felt. Dyson Hague, Registrar of Wycliffe College and editor of the *Evangelical Churchman*, was the leading Anglican fundamentalist in Canada in the 1920s. Hague established something of a reputation as a militant with his introduction to the 1917 edition of *The Fundamentals*, in which he assailed "the hypothesis-weaving and speculation . . . of the German theological profession." In the 1920s feuding between the two wings of the church in the Diocese of Toronto resumed, the Evangelicals once again asserting "the principles and doctrines of our Church established at the Reformation" and criticizing what they called the "crypto-Catholic teaching at Trinity College." Fundamentalism had an impact upon Presbyterians in Canada as well, though its effects were not nearly as divisive as they were among Presbyterians in the United States. William Caven, Principal of Knox College in Toronto, was yet another Canadian contributor to *The Fundamentals* and A.B. Winchester, also of Knox, was involved extensively in the World's Christian Fundamentals Association. As John S. Moir has noted, the theological militancy of fundamentalist Presbyterians was tempered by their need to join in common cause with other anti-unionists in the 1920s in the fight against church union. Little is known of the extent or influence of fundamentalism in the United Church of Canada in these years. The contention of Dr. Thomas Powell, United Church Superintendent of Missions for Alberta between 1925 and 1942, that 80 per cent of United Church membership in that province inclined toward fundamentalism suggests that the grip of modernism in the new church was far from secure.

IV

Fundamentalism reached well beyond the mainline Protestant churches in Canada. One of the most striking features of Protestant life in Canada in the years between the wars was the consolidation and growth of independent fundamentalist groups and the creation of new evangelical institutions. These sectarian movements were not new to Canada in the early twentieth century ——they had been a permanent feature of the Canadian frontier since the eighteenth century. Owing to the great tides of immigration that marked the Laurier years, however, the number and variety of these movements had begun to expand greatly. What was novel about sectarian Protestantism in Canada in the years after the Great War was its reorientation from a predominantly ethnic footing to one that was essentially theological. Here the influence of fundamentalism can hardly be exaggerated.

Until the Great War, religion served to shore up ethnicity among the large number of recent European immigrants. This was particularly true on the prairies, where the largest number of new arrivals were settling and where the forces of English-Canadian assimilation were relatively weak. Immigrants to Canada naturally brought with them whatever national and cultural identity they could carry. Understandably, the establishment of traditional religious observance in the new world mitigated the experience of culture shock. From the 1910s on, however, Protestant immigrants found themselves under increasing pressure from within and without to accommodate to the Anglo-Canadian mainstream.

Lutherans comprised the largest Protestant denomination among the non-English-speaking immigrant population in Canada in the early twentieth century. Norwegian, Swedish, Icelandic, Danish, and especially German Lutherans all established churches in Canada, often with the assistance of fraternal organizations in the United States. Between 1901 and 1911 the number of Lutherans in Canada had risen from 94,110 to a remarkable 231,883. In the three subsequent decades, growth was more modest but still substantial, with just over 400,000 Canadians listed as Lutheran in the census of 1941. In these years the Lutheran churches struggled to balance the desire of the first generation to maintain its traditional ethnic identity with that of the second generation to conform to Canadian society at large. The children of European immigrants to Canada recognized very early in life that English was the language of success. German-speaking Lutherans of even earlier Canadian origin found the pressure to "Anglicize" acute in the first half of the twentieth century. Patriotic fervour in English-Canada during the Great War, and again during World War II, translated into open suspicion of anything German, exacerbating the Lutherans' identity crisis. In the 1920s and 1930s Lutherans in both eastern and western Canada acceded to these pressures, introducing English-language services.

The religious life of Scandinavian immigrants to Canada was similarly disrupted after 1914. Under pressure from the English-speaking second generation, the Swedish Lutherans and the Dutch Christian Reformed Church began English-language services in the 1920s. However lamentable the passing of tradition was to some, it is apparent that church life was well served by this accommodation. The alternative became clear: the Norwegian Lutheran Church, which was the largest of the Scandinavian Lutheran churches in Canada and the least disposed to assimilate, lost one-half of its membership in the years 1920-1945. The United Church of Canada, like its antecedents, provided strenuous competition for these non-English denominations, welcoming individuals who preferred to move into the Anglo-Canadian mainstream. So too, ironically, did the sectarian movements that had sprung up at the turn of the century, many of which retained European languages in their services. Some German-speaking Lutherans defected to the German Baptist, the United Evangelical Brethren or German-language Pentecostal groups. Alienated Scandinavian Lutherans found a home in the Evangelical Mission Covenant and in the World Alliance of Evangelical and Missionary Churches.

To date, the only comprehensive study of Protestant sectarianism in Canada in the interwar period is W.E. Mann's *Sect, Cult and Church in Alberta* (1955). Mann identified 35 Protestant sects in Alberta in the early twentieth century, of which only the Salvation Army, the German Baptist Church, the Mennonites, and the Evangelical Mission Convenant were established before 1900. Many of those that came to the Canadian prairies later did so via the United States, including the Church of the Brethren (Dunkards), the Disciples of Christ, the Church of Christ (one of several splinters of the Disciples) and Christian Science. The German and the Scandinavian language groups arrived in the great wave of immigration before 1914. Among the holiness groups that also came at this time were the Free Methodists, the Nazarenes and a wing of Ralph Horner's controversial Holiness Movement. "Millennial" or "adventist" sects now established on the Canadian prairie included the Seventh-Day Adventists, the Brethren of Christ (Christadelphians), the British Israelites, and the Russellites (Jehovah's Witnesses).

The denominational histories of Canada's extant independent evangelical churches suggest that this explosion of dissent was national in scope, though clearly it was most pronounced on the prairies. Some significant differences and many lesser ones distinguished sectarian movements from each other but virtually all were self-consciously fundamentalist. They insisted upon Biblical literalism and the need for a climactic conversion experience in the life of the believer. Most practiced an ascetic and separatist moral code. Services tended to be "enthusiastic," a feature of sectarian worship that did not go unnoticed in the more reserved mainline churches. Participation of the laity was stressed. Polity was ostensibly congregational, though the tendency for these movements to unite around a single charismatic leader had the effect of circumscribing congregational authority. For all of their desire to maintain isolation, these sectarian groups showed a remarkable camaraderie with each other and with like-minded members of the large denominations. Local fellowships, pastoral associations, pulpit exchanges, Sunday schools, and annual rallies were organized cooperatively. Only the adventist groups shunned cooperative ventures.

The most enduring testimony to conservative evangelical and fundamentalist ecumenism in Canada in the 1920s and 1930s is to be found in the field of education. A host of Bible institutes and colleges were founded in these years. Although some closed and others barely made it through the lean years of Depression, they did provide the bedrock for evangelical Protestantism in Canada. These Bible schools were created primarily to train fundamentalist pastors, lay workers, and missionaries. The evangelical foreign missionary enterprise, spearheaded by organizations like the China Inland Mission, continued to grow. The pioneers of evangelical education in Canada also thought that lay church members ought to be made as Biblically literate as possible. Like the splinter groups from which these institutions were most often derived, these schools tended to be revivalistic in temperament, stressing personal religion, evangelism, and missions. They explicitly rejected what they called the sacramentalism, sacerdotalism, and secularism of the established church colleges. The founding of the non-denominational Winnipeg Bible Training Institute by Reverend H.L. Turner in 1925 was typical of these new Bible institutes. Turner, pastor of Glad Tidings Church and later president of the worldwide Christian and Missionary Alliance, was deeply troubled by life in Winnipeg in the twenties. Postwar economic and social problems, labour unrest, the radicalism of the social gospel and of liberal theology, and a growing indifference toward religion convinced him, as he put it, that "the Lord has laid upon my heart to open a Bible school." From modest beginnings the Institute blossomed into the preserve of evangelical Protestantism that Turner envisioned.

Several other institutions founded on the Canadian prairie in these years are worthy of mention. In 1921 the Bible training institute that would ultimately become the Canadian Nazarene College was founded in Calgary. After several changes of name and location the college settled in Winnipeg, where it is now affiliated with the University of Manitoba. In 1922 the Prairie Bible Institute was founded at Three Hills, Alberta. One decade later the Alberta Bible College was founded by the Church of Christ (Disciples) at Lethbridge, moving to Calgary in 1937. After a false start in 1932, the Alberta Bible Institute, now called Gardner Bible College, was founded in 1935 at Camrose. The following year the South Saskatchewan Bible Training School was founded by the Tennessee-based Church of God at Consul, Saskatchewan, moving to Moose Jaw in 1943 and ultimately to Estevan, where it was renamed the International Bible College. Two Rivers Bible Institute was founded in northeastern Saskatchewan in 1934, later moving to Nipawan where it became Nipawan Bible Institute. Briercrest Bible College was founded in Briercrest Saskatchewan in 1935 by Henry Hildebrand, a graduate of Winnipeg Bible Institute. The tiny Evangelical Mission Convenant of Canada ran short-term Bible institutes and camps in the 1920s and 1930s, finally establishing the Covenant Bible Institute at Norquay, Saskatchewan in 1941. This list, though not exhaustive, suggests something of the breadth and tenacity of the movement to establish durable evangelical educational institutions on the Canadian prairies.

The resolve to create a broadly based evangelical infrastructure in Canada in the years between the wars was also apparent in the creation of non-denominational fellowships. The most significant of these was the Inter-Varsity Christian Fellowship (IVCF). Inter-Varsity, or I-V, as it came to be known, had its origins in Britain in the early twentieth century. An annual conference of various British evangelical "unions" — each university having its own union — was begun in 1919. These meetings culminated in 1928 in the creation of the national Inter-Varsity Fellowship (IVF), a self-consciously conservative fraternity that was deliberately distinct from the liberal Student Christian Movement. In the late 1920s similarly styled unions were founded on Canadian campuses with the help of IVF members. In 1929 the three unions of the universities of Toronto, Manitoba, and Western Ontario met to create the IVCF. Among the students attracted to the new fellowship were those with evangelical backgrounds who found the liberal posture of the SCM uncongenial. From the outset the IVCF fashioned itself as an evangelical alternative to the SCM. It emphasized personal religion and evangelism, basing its statement of faith on that of the China Inland Mission. Inter-Varsity sought to serve evangelical conservatives from all denominations in the universities. As well it had a program of outreach in Canadian high schools: the Inter-School Christian Fellowship.

TABLE II: Founding of Prairie Bible Schools
1921-1947

Name	Location	Denomination	Date of Origin
Prairie Bible Institute	Three Hills	Non-denominational	1922
Western Bible College	Winnipeg	PAOC	1925
Winnipeg Bible Institute	Winnipeg	Non-denominational	1925
Canadian Nazarene College	Red Deer	Nazarene	1927
Christian Training Institute	Edmonton	German Baptist	1928
Miller Memorial Bible School	Pambrun	Non-denominational	1928
Calgary Prophetic Bible Inst.	Calgary	Prophetic Baptist	1929
Church of God Bible School	Moose Jaw	Church of God (Tenn.)	1930s
Moose Jaw Bible School	Moose Jaw	Free Methodist	1930s
Regina (Evangelical) Bible Inst.	Medicine Hat	United Evangelical	1930s
Saskatoon Bible College	Saskatoon	Non-denominational	1931
Alberta Bible College	Calgary	Disciples of Christ	1932
Alberta Bible Institute	Camrose	Church of God (Ind.)	1932
Peace River Bible Institute	Sexsmith	Non-denominational	1933
Bethel Bible Institute	Saskatoon	PAOC	1935
Briercrest Bible School	Briercrest	Non-denominational	1935
Two Rivers Bible School	Carlea	Non-denominational	1935
Western Holiness Bible School	McCord	Holiness Movement	1936
Grande Prairie Bible School	Grande Prairie	Non-denominational	1940
Covenant Bible Institute	Prince Albert	Mission Covenant	1941

Institution	Location	Affiliation	Year
Western Canada Bible Institute	Regina	Alliance	1941
Prairie Apostolic Bible	Saskatoon	Apostolic Church of Pentecost	1943
Full Gospel Bible Institute	Eston	Full-Gospel Missions	1944
Radville Christian College	Radville	Church of Christ	1945
Alberta Bible College	Edmonton	Apostolic	1946
Temple Bible Institute	Edmonton	Western Canada Alliance of Missionary and Evangelical Churches	1946
Canadian Northwest Bible Inst.	Edmonton	PAOC	1947

Source: W.E. Mann, *Sect, Cult and Church in Alberta* (Toronto: University of Toronto Press, 1955), p. 83.

Pentecostalism distinguished itself as the fastest growing branch of Canadian Protestantism in the early twentieth century. As sociologist Hans Mol has suggested, Pentecostalism is best understood as a movement rather than an institution, since denominational cohesion has never been especially important to its adherents. Although the first Pentecostals were fundamentalist in their opposition to modern theology and sectarian in their view of the world, they were best known for their emphasis upon "baptism in the Holy Spirit" as evidenced by glossolalia (speaking in tongues), so-called faith healing, and the gift of prophecy. The movement originated with a series of highly publicized revivals in Los Angeles in the first decade of the century. At the revivals the gifts of the spirit were said to be manifested. Robert E. McAlister of Cobden, Ontario, widely regarded the founder of Pentecostalism in Canada, was one of several Canadians to experience baptism in the Holy Spirit in Los Angeles in 1906. Some twenty-seven Pentecostal assemblies sprang up in Canada over the next decade, coming together during the war years in two fraternal organizations: the Pentecostal Assemblies of Canada (PAOC) and the Western Canada District Council of the Assemblies of God, USA. McAlister was the first national secretary of the PAOC; he also founded the *Pentecostal Testimony* in 1919. Believing the millennium to be imminent and the need for salvation urgent, Pentecostals quickly established themselves as one of the most aggressively evangelistic groups in Canadian Protestantism.

The enduring strength of Pentecostalism in Canada owes a good deal to the determination of one man to create a sound educational infrastructure for the movement in the years before World War II. A graduate of Wycliffe College in Toronto, James Eustace Purdie founded the first Canadian Pentecostal Bible school in 1925 and presided over the creation of five more before his retirement in 1950. That Canadian Pentecostals saw a need for institutions of higher learning in the 1920s was somewhat curious, since they showed little concern for matters of creed and they were convinced, moreover, that theological bickering was one of the distractions from which God had liberated them. Committed only to aggressive evangelism, Purdie and his fellow Pentecostal educators sought to establish a curriculum centred on the Word of God and the power of prayer. The schools emphasized, above all, practical training in preaching and evangelism. In the early years Purdie had to deal with chronic indebtedness: schools closed and reopened several times in the 1920s and 1930s. Libraries, classrooms, and even faculties were of dubious quality. Yet Purdie managed to train missionaries, evangelists, and field workers of deep conviction in these years;

these men and women would go on to become the backbone of the Pentecostal movement in Canada after World War II.

The war years and the 1920s also proved to be the heyday of one of Canada's most familiar sectarian movements, the Salvation Army. Between 1911 and 1921 the number of Canadians calling themselves Salvationists grew an astounding 82.5 per cent; the following decade growth was more modest but still significant at 31 per cent, testimony to the evangelistic strength of the Army. It was during the Great War that the Salvation Army in Canada established its reputation for vital *social* outreach. Apart from their day-to-day visitations among the families of departed soldiers, Salvationists inaugurated a War Services drive in 1918 that raised $1.5 million in aid of hostels for returning soldiers, assistance to war brides, and other forms of social assistance. The now-familiar Red Shield of the Salvation Army was first invoked at this time. The social service wing of the Army expanded into the 1920s. "Army Chariots" (motor vans) were used in rural evangelism on the prairies, while in the urban centres Salvationists widened their already considerable work among the destitute, building a host of new senior citizens homes, Grace hospitals, and hostels. So impressive was the work of the Salvation Army that a branch of the Anglican Church Army, itself inspired by the success of the Salvationists in Britain in the early 1880s, was established in Canada in 1929 with the cooperation of the Council of Social Service.

The 1920s and 1930s also witnessed the emergence of a new phenomenon in Canadian Protestantism: the rise of non-denominational evangelical churches. Of these the most significant and enduring was led by Oswald J. Smith, and it is known today as the Peoples Church. In many ways, Smith's life mirrors the state of flux in which evangelical Protestantism in Canada found itself in the years between the wars. He was born in 1889 to an average western Ontario family. A deeply introspective youth, Smith was converted at age sixteen at one of many evangelistic rallies staged at Toronto's Massey Hall. From there he embarked on a life of service to God, and one that saw him immobilized more than once by deep depression, uncertainty, and guilt. He eventually attended the Toronto Bible Training School (late the Ontario Bible College). After a course of study at McCormack Theological Seminary in Chicago, he was ordained. At age 22 he was called as an assistant pastor to J.D. Morrow at Toronto's Dale Street Presbyterian Church. Though the evidence is sketchy, it would appear that Smith was too "enthusiastic" for the congregation at Dale Street. He left the church in 1918 and, after testing his hand at editorial work for the *Evangelical Christian*, he embarked on the first phase of the career for which he is best remembered: the creation of an evangelical, non-denominational, and missions- oriented ministry.

Smith's theology, however unsystematic, was doggedly pietistic and evangelistic: during his brief stay at Manitoba College, he later recalled, his sobriety was ridiculed by the liberal theology students and from the moment of his conversion he showed an extraordinary passion for missions. His first attempt at a non-denominational evangelical ministry, which he called the "Gospel Auditorium," was begun in 1920 and occupied the 750-seat Royal Templar Hall in Toronto. Owing primarily to financial pressures he merged his group the following year with the fledgling Parkdale Tabernacle, a church of the Christian and Missionary Alliance. It would appear that by this time Smith had accepted the militant anti-modernism of fundamentalism and most of the tenets of Pentecostalism. At a 1921 Alliance rally at Massey Hall, at which miracles of healing were said to have been performed, he claimed to have had his vision corrected and subsequently threw away his eyeglassess. Smith attracted adherents by spicing up his services with guest speakers and musicians. By the summer of 1921 he had outgrown Parkdale and was conducting evangelistic campaigns in a 1500-seat tent; within a year he built, on-budget and debt-free, the Alliance Tabernacle at 85 Christie Street, earning a name for himself as one of Toronto's greatest ministers. By 1926 the Tabernacle had been expanded to seat 2500. It also had built two branch churches, a Bible institute, a bookstore, a newspaper and a publishing house, and it was raising some $38,000 annually for foreign mission work.

A falling out with the Alliance led Smith to leave the Tabernacle in 1928, whereupon he immediately inaugurated the similarly-styled Cosmopolitan Tabernacle, later the Peoples Church. After several moves the building which housed the former Central Methodist Church on Bloor Street was chosen as the site of the new Tabernacle. Smith had by this time enlarged his outreach to include radio and was broadcasting his "Back Home Hour" on forty-six radio stations across Canada. The crowds at the Tabernacle exceeded 2000 in the early 1930s and Smith reluctantly implored his radio hearers not to try to attend the live service! Though it is difficult to codify Smith's theological evolution, it is clear that he was drawn in the 1930s toward a Dispensationalist view of Biblical prophecy. Called "the modern Moody" by his followers, Smith's popularity in Canada and the United States persisted into the 1940s and 1950s and, as a keen supporter of missions, he spent much of his mid-life travelling abroad. In 1959 his son, Paul B. Smith, was inducted into the Peoples Church as a pastor and several years later assumed full responsibility for the operations of the church, which is now situated north of the City of Toronto.

V

By the end of the 1920s a certain degree of stability had returned to Canadian Protestantism. The United Church of Canada was an established fact of life and, despite ongoing tension between the new church and the continuing Presbyterians, the place of each in the future of Canadian Christendom was acknowledged. A similar kind of equilibrium existed between the dissenting fundamentalists and the mainline churches, though this was based less on veneration of diversity than on resignation to the idea of separate spheres. In some minds the seemingly limitless prosperity of the era had done more to hinder religion in Canada than to inspire it but in general there was relief that the world had settled back into something resembling "normalcy," a favoured aphorism of the day.

For Canada's religious leaders and for church-going public alike, the Crash of 1929 and the ensuing economic decline came as a rude awakening. Even as markets for resources began to slump in the late 1920s, bankers and businessmen persisted in their optimism about the ability of the Canadian economy to sustain growth indefinitely. The global economic downturn was especially hard on exporting nations like Canada. Increased American tariffs meant vastly reduced sales of grain, pulp and paper and minerals for Canadian producers; businesses that had not been dashed by the collapse of the stock market were forced to cut costs and staff, while nervous bank officials called in loans and slowed credit to a trickle. Not until World War II would the Canadian economy recover,and even then it was widely feared that the depression would resume once the wartime stimulus ebbed.

The impact of the Great Depression on the lives of ordinary Canadians varied. On the prairies, plummeting wheat prices were accompanied by an unprecedented ten year drought. This unfortunate coincidence tested the faith of many farm families and ruined more than one. Rudimentary, municipally-funded relief programs provided assistance only to needy families, making the prospects of the single, unemployed male singularly bleak. Some middle class Canadians who had jumped on the speculation bandwagon in the late 1920s were also ruined but, as the Rowell-Sirois Commission Report of 1937 pointed out, "Most of the workers in the skilled trades, the professions and the white collar occupations who retained their jobs actually enjoyed a considerable improvement in their real [income] position."

For administrators in the mainline denominations, the watchword in the 1930s was "cuts": office and college staffs were thinned, ministers' salaries were reduced by as much as one-half, and sizeable operating deficits were incurred. In the United Church, the Board of Foreign Ministers suffered the largest cutback; with funding halved between 1928 and 1935 it had no choice but to recall missionaries from foreign fields. Other mission boards and societies were less seriously afflicted. Not surprisingly, the churches' overriding concern was for those Canadians most debilitated by the depression. Relief work assumed a new urgency. Local clergy dedicated themselves to the collection and distribution of clothing and food, and interdenominational relief drives were conducted in aid of desperate prairie communities. In central Canada, the work of inner-city missions for the unemployed and the homeless were expanded as much as resources allowed. Of the Protestant denominations, the United Church assumed most of the responsibility for relief. In 1931 it created an umbrella agency, the National Emergency Relief Commission, to coordinate the work of the regional conferences. However much Canadian fundamentalists may have disdained social gospel ideas, they understood the meaning of Christian charity and showed deep sympathy for the plight of the impoverished. T.T. Shields spoke for many conservative evangelicals and fundamentalists in Canada when he said that "no sort of moral reform can take the place of individual regeneration; but that certainly does not relieve us of the obligation to do what we can to further such reforms as make for righteousness." The churches' greatest efforts notwithstanding, private contributions for relief work inevitably shrank with the economy while the need grew.

Similar constraints bound the small evangelical churches during the depression decade. In spite of the growing popularity of sectarian religion, these were years of mere survival for many of these newer groups. Like the large denominations, they had barely sufficient resources to maintain the institutions and programs they had established in the previous decade; little remained to meet new needs. Owing to internal problems, the economic fortunes of the Salvation Army, by now recognized as one of Canada's foremost agencies of Protestant philanthropy, had begun to sag even before the Crash. In 1928 the Army's High Council had challenged the traditional right of the General to name his successor. The news media turned what was a legitimate disagreement over jurisdiction into a sensational feud between the Council and General Bramwell

Booth, son of the founder. In the end, the Council successfully asserted its authority and only limited dissent within Army ranks surfaced. The damage to public opinion, however, was serious: many Canadians became disillusioned by such manoeuvering in an organization dedicated to Christian charity. Consequently, donations were withheld.

Through the 1930s were years of austerity for church administrators and social service workers, they were also years of renewal and experimentation in Protestant church life. Fired by the disparate economic and psychological effects of the Depression, the search for religious meaning assumed an urgency in the early 1930s unparalleled since the Great War. For those church leaders who had been troubled through the 1920s by what they perceived as the spiritual decline of Canadian society, the possibility that the economic downturn might occasion a revival of personal piety and evangelism was actually encouraging. What Canada desperately needed, according to the likes of George Pidgeon of the United Church, was a movement to bring both individuals and churches back to the Cross. Such exhortations were answered in the early years of the depression first by an extraordinary revival in Japan at the hands of the evangelist Toyohiko Kagawa and then, by the arrival in Canada of Frank Buchman's Oxford Group Movement.

Toyohiko Kagawa was a Princeton-educated Presbyterian minister who lived and worked in the ghettoes of Kobe, Japan. An indefatigable evangelist, social reformer, labour activist, and writer, Kagawa first came to the attention of Canadian missionaries in Japan in the mid-1920s. In 1928 he embarked on an evangelistic campaign called "A Million Souls for Christ" in which thousands of Japanese were converted. Stunned by Kagawa's success, Canadian missionaries, two thirds of whom were supported by the United Church, mobilized to offer him their full moral and bureaucratic support. The Million Souls campaign was renamed the Kingdom of God Movement, a newspaper was founded, and a "Kagawa Fellowship" was created with a Canadian missionary as its head to supervise the translation and mass publication of the evangelist's works. Back in Canada, where George Pidgeon himself had organized a "Kagawa Cooperating Committee," Kagawa's popularity as an evangelist was unrivaled. Spokesmen for all of the mainline denominations called him a modern prophet; many would have agreed with retired Methodist missionary J.K. Unsworth that he was "the Nipponese embodiment of Christ of Palestine."

Kagawa's reputation and influence in Canada climaxed, prematurely, in 1931. In that year the evangelist undertook a three-month tour of North America that included stops at major

Canadian cities. He was accorded celebrity status that included front page stories and photographs in the church presses and his addresses consistently drew capacity crowds. In response both to Kagawa's success in Japan and to his popularity in Canada, the General Council of the United Church resolved to "seek conference with the Churches of Canada, in the hope that a Kingdom of God movement in Canada may eventuate." The aim of such a movement, according to the Council, would be "to make our religion more vital and sincere and practical." In yet another of the cruel ironies of the 1930s, however, Japanese forces occupied Manchuria in 1931, bringing the worst in North America xenophobia to the fore. Although Kagawa had always preached pacifism and was a determined critic of the "militarists" in Japan, his stature in the West suffered immeasurably by these events. In the end, despite the continuing loyalty of prominent Canadian church leaders and virtually all of the United Church missionaries in Japan, nothing came of the idea of a Kingdom of God Movement in Canada.

For those who had taken Kagawa's popularity in Canada as a sign that the nation was poised for revival, the vacuum left by the precipitous drop in that popularity might have been agonizing. It was not. This was because the impulse behind the embryonic Kingdom of God Movement in Canada was sublimated by the revival brought to Canada in 1932 by the Oxford Group Movement. The connection between the two movements can be illustrated by noting that many of the arrangements for the visits of the Oxford Group team to Canada were made by the Kagawa Cooperating Committee of Toronto.

The Oxford Group Movement was a movement of personal, pietistic religion that operated, for the most part, within the mainline churches of the English-speaking countries. Its founder was Frank N.D. Buchman, an American-born Lutheran of great devotion, determination, and energy. "Buchmanism" began in the postwar years as a novel approach to evangelism among university students in Britain and the United States. The movement coopted the name of Oxford University in the late 1920s even though there was never any official affiliation. The most intriguing aspect of the Oxford Group Movement was its use of contemporary, quasi-bureaucratic jargon to express what were essentially traditional evangelical concepts. Buchman and his followers were adamant about the need of the individual for salvation through conversion, a process they called "changing." One was changed by embracing the "Five Cs:" Confidence, Confession, Conviction, Conversion and Continuance. Once changed, one became a "life - changer."

confessing one's own sin or "sharing" as a means of changing others. The process emulated the traditional evangelical rituals of confession and exhortation. The Oxford Group Movement stressed daily meditation in which the will of God, or "guidance," could be discerned by the believer in a spirit of complete surrender and obedience to Him. One could "check" guidance by testing it against "the Four Absolutes" of Honesty, Purity, Unselfishness, and Love. Conferring with more experienced Group members was encouraged. Another distinguishing feature of the Movement was its preferred mode of congregation, the "House party," an informal and opulent gathering usually held at a private mansion or luxury hotel. House parties gave the Movement a reputation for attracting the wealthy and powerful, making its slogan, "First Century Christian Fellowship" something of a misnomer. Buchman also worked to bring the message of personal salvation to smaller local churches, however, holding more modest meetings and attracting many believers with his simple evangelistic faith.

A "team" of life-changers, including Buchman himself, arrived in Canada for the first time in the fall of 1932. News of the great number of conversions that were accompanying Oxford Group meetings elsewhere had preceded the team and anticipation ran high. At the first stop of the tour, Montreal, many church leaders were changed, including Dean D.L. Ritchie of Montreal Theological College, Reverend Leslie Pidgeon, and Bishop J.C. Farthing. In Ottawa the team was greeted by Prime Minister R.B. Bennett and by many of the city's leading clergy. By the time the team arrived in Toronto, the third stop on the tour, George Pidgeon was calling the Oxford Group Movement "the greatest spiritual movement in the history of Canada." From Toronto the team went West, holding meetings in Vancouver, Victoria, Edmonton, Calgary, Winnipeg, and Regina. It wound up its visit with an enormous House party at the Banff Springs Hotel. Wherever it went, the Group attracted large numbers of politicians, businessmen, and church officials. Thousands of Canadians were converted. The team left for England in the summer of 1933, but not before helping to establish Oxford Groups in every Canadian city west of Montreal. Some churches, like Bloor Street United in Toronto, sponsored as many as four separate Groups. As Robert G. Stewart has shown, these organizations provided Canadians with intimate fellowship and with assurance of their salvation. Many entered lives of Christian service and the spiritual life of more than one church was invigorated.

In Canada as elsewhere, however, the Oxford Group Movement and the "revival" it had inspired were the locus of considerable controversy. Some observers, W.B. Creighton most notably, were suspicious that "sharing" abetted subliminal perversion, since it frequently centred on explicit discussions of sex; others, including T.T. Shields, expressed the view that the theology of the Movement was superficial and unscriptural. The harshest criticism of the movement came from the ranks of social gospellers. For the likes of Richard Roberts of the United Church, the Group's apparent neglect of the social context of sin, epitomized by its lavish parties during the worst months of the depression, was unconscionable. It is difficult to know precisely where Buchman stood on the social question but one of his slogans is suggestive: "When everybody cares enough, and everybody shares enough, then everybody will have enough." He seems to have taken the view that if all men were changed then economic, social, and political change would be superfluous. All interests, he liked to say, including those of capital and labour, could be brought into perfect harmony and honesty under God's guidance. In the early 1930s, when Canadians were increasingly receptive to the idea of a new economic and social order, it is not difficult to see why some social activists in the churches disdained Buchman's apparent acquiescence in the status quo. From their perspective, the movement not only failed to articulate a credible social vision, but it soothed the guilt of upper and middle class Canadians during the depression by promulgating an ethos of paternalism and personal charity that actually shored up the capitalist system.

Buchman and his team returned to Canada in 1934 but by then the popularity of the movement had begun to ebb. Crowds were much smaller than they had been in 1932-3 and meetings were said to have lacked freshness. Only in the Maritimes, where the team had not travelled during its first Canadian tour, did enthusiasm for the revival reach fever pitch. International tensions had by this time become a matter of grave concern and the Oxford Group had modified its language accordingly: Buchman spoke of the need for a "Dictatorship of the Holy Spirit" and a "world-changing army." Such ideas foreshadowed the recasting of the Oxford Group Movement as Moral Re-armament in the late 1930s, but like his earlier social pronouncements these slogans lacked substance. After 1934, the number of Oxford Group House parties and church organizations dwindled rapidly. By the end of the depression decade, the Movement in Canada had disappeared almost entirely.

There was no denying, however, that the impact of the Oxford Group Movement had been dramatic. However much it may have absolved guilt-ridden upper and middle class Canadians, it had also given them a forum for the kind of pietistic and evangelistic experience that many had come to regard with condescension. Indeed, the available evidence suggests that it had provided mainline Canadian Protestantism with its greatest revival of personal evangelism since the nineteenth century.

VI

Many Canadians suspected that the depression of the 1930s represented not merely a downturn in the cyclical Canadian economy but the outright collapse of profit-oriented, competitive industrial capitalism. This sentiment was most obviously apparent in the ideology of the Cooperative Commonwealth Federation (CCF). a coalition of labour and farmer interests that banded together in the early 1930s to form a national political party. The CCF established as one of its central objectives the creation of an economy founded on the social gospel ideal of "supplying human needs instead of the making of profits." A large number of CCF leaders had once been, or were currently, ordained clergy: Notable among them were the Methodist J.S. Woodsworth, the Anglican Reverend Robert Connell, and the Baptists T.C. 'Tommy' Douglas and Stanley Knowles. For these men, democratic socialism was but the natural extension of the social teachings of Christ in an industrial age.

Similar sentiments were being expressed from within the churches themselves. As early as 1931 a movement was afoot in the United Church to mobilize the resources of the national church in the cause of radical social reconstruction. This campaign was led by a group of Toronto clergy calling themselves the Movement for a Christian Social Order. They believed that Christianity was incompatible with capitalism and called for "the socializing of the organized agencies of production." Initially it seemed that they were expressing ideas that held common currency in the church. Virtually all of the conferences of the United Church issued resolutions in the early 1930s favouring the redistribution of wealth and the collectivization of the nation's economic resources for the common good. Even more promising was the decision of the General Council to appoint a commission headed by Sir Robert A. Falconer to study "the Christian standards and principles which effect or should govern the social order." According to the Report of the Commission, released in September 1934, the depression and its attendant social ills were outgrowths of the modern industrial economy and, more specifically, of the exclusive concern of business for profit. Private gain could be subordinated to the social good, it concluded, only if the right of industrious working people to decent living and working conditions was affirmed and upheld. As for the responsibility of the individual Christian the Report exhorted its readers to renounce their own selfish desires in favour of the promotion of the greater social good. However, the Falconer Commission and the leadership of the United Church were divided on the question of social reconstruction, as the release of a dissenting minority report made clear. Anonymously written, this addendum charged that the offical Report had not gone far enough in its call for change. The Commission's emphasis on "Christian conscience," according to the dissenters, was laudable but inadequate. What was needed were concrete strategies for rectifying the defects that were inherent in the economic system, starting with the transfer of the means of production to communal ownership and control. Remarkably, there was no public debate over the findings of the study.

Disappointed by the moderate tone of the Falconer Commission majority Report and by the noncommittal attitude of the United Church leadership, the "radicals" in the church undertook to create a national fellowship dedicated to social reconstruction. The resulting organization was inaugurated in 1934 as the Fellowship for a Christian Social Order (FCSO). The Basis of Agreement of the FCSO entrenched two essential principles, namely that "the capitalist economic system is at variance with Christian principles" and that "the creation of a new social order is essential to the realization of the Kingdom of God." All of the founding members of the Fellowship were ordained United Church clergy; several, including R.B.Y. Scott, John Line, Gregory Vlastos, R. Edis Fairbairn, and J. King Gordon, had been founding members of the League for Social Reconstruction, an intellectual fraternity of liberals and socialists allied with the CCF. Although the FCSO did not become officially ecumenical until its Constitution was revised in 1938, at least one Anglican —— Andrew Brewin —— played a prominent role in the organization from the outset.

The founding of the Canadian Fellowship for a Christian Social Order did not constitute a wholesale revival of the turr-of-the-century Protestant social gospel. Though FCSO members often borrowed the rhetoric and idealism of the social gospel, they were far more realistic than their forebears about the rigidity of social and economic structures and the place of power in human relationships. This realism arose out of the disillusionment these reformers had themselves experienced during the 1920s. As well, so-called neo-orthodox ideas from Europe and the United States had challenged the foundations upon which the traditional social gospel had been built.

Neo-orthodoxy is commonly said to have had its origins in the thought of Karl Barth, a Swiss-born minister who taught theology in Germany in the 1920s. Like a good many European and North American theologians of his age, Barth started out as a liberal, believing that devoted Christians could build the Kingdom of God on earth. The Great War dashed this vision and caused him to reconsider all of the premises on which his own and most of Western liberal Protestantism had been fashioned. He came to believe that theology had been pursuing false goals for the better part of a century. At the core of Barth's critique was his strikingly simple perception that men had been preoccupied with seeking God when they ought to have been concerned with God's search for man. By this reasoning he rejected the twin pillars of liberal Protestantism: the immanence of God and the perfectibility of man. In their place he reasserted the transcendence of God and the reality of sin. Because of his stern insistence that God and man were essentially separate and, therefore, that man could know God only be revelation and grace, Barth's ideas came to be known by the term "crisis theology." There is little evidence to suggest that Barth exerted a great influence directly upon Canadian Protestantism prior to World War II, even though his writings were available in translation after 1929. Apparently, only one faculty member of a Canadian theological college, Walter W. Bryden of Knox, described himself as a Barthian in the 1930s. It is likely, as Michael Gauvreau has intimated, that the Kantian tradition in Canada was too strong to permit the complete separation of history and theology; there is also evidence to suggest that Canadian liberals failed to appreciate the difference between crisis theology and fundamentalism.

Indirectly, however, Barth's influence in some quarters of Canadian Protestantism during the depression was profound. The crucial conduit of European neo-orthodox ideas in Canada, as in the United States, was Reinhold Niebuhr of Union Theological Seminary in New York. Fluent in the theological language of neo-orthodoxy but also concerned with its implications for social, economic, and political reform, Niebuhr gave essentially Barthian ideas a form tailored to North American Protestantism. Writing for journals like the *Atlantic Monthly* in the late 1920s and early 1930s, Niebuhr attacked the naivete of liberal Protestantism and the social gospel, stressing instead the reality of human sinfulness and the role of power in human relationships. He developed these ideas fully in *Moral Man and Immoral Society* (1932), a book widely considered to have been the most important to come out of North American Protestantism in the interwar years. Like Barth, Niebuhr believed that the Kingdom of God on earth was an unattainable ideal, since man's sinfulness prevented him from realizing the perfection of Christ. Further, he said, justice could not be achieved by moral appeal but only by the establishment of an equilibrium of power between groups with conflicting interests. In light of this, the Christian was to work for social improvement, yet without any illusion that it would eventually lead to perfection.

The Niebuhrian strain of neo-orthodoxy thus represented a rejection of the traditional social gospel; yet it was also a call to radical social action. Niebuhr's own activism bore this out. He had been one of the founding members of the Fellowship for a Christian Social Order in 1922 but with the onset of the depression he had lost confidence in its moderate platform. He founded the quasi-Marxist Fellowship of Socialist Christians in 1931 in the belief that the Christian had a responsibility to engage directly in the struggle for power that lay at the heart of true reform. Throughout the 1930s Niebuhr served as a linch-pin between American Protestantism and the democratic left, openly supporting the Socialist party and organized labour. The American FCSO, by contrast, led by Harry Emerson Fosdick, remained the locus of the moderate wing of the Protestant social gospel, supporting Franklin Roosevelt's New Deal.

The Canadian Fellowship for a Christian Social Order owed more than its named to the Christian Socialist movement in the United States. J. King Gordon, who had studied under Niebuhr and fellow radical Harry F. Ward at Union Theological Seminary in the 1920s, recalled recently that "some of us [in the FCSO] had been in touch with the Fellowship of Socialist Christians in the United States and at first this appears to have been the model we sought to use." Although they rejected the Barthian duality of relationship between God and man, FCSO spokesmen took great pains to forestall the accusation that they represented yet another manifestation of "the utopian optimism of modern liberalism." The leading theologian for the Fellowship, Professor John Line of Emmanuel College at the University of Toronto, repudiated earlier social gospel principles by denying both the imminantism of God and the notion that any new economic or social order might be equal to the Kingdom. Nonetheless, he asserted, it was not necessary to supplant the ideal of community with 'anxiety' in the search for ethical and theological legitimacy as Niebuhr seemed to be doing. As Roger C. Hutchinson has suggested, then, the Canadian FCSO was decidedly "post-Niebuhrian" in its theological and reformist agenda.

The Fellowship established branches in all of the conferences of the United Church, where members dedicated themselves to the resolution of community social problems and to spreading the word about radical social reconstruction. FCSO members wrote prolifically. Their articles and essays appeared in academic journals, church newspapers, and secular magazines throughout the 1930s. FCSO literature called for state control of essential industries and demanded that the locus of political power be transferred from the capitalist class to the working people. These reforms were somewhat inspired by tours of the Soviet Union that had been undertaken by prominent Fellowship members in the early 1930s. More pragmatically, the FCSO defended the rights of workers to collective bargaining and argued for the introduction of social welfare measures, including unemployment insurance and old age pensions. Though the FCSO maintained cordial relations with the CCF, it was nominally apolitical through the 1930s. The Fellowship is best remembered for its 1936 anthology, *Towards the Christian Revolution*, a book that has since seen many reprintings, most recently in 1987. The main objective of this work was, ostensibly, to persuade Canadians of the potential of Christian socialism to make a better society. Its defensive tone evoked, however, a movement already in retreat. The authors' need to distance themselves and Christian socialism from Communism and Fascism, in particular, strained their thesis that capitalism was the worst evil facing modern man.

Practically from the outset the Fellowship was at odds with the United Church hierarchy. George Pidgeon and J.K. Mutchmor, in particular, espoused a conservative philosophy of Christian social service and were openly hostile to the idea of radical social change. Occasionally FCSO members were removed from the faculty of church colleges, though never explicitly for their social radicalism, and young ministers with socialist leanings were frequently consigned to isolated churches. During World War II, control of the FCSO passed from the founders to a younger, more radical generation led by J. Morton Freeman. Believing that direct political action was essential to the achievement of social justice the new leaders politicized the Fellowship and pushed it decidedly left. Their rapport with some prominent Communist party members raised the spectre of Communist infiltration alienating not only social reformers in the churches but the democratic socialists that had comprised the backbone of the Fellowship since its inception. The FCSO could not withstand this internal pressure and in October 1945, no doubt to the satisfaction of many in the Canadian churches, the Fellowship was officially dissolved.

VII

Notwithstanding the fiscal austerity under which Canadian fundamentalists and conservative evangelicals were forced to labour during the 1930s, the popularity of so-called "old time religion" rose considerably in these years. Bible institutes and nondenominational fellowships continued to provide Canadian evangelicalism its essential infrastructure and new ground was broken in the peripheral rural communities. This expansion was due to the emergence of powerful radio ministries and invigorated programs of itinerant evangelism that took advantage of the retreat of the mainline denominations from these areas.

The increasing popularity of fundamentalism in Canada in the depression years owed something to a revival of interest in Biblical prophecy. Not since the gloomiest days of the Great War, in fact, had Canadians outside of the separatist sects shown more than a passing interest in the end-times as prophesied by the Scriptures; generally speaking, the prosperity of the 1920s had not lent itself to apocalyptic interpretations of history. Virtually all self-styled fundamentalists continued to subscribe, nonetheless, to premillennial eschatologies. From this perspective, the world would grow progressively worse until, ultimately, Christ would return to establish His Kingdom. For those who were saved, according to most premillennial theorists, escape would come in the form of the Rapture, when Christ Himself would sweep His followers from the earth and deliver them from the Tribulation. Liberal Protestants, by contrast, at least until the advent of neo-orthodoxy, were most often postmillennial eschatologically, believing that Christ would return to earth after the millennium had been established. Viewed against the cataclysm described in the Books of Daniel and Revelation, the depression at home and the increasingly chaotic state of the outside world seemed not only comprehensible but pregnant with meaning. Books like Oswald J. Smith's *Studies in Prophecy* (1938) warned of "terrible catastrophes" in the immediate future, specifically equating the Tribulation with the rise of dictatorship. Adventism, Dispensationalism and "Scofieldism" attracted new adherents. Their elaborate schemata to systemize history and predict the future according to Biblical prophecy even sparked the curiosity of many on-lookers. Liberal modernists attacked premillennarians for their "pessimism" but the truth was that for subscribers to such eschatologies, the final downward spiral of the world brought ever greater anticipation of the Rapture and the Second Coming.

Among those Canadian Protestants who appreciated pre-millennialism was William Aberhart, the controversial Social Credit premier of Alberta between 1935 and 1943. Aberhart was born in 1878 in Egmondsville, Ontario into a Presbyterian family. A gifted student in his youth, he became a secondary school teacher and principal of great repute. In 1910 he left Ontario for Calgary, where he became principal of the city's leading high school. Aberhart left no detailed record of his early theological development but the broad outlines are clear. He underwent a conversion experience at the age of nineteen, thereafter moving from the Calvinism of his Presbyterian heritage to Arminianism and finally, around the turn of the century, to the dispensational theories of the Plymouth Brethren. In 1918 he established the Calgary Prophetic Bible Conference, which began with modest Sunday afternoon Bible classes at Westbourne Baptist Church. Quickly it expanded to included lectures at the city's Palace Theatre. With the inauguration of his immensely popular radio broadcasts in 1925, Aberhart's audience were said to have numbered in the hundreds of thousands. Recordings of his broadcasts that have survived to the present evince his extraordinary media charisma: their impact on a culture only newly acquainted with electronic media can only be estimated. In 1927 Aberhart built his own 1200-seat structure, the Bible Institute Baptist Church, where, though unordained, he assumed ministerial duties himself. He seems to have commanded far greater loyalty as a radio evangelist than as a local pastor, for in 1929 a sizeable minority of his church group defected to form the first Alberta congregation of T.T. Shield's Union of Regular Baptists.

Though he showed a remarkable flair for mixing the traditional and the unconventional, Aberhart's theological message was always the same: the Rapture and Christ's Second Coming were imminent, therefore the need of the individual for rebirth was immediate. This accorded well not only with the sectarian style of Protestantism that had grown up in Alberta but also with the fundamentalist orientation of many of the mainline churches in the province. As Hans Mol has suggested, Aberhart provided Albertans with a sense not only of their place in the fulfillment of God's prophecy but of their collective destiny. He believed that Alberta was favoured by God and, therefore, that the Rapture was likely to begin there; it was said, in fact, that he slept with his blinds open in the hope that he would be the first to see Christ upon His return. Like Henry Alline, whose New Light revival had provided Nova Scotians with a "feeling of fragile oneness" during the American Revolution, Aberhart provided charismatic leadership and a message of salvation that transcended Alberta's ethnic and denominational divisions. Even for those Albertans who could not swallow Aberhart's prophetic teachings whole, his weekly addresses provided much-needed reassurance at a time of widespread hardship.

Aberhart's ministry was transformed in 1932 by his discovery of
Social Credit, a monetarist salve for the depression. Devised by a
Scottish engineer and amateur economist, Major H.C. Douglas, the
theory taught that because the wages of workers represented only a
portion of the total cost of production, the capitalist system faced a
chronic shortage of purchasing power. To remedy this defect,
Douglas reasoned, one need not overthrow capitalism, as the
communists and socialist directed, but merely provide consumers
with credit equal to the discrepancy between wages and prices.
Although erroneous, this modest theorem struck Aberhart as an
"economic movement from God Himself" a panacea for the
Alberta's economic woes. As David R. Elliott and Iris Miller have
argued in their recent biography of Aberhart, *Bible Bill*, his unlikely
transition from the separatism of dispensational fundamentalism to
the liberal reformist elements of Social Credit can be explained by
the eclectic and sometimes self-contradictory theological views he
had adopted over the years. Aberhart's turn to Social Credit in the
1930s was not so much an abandonment of his dispensationalist
views but a return to the Methodist and Presbyterian social ideals he
had encountered as a young man. Certainly the inner logic and the
seemingly self-evident truth of Douglas' theories might be expected
to strike a resonant chord in one accustomed to the intellectual
rigidity of dispensationalism; Aberhart's Social Credit flow-
charts bore more than a passing resemblance to his pictorial
representations of dispensationalism. He began immediately to
supplement his evangelistic outreach with his own version of Social
Credit theory, advocating the allocation of a "social dividend" of
twenty-five dollars monthly to each Albertan. His rudimentary ideas
were ridiculed by the provincial political establishment, even by
those politicians who were attracted to Douglas' theories.
Undaunted, Aberhart moved to form his own political party. To his
central platform of monetary reform he added such CCF-styled
planks as medicare and labour reform, even borrowing the old social
gospel rhetoric about building "a new social order."

Disillusioned by the depression and fed up with the scandal-
ridden UFA government, Albertans voted overwhelmingly in favour
of Aberhart and his Social Credit party in the election of 1935. In
truth, they were voting not so much for the "funny money" theories
of Social Credit as they were for a man they had come to regard as a
pillar of honesty and strength in a world of corruption and disorder.
This became obvious in 1940 when Aberhart and his party were re-
elected with a reduced majority, even though some of their key
monetary policies had been pronounced *ultra vires*. Aberhart's fire-

and-brimstone evangelism and his monetarist flights of fancy may have seemed incongruent to outside observers but for a majority of Albertans his determination to shoulder their burdens was clear. Whether calling for personal regeneration in Christ or attacking eastern Canadian bankers, he provided ordinary people in the province a measure of self-esteem and control in their lives that had been all but sapped by the depression.

It is important to note, as well, that William Aberhart was not led into the cul de sac of anti-semitism. The same cannot be said of other dispensationalists. Some American fundamentalists, including the extension secretary of the World's Christian Fundamentals Association, Gerald B. Winrod, were drawn by their study of dispensationalism in the 1930s to view Biblical prophecy through the prism of pernicious Jewish conspiracy theories. Mussolini's rise to power in "Rome," the rise of Communism, the migration of Jewish settlers to Palestine, the collapse of the American banking system, and the visibility of Jews in the New Deal administration all confirmed, according to these alarmists that the rise of the Anti-Christ, himself probably a Jew, was imminent. The spectre of an international financial conspiracy run by Jews accorded equally well with many of the monetarist economic solutions put forward in the United States and Britain during the depression. Major Douglas was himself an anti-semite. There is little evidence to suggest, however, that the Canadian Protestant clergy were attracted in the 1930s to Jewish conspiracy theories or that they became any more anti-semitic than they had previously been. The Ku Klux Klan had been active in some parts of Canada in the 1920s: in Saskatchewan the Klan was said to have had some twenty-four Protestant clergymen as members. However, the Canadian Klan more closely resembled the Orange Order in its prejudices than its American counterpart. As for Aberhart, he recognized the crucial role of the Jews in the realization of Biblical prophecy while explicitly distancing himself from the anti-semitism of both the Winrod and the Douglas varieties.

VIII

Following close on the heels of the collapse of the world economy came the collapse of the "international order," a euphemism for the uneasy stand off that had characterized relations between the major powers since the Armistice. Like the Crash of 1929, the unravelling of the postwar peace came as a shock to many Western observers in spite of the foreshadowing events of the 1920s. Few Canadians had expressed reservations about the punitive tenor of the Versailles

Treaty at the time of its signing in 1919. Before long, however, calls for revision arose. Some feared that the allies' harsh treatment of Germany had made war more, rather than less, likely. The idealism that had given rise to the League of Nations proved stillborn; the hope that peaceful negotiation might supplant armed conflict in the resolution of international differences faded. For all of the human suffering the League had alleviated in the aftermath of the war, even member nations remained unwilling to submit their grievances to a supranational authority. Some, including Canada, failed to articulate a clear position on collective security in the event that the League Charter was invoked to mediate international conflict. The expansion of the world's great navies was brought under control by a series of disarmament conferences but these agreements were between former allies and thus brought little in the way of true international security.

The bubble burst in September 1931 when Japanese forces in Manchuria bombed a portion of the South Manchurian Railway and subsequently declared their lawful occupation of the province. Fearing that economic sanctions might lead to war, Western governments responded to the Japanese actions only with expressions of disapproval. However sensible this posture may have seemed on strategic grounds, the refusal of the great powers to act in a manner consistent with the principle of collective security effectively emasculated the League of Nations. Not surprisingly, given the large number of Canadian missionaries stationed in Asia, these events were of acute concern in the churches. In the Methodist and the Anglican denominations, which maintained missionaries in both China and Japan, considerable effort was taken in the consideration of the claims of either side. China missionaries were openly hostile toward what they perceived as Japan's ruthless expansionism. Missionaries in Japan, on the other hand, who for twenty years had been preparing the West for the day when the Japanese, like the British, would outgrow their tiny island, were neither surprised nor outraged. They were far less concerned with Japan's claim to Manchuria than they were with the usurpation of power in Japan by the increasingly popular "militarists."

Any doubt about Japan's objectives in China was put to rest in July 1937 when Japanese forces undertook a merciless full-scale assault upon North China. Deploying troops in the hundreds of thousands as well as modern aircraft capable of saturation bombing, the Japanese promised to "beat China to her knees in three months." For a time it appeared as though they might succeed. Between twenty-five and forty million Chinese, including Generalissimo Chiang Kai-shek, migrated eastward in the first year of the conflict; untold millions, most of whom were civilians, were killed. Not until late 1938, when Chinese guerrillas began to beat back the Japanese in the countryside, was there any relief from the onslaught. Missionaries, particularly those in the occupied fields of eastern China, found their lives utterly disrupted. Some took their chances behind Japanese lines: until Pearl Harbour they were granted a measure of autonomy by the invading generals. Others evacuated the mission fields along with the Chinese. Remarkably, some missionaries in Japan continued to express sympathy for the imperial policies of the Japanese even after the invasion. Back in Canada, the barbarity of Japanese conduct in China turned the churches, and the Canadians population at large, decidedly against Japan. This sentiment would later be manifested in the refusal of most church representatives to criticize the government's internment of Japanese-Canadians.

By 1937, however, Asia was no longer the only trouble spot in the world, nor did it seem to most Canadian observers to be the worst. Hitler's rise to power in Germany, his rearmament of the Reich, and his mesmerizing rhetoric about avenging the humiliations of Versailles were cause for grave concern. Since coming to power in 1922, the Italian dictator Mussolini had been regarded as a curiosity in the West, but this changed when he launched a brutal invasion of Abyssinia (Ethiopia) in 1935 to secure himself a measure of imperial glory. In Spain General Francisco Franco launched a coup in the summer of 1936 to overthrow the leftist Republican government. Franco was aided by Hitler's planes and Mussolini's troops. Church leaders in Canada responded to the rise of European fascism with apprehension and revulsion: apprehension because the seemingly inexorable concentration of power in the hands of the dictators seemed to ensure the inevitability of war; revulsion due to the fascists' curtailment of civil liberties and the Nazis' treatment of the Jews. A pro-Nazi German Christian Movement arose. Its founders were all ordained Protestants whose rallying cry was "One Nation! One God! One Reich! One Church!" This development prompted a sustained campaign of opposition in the conferences and presses of the Canadian churches, and the anti-Nazi Confessing Church led by pastor Martin Niemoller received their unwavering moral support.

Not surprisingly, the rise to power of the extreme right in Europe and in Japan tested the mettle of the antiwar movement in Canada. In 1937 world war no longer seemed a remote possibility; indeed, it seemed probable that Anglo-American "pacifism" might make the dictators' drive for world domination easier. Faced with the choice between the evil of war and the evil of Fascism, many liberal

Protestants reluctantly abandoned the pacifism they had embraced in the 1920s. Absolute pacifists, like those in the Society of Friends and the Fellowship of Reconciliation, responded to the disintegration of the antiwar coalition by allying themselves with isolationists and by girding themselves for yet another struggle over conscientious objection. The majority of church leaders and Protestant laymen in Canada, for whom a love of peace had never translated into pacifism, nonetheless shared the hope that means could be found to avert the war. Two decades of literature on the destructive capacity of the newest generations of weapons had raised the spectre of a conflict more barbaric and protracted even than the Great War; some pundits had even speculated on the possibility that the next great war might hearken the end of civilization. Little wonder, then, that praise for the 1938 Munich agreement granting Hitler the Sudetenland portion of Czechoslovakia rang from virtually every Canadian pulpit.

When war finally came, in September 1939, it prompted the patriotic support of the Canadian churches. However, the millennial enthusiasm that had marked the outbreak of hostilities in 1914 had not reappeared. From the perspective of most clergy, Hitler was at least as great an evil as the Kaiser ever had been but there was no sense that his defeat would usher in the Kingdom. As John Webster Grant had surmised, they viewed the war as "a messy but necessary job."

Fearing that the unanimous endorsement of the war effort by the presbyteries of the United Church might mean a repeat of the crusading zeal of 1914, sixty-eight United Church ministers with pacifist leanings issued "A Witness Against the War" in October 1939. This document sought not to turn the United Church against the war effort but rather to temper the church's patriotism and remind it of its responsibility to those within its fold for whom war was unconscionable. The debate in the United Church that followed the publication of this petition was acrimonious but influential: the General Council, which was by no means pacifist, declined to support conscription in 1942. With the exception of some highly patriotic ministers, notably T.T. Shields, who once again demanded an "all-out war effort" including conscription, the Protestant clergy in Canada attempted to accord conscientious objectors the same respect as they did those Christians for whom fighting in a "just war" was a grave personal responsibility. Dissension about pacifism flared up occasionally, with more than one anti-war advocate being removed from the pulpit, but there was generally far less tension between the poles of pacifism and patriotism than there had been during the Great War.

The day-to-day role of the clergy during the Second World War was much the same as it had been in the first: chaplains were dispatched and pastoral duties were once again enlarged to encompass the task of providing comfort on the home front. Perhaps surprisingly, the most dramatic alterations in liberal Protestant church life in Canada in these years came in the realm of theology. To the extent that conservative evangelicals and fundamentalists were concerned with the war, the conflict seemed to confirm beyond any doubt the error of liberal modernism and its absurd notions of evolution and human perfectibility. In the ranks of the liberals themselves, there was a distinct movement in the direction of orthodoxy, as reflected in the rising popularity of the writings of Barth and Niebuhr and in the movement of seminarians "back to the Bible." Man's inability to remedy the Depression, thwart an Adolf Hitler, or prevent a second global war mocked the idea of human progress and confirmed the hard reality of human sin.

Wartime sacrifice once again had the effect, nonetheless, of bringing social reform to the top of the churches' agenda. Following the lead of British Archbishop William Temple, the General Synod of the Anglican Church in Canada abandoned its dogged aloofness to the reform question and called in 1943 for a national program of social security. Other church councils issued similar pronouncements. However radical they may have appeared, these appeals were not typical of the utopian social gospel nor of the radical social reconstruction envisioned by the Fellowship for a Christian Social Order. On the contrary, they were thoroughly "Niebuhrian," both in the modesty of their objectives and in the emphasis they placed upon government protection of the powerless from the powerful. Church leaders applauded Mackenzie King's introduction of the Family Allowances Act in 1944 and his promise of similar assistance for veterans, homeowners, farmers, the ill, and elderly during the election campaign of 1945.

Ironically, the new reformist orientation of the federal Liberal party had its genesis in King's worries about competition from the CCF. The man whom King feared the most was T.C. "Tommy" Douglas, an ordained Baptist minister who carried into politics the social gospel he had embraced at Brandon College in the 1920s. Douglas's political career began in 1934 when he was elected to the House of Commons as the member for Weyburn, Saskatchewan. In 1942 Douglas assumed the leadership of the Saskatchewan CCF and in the provincial election of 1944 he swept the party to victory on a campaign promising a moratorium on farm debt and the implementation of public health care. Ever sensitive to the winds of change, King adjusted the federal Liberal platform. Just as he had done in the early twenties with the Progressives, he borrowed many of the reforms emanating from the CCF, thereby undermining its strength as a national party.

The continuing association of the social gospel with the Cooperative Commonwealth Federation may have provided reform-minded Protestants in Canada with a vehicle for their reformist energies in the 1930s and the 1940s; but thereafter, as Hans Mol has argued, the secularization of social reform in Canada rendered the CCF and its successor, the New Democratic party, the preferred political affiliation of non-churchgoers. With the demise of the FCSO in 1945 the once-powerful idea of building the Kingdom of God on earth was dead in the Canadian Protestant churches, supplanted once and for all by a more limited, "realistic" and secular agenda for social reform.

IX

Horrific though they were, the atomic bombings of Hiroshima and Nagasaki brought an end to World War II. Canadians entered the nuclear age in an ambivalent mood, torn between their fears of both renewed economic depression and international tension but buoyant about their return to civilian life and the possibilities that stretched before them. Church leaders had every reason to hope that, after ten years of depression and six years of war, the nation was poised for revival; they also had ample reason to fear that Canadians would slip from the spiritual moorings that had seen them through these long years of turmoil and sacrifice.

Census statistics for 1941 revealed that religion in Canada was diversifying and that the traditional dominance of the mainline Protestant churches among non-Francophones was waning. Church union had altered the demographic profile of Canadian Protestantism most dramatically. Presbyterianism had been the largest Protestant denomination in Prince Edward Island, Nova Scotia, Manitoba, Saskatchewan, and Alberta since Confederation; after union the United Church of Canada became the largest denomination in each of these provinces. The Presbyterian church in Nova Scotia felt the impact of church union most dramatically, being reduced to the fourth largest denomination in the province after 1925. In each of the prairie provinces Presbyterianism fell to third, behind the United Church and the Church of England. In Prince Edward Island the strength of the continuing Presbyterian church was sufficient to maintain a rank of second largest. In Ontario, where Methodism had always been the largest denomination, the United Church naturally became predominant. The position of neither the Baptists nor the Anglicans was affected by church union. Baptists remained predominant in New Brunswick, as they had been historically, and the Church of England remained the largest Protestant denomination in British Columbia, the Yukon Territories, and Northwest Territories.

The census of 1921 had been the first to show that industrialization had rendered rural dwellers in Canada a minority. By 1941, 54.3 per cent of the Canadian population was classified as urban. Of the mainline Protestant denominations in Canada, the urban-rural profile of the Baptist denomination and the United Church most closely resembled the national average in 1941: the proportion of Baptists living in urban areas was cited as 48.9 and that of United Church members as 50.9. Approximately 62 per cent of Anglicans and Presbyterians in Canada, by contrast, were listed as urban. Many of the smaller denominations in which ethnic identity and agricultural tradition remained strong, such as the Doukhobors, Lutherans, and Mennonites, remained almost entirely rural in 1941. Other movements, most notably the Salvation Army and Christian Science, remained predominantly urban. Of the smaller Protestant groups in Canada, only the Pentecostals' demographic profile resembled that of the nation at large in 1941, with 47.3 per cent listed as urban.

One of the most significant revelations in the 1941 census data was the discrepancy between the median age of the membership of the mainline churches and that of some of the new Protestant groups. Only 22.6 per cent of Canadian Anglicans, 26.1 per cent of Baptists, 24.5 per cent of United Church members and 20.3 per cent of Presbyterians in Canada were under the age of fifteen in 1941. The proportion of Pentecostals and Adventists under the age of fifteen, by contrast, was 32.7 and 30.3, respectively. These figures suggested all too clearly that the growth potential for the major Protestant denominations in Canada was well below that of the new charismatic groups, a situation that had begun to worry some of Canada's mainline Protestant leaders as early as the 1920s.

Above all, the census of 1941 revealed that Canada was becoming increasingly pluralistic in matters of religion and that the once powerful vision of a Christian Canada was under strain. The average percentage increase for all religious groups in Canada in the years 1871-1941 was 221.4 per cent. Of the mainline Protestant churches only the Anglicans could boast higher than average rate of growth in these years, with 247.8 per cent. The combined growth rate of the Presbyterian, Congregationalist, Methodist, and United Church in this period was only 157 per cent; the Baptists, with a mere 97.9 per cent rate of growth, fell short of the national average and, indeed, were unable even to double their numbers in this period. The rate of growth in the Roman Catholic Church in Canada in the same period was just over the national average at 224.9 per cent.

The expansion of non-Christian religions in Canada in the years 1871-1941, by contrast, was shown to have been dramatic. The number of Jews in Canada rose by a remarkable 13,572 per cent, and the average rate of increase for those Canadians listed in the category, "Other Religions," was 825.7 per cent. Taken as absolute members, of course, these non-Christian groups remained small. In 1941 there were still only 168,585 Jews in Canada of a total population of 11.5 million, and only 183,741 Canadians were classified as Buddhist, Confucianist or "Other." Nonetheless, some of the leaders of the Canadian churches saw in this trend cause for concern. Since the turn of the century the churches had been among the most outspoken advocates in Canada of controlled immigration of non-Christan peoples; the flow of "new Canadians," they had argued, should be governed solely by the capacity of the Canadian churches to convert, train, and assimilate immigrants. By the 1930s it had become clear that non-Christian immigration had outpaced the capacity of the churches for proselytization and Canadianization. Some churchmen, like J.I. MacKay, superintendent of the Church of All Nations in Toronto, had begun by this time to embrace the notion of an ethnic "mosaic" and to speak of a future in which "multiculturalism" would provide the core of a new Canadian identity. For others, however, the census of 1941 simply confirmed that the greatest era in Canadian national and religious life — the era of "His Dominion" — had closed.

SUGGESTIONS FOR FURTHER READING

While some of the best scholarship in Protestant church history in Canada has dealt with the period 1914-1945, significant gaps in the literature remain. Apart from the relevant sections of John Webster Grant, *The Church in The Canadian Era: The First Century of Confederation* (Toronto: McGraw-Hill Ryerson, 1972) and Robert T. Handy, *A History of the Churches in the United States and Canada* (New York: Oxford University Press, 1976), no survey of Canadian Protestantism in the period between the world wars exists. The most useful sociological study of religion in Canada in these years remains Hans Mol's *Faith and Fragility: Religion and Identity in Canada* (Burlington: Trinity Press, 1985). A host of denominational and sectarian histories cover this period, including John S. Moir, *Enduring Witness: A History of the Presbyterian Church in Canada* (Toronto: Bryant, 1975); Philip Carrington, *The Anglican Church in Canada* (Toronto: Collins, 1963); J.K. Zeman, ed., *Baptists in Canada: Search for Identity Amidst Diversity* (Burlington: G.R. Welch, 1980); and Leslie K. Tarr, *This Dominion His Dominion* (Willowdale: Fellowship of Evangelical Baptist Churches in Canada, 1968). Similarly, there are many histories of Canada's Protestant church colleges that encompass this period, the most general of which is D.C. Masters, *Protestant Church Colleges in Canada: A History* (Toronto: University of Toronto Press, 1966).

The social gospel has dominated the study of Protestantism in Canada in the early twentieth century. This is due largely to the influence early in the life of religious history as a distinct field in Canadian scholarship of Kenneth McNaught's *A Prophet in Politics: A Biography of J.S. Woodsworth* (Toronto: University of Toronto Press, 1959), Stewart Crysdale's now outdated *Protestant Ethics in Canada: A Survey of Changing Power Structures and Christian Social Ethics* (Toronto: Ryerson Press, 1961) and especially Richard A. Allen's *The Social Passion: Religion and Social Reform in Canada, 1914-1928* (Toronto: University of Toronto Press, 1971). Allen's looming presence in Canadian religious history has been felt down to the present. He chaired an excellent panel of papers published as *The Social Gospel in Canada* (Ottawa: National Museum of Canada, 1975), which includes J. King Gordon's fascinating memoir, "A Christian Socialist in the 1930s," and recently he has produced several articles on the life of Salem Bland. Theses written under Allen's supervision have included Donald L.Kirkey, "Building the City of God: The Founding of the Student Christian Movement of Canada" (M.A. thesis, McMaster University, 1983) and Thomas P. Socknat, "Witness Against War: Pacifism In Canada, 1914-1945" (Ph.D. thesis, McMaster University, 1981). The latter has recently been published in book form (Toronto: University of Toronto Press, 1987) and stands as the definitive treatment of pre-Cold War pacifism within and without the Canadian churches, though David R. Rothwell's "United Church Pacifism, October, 1939," Bulletin 22 (1973) and Donald M. Page's "The Development of a Western Canadian Peace Movement," S.M. Trofimenkoff, ed., *The Twenties in Western Canada* (Ottawa: National Museum of Canada, 1972) remain insightful. Other important contributions to the study of the social gospel in Canada include E.R. Forbes' important essay, "Prohibition and the Social Gospel in Nova Scotia," *Acadiensis I* (1971); Brian Fraser, "Theology and the Social Gospel Among Canadian Presbyterians: A Case Study," *Studies in Religion 8* (1979);

Sheila P. Mosher, "The Social Gospel in British Columbia: Social Reform as a Dimension of Religion, 1900-1920" (M.A. thesis, Victoria University, 1974); Marilyn Joan Harrison, "The Social Influence of the United Church of Canada in British Columbia, 1930-1948" (M.A. thesis, University of British Columbia, 1975); Douglas H. Ross, "A Theological Analysis of the Socio-Critical Role of the United Church of Canada between 1925 and 1939" (Ph.D. thesis, University of Ottawa, 1982); and John Edward Hart, "William Irvine and Radical Politics in Canada" (M.A. thesis, University of Guelph, 1972).

A growing body of work exists on the impact of the world wars and of the international crises of the 1920s and 1930s upon Canadian Protestantism, apart from the subject of pacifism. J.M. Bliss, "The Methodist Church and World War I," *Canadian Historical Review 49* (1968), David B. Marshall, "Methodism Embattled: A Reconsideration of the Methodist Church and World War I," *Canadian Historical Review 66* (1985), and Michael Gauvreau, "War, Culture and the Problem of Religious Certainty: Methodist and Presbyterian Church Colleges, 1914-1930," *Journal of the Canadian Church Historical Society 29* (1987) attempt to ascertain the impact of the First World War on the churches, while Charles Thompson Sinclair-Faulkner, "For Christian Civilization: The Churches and Canada's War Effort, 1939-1942" (Ph.D. thesis, University of Chicago, 1975) gauges their responses to the Second. The churches' cultivation of new international roles in the 1920s and 1930s has been documented in Robert A. Wright, "Canada's Share in World Tasks: Aspects of Internationalism in the Mainline Protestant Churches in Canada, 1918-1939" (Ph.D. thesis, Queen's University, 1989). N.W. Rowell's crucial role in the cultivation of Christian internationalism in Canada has been documented in Margaret Prang, *N.W. Rowell: Ontario Nationalist* (Toronto: University of Toronto Press, 1975). Protestant missions have been the subject of several excellent studies. Among the most useful for the period 1914-1945 are Alvyn J. Austin, *Saving China: Canadian Missionaries in the Middle Kingdom, 1888-1959* (Toronto: University of Toronto Press, 1986); John William Foster, "The Imperialism of Righteousness: Canadian Protestant Missions and the Chinese Revolution, 1925-1928" (Ph.D. thesis, University of Toronto, 1977); and Andrew Hamish Ion, "British and Canadian Missionaries in the Japanese Empire 1905-1925" (Ph.D. thesis, University of Sheffield, 1978). Ion's revised thesis was published under the title *The Cross and the Rising Sun* (Waterloo; Wilfrid Laurier University Press, 1990).

Church union has been a preoccupation of denominational and

professional historians practically since the turn of the century. C.E. Silcox, *Church Union in Canada: Its Causes and Consequences* (New York: Institute of Social and Religious Research, 1933), John Webster Grant, *The Canadian Experience of Church Union* (London: Lutterworth, 1967) and Mary J. Vipond, "Canadian National Consciousness and the Formation of the United Church of Canada," Bulletin 24 (1975) suggest something of the evolution of this historiography. The story of the opposition of one-third of Canadian Presbyterians to church union has been told several times, most recently by N. Keith Clifford in *The Resistance to Church Union in Canada, 1904-1939* (Vancouver: University of British Columbia Press, 1985).

Relative to the liberal Protestant tradition in Canada, serious study of evangelical tradition lags considerably. For instance, there is no equivalent in Canada of George M. Marsden's *Fundamentalism and American Culture* (New York: Oxford University Press, 1980) even though Canadians have been well represented in the fundamentalist movement from the outset. The only general surveys of the evangelical tradition in Canada are John Stackhouse, "Proclaiming the Word: Canadian Evangelicalism Since World War I" (Ph.D. thesis, University of Chicago, 1987) and David R. Elliott's controversial study, "The Intellectual World of Canadian Fundamentalism, 1870-1970" (Ph.D. thesis, University of British Columbia, 1989). Largely because of the dominating presence of T.T. Shields, Canadian Baptist scholars have assumed the lead in the study of conservative evangelicalism. Leslie K. Tarr's sympathetic biography, *Shields of Canada: T.T. Shields, 1873-1955* (Grand Rapids: Baker, 1967) and his more scholarly "Another Perspective on T.T. Shields and Fundamentalism," in Zeman, ed., *Baptists in Canada*, noted above, are complemented by the clinical objectivity of Walter E. Ellis, "Gilboa to Ichabod: Social and Religious Factors in the Fundamentalist-Modernist Schisms Among Canadian Baptists, 1895-1934," *Foundations 20* (1977) and C. Allyn Russell, "Thomas Todhunter Shields: Canadian Fundamentalist," *Ontario History 70* (1978). G. Gerald Harrop's "The Era of the 'Great Preacher' Among Canadian Baptists." Robert T. Handy's "The Influence of Canadians on Baptist Theological Education in the United States" and Winthrop S. Hudson's "The Interrelationships of Baptists in Canada and the United States" all of which appear in *Foundations 23* (1980), are also insightful, as is G.A. Rawlyk, "A.L. McCrimmon, H.P. Whidden, T.T. Shields, Christian Higher Education, and McMaster University," in Rawlyk, ed., *Canadian Baptists and Christian Higher Education* (Montreal/Kingston: McGill/Queen's University Press,

1988). The impact of fundamentalism on Baptists in the Canadian West has been described in John B. Richards, *Baptists in British Columbia: A Struggle to Maintain 'Sectarianism'* (Vancouver: Northwest Baptist Theological College and Seminary, 1977) and in Karel D. Bicha, "Prairie Radicals: A Common Pietism," *Journal of Church and State 18* (1976). The fundamentalist stir in the ranks of eastern Canadian Baptists is documented in G.A. Rawlyk, "Fundamentalism, Modernism and the Maritime Baptists in the 1920s and 1930s, *Acadiensis 16* (1987). An enlightening and witty view of the controversy over higher criticism in Toronto in the 1920s is provided in John S. Moir, "Mildewed with Discretion : Toronto's Higher Critics and Public Opinion in the 1920s," *Studies in Religion 11* (1982). With only a few exceptions, the study of independent evangelical and fundamentalist churches (or sects) in Canada has been the domain of sociologists and sectarian historians, W.E. Mann, *Sect, Cult and Church in Alberta* (Toronto: University of Toronto Press, 1955) is a dated source for the explosion of dissent that occurred on the Canadian prairies in the early twentieth century. For a more recent examination of the phenomenon, see Donald A. Goertz, "The Development of a Bible Belt" (M.A.; St. Michael's, 1984). Oswald J. Smith is the subject of Lois Neely's 'official' but nonetheless insightful biography, *Fire in His Bones* (Wheaton: Tyndale House, 1982). James Eustace Purdie's role in Pentecostal education in Canada is documented in Brian Ross, "James Eustace Purdie: The Story of Pentecostal Theological Education," *Journal of the Canadian Church Historical Society 17* (1975).

Radical Christian socialism in Canada in the 1930s has been the subject of two theses, Roger C. Hutchinson's "The Fellowship for a Christian Social Order: A Social Ethical Analysis of a Christian Socialist Movement" (Th.D. dissertation, Emmanuel College, University of Toronto, 1975) and Margaret R. Sanders, "The Fellowship for a Christian Social Order" (M.A. thesis, Trent University, 1979). The link between the radical social gospel and democratic socialism in Canada has been probed in Michiel Horn's *The League for Social Reconstruction: Intellectual Origins of the Democratic Left in Canada, 1930-1942* (Toronto: University of Toronto Press, 1980). Too little is known about the influence either of Karl Barth or of Reinhold Niebuhr upon Canada; however a recent study of W.W. Bryden's theology, its relation to neo-orthodoxy, and its influence upon the Presbyterian Church in Canada is found in John Visser's "The Conception of Revelation in the Theology of Walter W. Bryden" (Th.D.: Toronto School of Theology, 1988). The influence of Toyohiko Kagawa has been documented in Robert A. Wright, "A New Spirituality: The Impact of Mahatma Gandhi and Toyohiko Kagawa on the Canadian Protestant Churches in the Years between the Wars," Canadian Historical Association, Historical Papers (1988, microfiche edition), while that of Frank N.D. Buchman has been described in an important study by Robert G. Stewart, "Radiant Smiles in the Dirty Thirties: History and Ideology of the Oxford Group Movement in Canada, 1932-1936" (M.Div. thesis, Vancouver School of Theology, 1974). Scrutinizing William Aberhart and Social Credit has become something of a cottage industry in the historical profession, spawning, among other projects, a series of books sponsored by the Canadian Social Science Research Council under the heading "Social Credit in Alberta." David R. Elliott and Iris Miller, *Bible Bill: A Biography of William Aberhart* (Edmonton: Reidmore, 1987) is without question the finest treatment of Aberhart's religious life to date.

THE PROTESTANT EXPERIENCE
IN CANADA SINCE 1945

John G. Stackhouse, Jr.

Plus c'est la meme chose, plus ca change. Forty-five years after the
end of the Second World War, Canadian Christianity looked
superficially the same as it had a generation before. Canadians told
census-takers that basically the same denominations held their
allegiances as had held them in the 1940s. Christian churches still
dominated the skylines of most small towns and villages, and were
by far the most common houses of worship. Clergy continued to hold
positions of respect, and many newspapers maintained "Religion"
sections, some of which went considerably beyond mere
advertisments of weekly church services.

For all the apparent similarities and continuities, however, the
years since World War II saw significant changes in the Christian
churches. Canadians might have maintained allegiances to the
same denominations, but the nature of those allegiances had
changed. Churches might predominate in size or number over other
religious buildings, but many stood no more than half-full on
Sunday mornings, and some now had signs outside identifying
them as house of worship for different denominations and religions.
Clergy might continue to be respected as honest, hard-working
community servants, but now increasingly they were seen as social
workers and counsellors rather than as leaders in church and
society. More of their number spoke in soprano and alto voices,
rather than tenor and baritone. Newspapers and other media might
monitor Canadian religion for the occasional unusual story, but for
the first time in Canadian history, questions of public policy — even
French-English relations — normally would be discussed and
resolved without substantial reference to religion.

Interpreting the story of recent Canadian religion in general, then, and of Canadian Protestantism in particular, is fraught with the danger of concentrating too much on the obvious continuities at the risk of ignoring the real changes often discernible only beneath the surface or around the edges. On the other hand, since historians often thrive on novelty, the opposite danger looms of exaggerating the new and different so as to distort the basic patterns of Canadian Protestantism which characterize the whole period.

The first fifteen years after the war (1945-1960) were seen by contemporaries and later observers as generally good years of growth and prosperity for Canada and her churches. While considerable evidence supports this impression, closer analysis reveals fault lines and even actual shifts which pointed ahead to the upheaval of the brief but crucial period in Canadian history known in the vernacular as the "sixties." After this decade, the still familiar landscape of Canadian religion was altered in unmistakeable and important ways. The consequences of some profound changes were yet to be clearly seen.

Boom: 1945-1960

As the "orderly decontrol" of the huge Canadian war effort began late in 1945, pundits differed in their predictions regarding Canadian society. Some had great expectations. The Canadian economy, revved up to produce one of the world's best-equipped fighting forces, would switch over to peacetime production of goods most Canadians had never been able to afford. With this aim, as federal Cabinet Minister C.D. Howe, head of the Department of Reconstruction, presided over a series of programs to benefit Canadian industry. War-time brought the institution of unemployment insurance and family allowances. These advances in social security and the growing influence of labor unions promised a higher standard of living and greater social stability than Canadians had previously enjoyed.

Some who looked particularly at the nation's Protestant churches had reason for high hopes as well. Men in uniform, glad in times of crisis for the ministrations of a padre of any denomination, probably would now support the ecumenical ventures some of their church leaders had been pursuing. The anticipated economic growth would provide resources for replenishing the depleted supply of pastors and erecting new church buildings. Further, the combination of wartime exposure to suffering and death and the exhilaration of peace might well provoke many to seek out their churches afresh: a religious revival might even break out across the nation.

Some observers, on the other hand, had lesser expectations. The end of World War I had seen Canada plunged into a serious depression, both economic and religious, and perhaps things would never be the same again. Churches across Canada had suffered for lack of pastors during the Second World War and it was unclear how many veterans would seek such sacrificial posts after the demands of combat. Moral decline threatened as many soldiers left behind war-time lovers and self-indulgent recreational habits, returning home to strained or broken marriages and children they had not seen in years. Sunday-school faith often had failed to help men and women deal with the usual horrors of war, much less with Auschwitz or Hiroshima. The abandonment of traditional Christianity was, for many, the result.

Both hopes and fears were realized in the years ahead, although not necessarily in the ways expected. The Canadian economy *did* boom after the war and many Canadians experienced a dramatically increased standard of living. For their part, the Canadian Protestant churches grew beyond the expectations of all but the most sanguine of their prophets. The growth, however, did not necessarily indicate increased influence for the churches in Canadian society and culture. The question would later arise as to whether, in relation to the growth of the Canadian population at large, the Protestant churches had really "grown" at all. Some of the apparent achievements were often ambiguous and decidedly ironic. For, to use a Canadian pun, while industries and churches can boom with success, so does lake and river ice boom as it begins to break up in the spring.

I

Even to the careful observer, the later 1940s and 1950s looked like a glorious time for Canadian Protestantism. Sunday school enrollments rose and where the children went, so soon went their parents to produce the largest rate of growth the churches had seen in the twentieth century (see Figure 1). The United and Anglican Churches, for instance, saw their memberships rise by about 25% between 1951 and 1961. This increase represented an understandable post-war desire to "get things back to normal." "Going to church" was a natural part of the overall conservatism of Canadian society in the 1950s. It also reflected, however, the many social and service opportunities available in churches. Society had been fragmented by war-induced separations and made more conscientious, perhaps, by experiences of wartime suffering at home and abroad. Men's and women's church groups flourished; the men's groups now rivalling traditionally popular societies like the Kiwanians and Lions. Service projects proliferated in all of these organizations. Study groups formed and retreats were organized to deal with questions raised by the experiences of war or just to educate laypersons who had not taken Sunday School or sermons seriously before. The sales of religious books and periodicals rose tremendously: Protestant church papers alone passed the one million mark in total circulation.

Two more reasons for the numerical increase in at least some groups, to be sure, had nothing to do with the churches' efforts and program per se. After the war, and especially in the 1950s, Canada received a stream of immigrants which was rivalled in size only by the influx during the early decades of the twentieth century. The other reason for greater numbers was the increased Canadian birth rate, an increase which had begun just before the war and continued well into the 1960s.

To accommodate an increase in both numbers and activities, congregations found themselves needing bigger and sometimes more versatile buildings. Larger sanctuaries were built, especially in the burgeoning suburbs, and additions of classrooms, dining halls, and gymnasia were common. Between 1945 and 1966, for example, the United Church alone built 1500 new churches or halls and 600 new manses.

All of this, naturally, had to be financed. Fortunately, generally steady growth in the Canadian economy was felt, especially in the urban and suburban areas, and it was also these areas that saw the most church growth. There was more money that could be collected, and professional fund-raisers increasingly helped churches collect it. One American group, the Wells Organization, doubled the receipts of 92 per cent of the 2000 churches it served before the organization collapsed in 1960, and some of the Wells techniques were appropriated by others. The Presbyterian Church provides one example of the financial boom: in 1945 it raised $3.2 million for all purposes; in 1949 it increased this to $4.8 million; and a decade later it collected $11.3 million.

The conservative attitudes of the time tended to favour familiar denominational "labels" and "products" rather than uncertain ecumenical ventures, and the boom in numbers and resources tended to encourage denominational independence, if not outright competition, rather than cooperation. This only served to underscore the point observed elsewhere that Canadian ecumenism was at least as much a matter of prudent use of limited resources in the interest of common objectives than of deep theological concern over a fragmented church. Indeed, some observers believed that a stronger effort toward developing a theological rationale for union would have kept some projects from failing, since sometimes when the practical need for combining resources disappeared, so did the interest in cooperation.

Nonetheless, certain ecumenical dreams were pursued and some were fulfilled, while others seemed on the verge of being realized. These ventures were of various kinds. Some institutions, such as the Canadian Lutheran Council established in 1952, brought together for joint action denominations of the same tradition. Many of these groups were formed to funnel relief funds to post-war Europe or to care for the "displaced persons" now in Canada. Some were dialogues toward organic union between churches of different traditions: this was the aim of interaction between the United Church, the Anglicans, and Disciples. The Canadian Council of Churches embodied the dream of an organization which would coordinate the work and witness of all the churches of Canada. The CCC, established in 1944, became a component of the new World Council of Churches, itself not formally constituted until 1948.

The spirit of independence and nationalism encouraged by Canadian's participation in the war and subsequent growing economic prominence was echoed in some ecclesiastical developments as well. Some denominations began to draw away from their American counterparts into autonomous Canadian units. For example, the Lutherans formed both their individual denominations and the Canadian Lutheran Council. The Church of England in Canada became in 1955 the Anglican Church of Canada with its own distinctively Anglo-Canadian flag.

In all, then, the era seemed a bright one for the churches who together held the allegiance of the vast majority of Canadian Protestants: United, Anglican, Presbyterian and Lutheran. Furthermore, the period saw some important developments in Canadian Protestant life outside these traditionally mainline churches.

II

Canadian Baptists were one of the few sizeable groups that did not experience significant growth overall since 1945. This was at least partly because their region of greatest strength, the Maritimes, was in a general state of decline throughout the twentieth century compared with central and Western Canada. The consequences of this concentration of Baptists in New Brunswick and Nova Scotia caused one prominent historian to muse, "If the future of Canada had been a Maritime future rather than a Western one, the Baptist denomination would have been as important to Canada today as it is in the United States." As other churches grew much more quickly than the Baptists, the identity of Baptists as a "mainline" denomination seemed imperilled (see Figures 1 and 2). One notable development in Baptist history did occur, however, in the decade after the war. The two main groups formed out of the fundamentalist side of the controversies of the 1920s, especially those involving T.T. Shields and McMaster University, joined together in 1953 to form the Fellowship of Evangelical Baptist Churches of Canada. This was intended to be a national alliance which would stand as a more decidedly conservative counterpart to the Baptist Federation of Canada (founded in 1944).

Various Mennonite groups also explored closer relationships which had begun in wartime. The Mennonite Central Committee, established in 1964, finally joined together various regional relief organizations begun in previous decades. In the 1940s and 1950s Mennonites founded at least seven high schools and several Bible institutes and colleges. Some also supported transdenominational institutions like Prairie Bible Institute in Alberta. The considerable number of Dutch immigrants strengthened the ethnic and theological distinctiveness of the Christian Reformed Church in Canada. Various independent evangelical congregations grew up, especially in Ontario and on the prairies, and the Pentecostal churches continued to manifest the vigour which would result in their experiencing significant numerical increase in each of the succeeding decades (see Figures 1 and 2).

The Salvation Army found itself in a unique position. Its wartime services had earned it the respect of a large number of Canadians and many Salvationists clearly enjoyed this welcoming into the mainstream of Canadian life. At the same time, however, their zeal for evangelism and zest in worship seemed remarkably diminished to observers within and without who recalled the days of street parades and "holy cartwheels" in Sunday morning services. The "Blood and Fire" seemed thinner and cooler than before. This development indicated the increasing similarity between the Army and other formerly more enthusiastic revivalist traditions, most notably Methodist revivalism in the United Church.

Those Protestant Christians in various denominations, mainline or otherwise, who held to a "high" view of the inspiration and authority of the Scriptures, the importance of personal conversion, and the centrality of evangelism in the mission of the church felt more and more estranged from others in their denominations concerns seemed disturbingly different. Presbyterian like W. Stanford Reid and pastors like Perry F. Rockwood, ance, spoke of their fears of "modernism" in the church, hich echoed both those of anti-unionists of a generation before and those now of contemporaries in other pluralistic churches. At the same time, these Protestants began to see themselves as part of a transdenominational fellowship of like-minded Christians in a wide range of denominations. They would come to identify their fellowship as "evangelical" despite the different religious categories this adjective had denoted in the past. This sense of being part of an evangelical movement would be much stronger at this time in the United States, especially in the institutions associated with Billy Graham. Nonetheless, the formation of certain institutions in Canada indicated that Christians of a variety of traditions recognized in each other key commitments and were willing to work together to advance them.

For instance, the Inter-Varsity Christian Fellowship of Canada (IVCF), begun in 1929, recovered from the loss of male staff to the war effort and began after 1945 to extend itself across Canada. Its older counterpart, the Student Christian Movement (SCM), continued to debate its own identity and purpose, especially in the light of neo-orthodox theology. The SCM did maintain its basic liberal commitments to provide a forum for questions from Christians and non-Christians alike and to work for the social betterment of humanity. IVCF, on the other hand, articulated the traditional evangelical concern to nurture spirituality among Christian students in secondary schools, vocational and professional colleges, and universities and to help them evangelize their peers. It was in IVCF that many evangelicals encountered for the first time Christians from other denominations that shared these basic convictions. Bonds began to form that would result in other ecumenical projects with an evangelical emphasis.

The proliferation of Bible schools and colleges in the 1930s and 1940s, especially on the prairies, demonstrated as well the willingness of evangelicals to work together in a common cause, in this case the training of young people for domestic church service and foreign missionary work. By the 1940s there were thousands of students enrolled in Bible schools across Canada while the numbers in the mainline theological colleges declined to a far smaller number.

Most important of these Bible schools was the Prairie Bible Institute, in the little town of Three Hills, Alberta, some eighty miles from Calgary in the heart of wheat country. Prairie had grown dramatically since its founding in 1922. Under the powerful leadership of American L.E. Maxwell, the school had added a high school program to its offerings, and the combined attendance reached a peak of 900 in 1948-49 as Prairie enrolled servicemen who had delayed education during the war. Many of these were Americans, and Prairie exemplified the cultural ties between Canadians and Americans on the plains. Prairie Bible Institute became the largest Bible school in the world, and while its enrollment declined to 560 by the mid-1950s, it rebounded to 671 by 1960-61. Prairie's stature as an international center for the training of evangelical missionaries and church workers was well established.

This was still too early, however, for many evangelicals to have any sense of a national fellowship or network. Occasionally the circles around some of these transdenominational institutions would intersect (especially those headquartered in Toronto, like the large Sudan Interior Mission, Toronto Bible College, and IVCF), but they were not linked in any ongoing, deliberate fashion. Indeed, one observer of the Christmas missions conference sponsored by IVCF at the University of Toronto in 1946-47 noted that while L.E. Maxwell was on the program as one of several prominent speakers, the IVCF leaders from Toronto and the Prairie folk who accompanied Maxwell found each other distressingly alien in outlook on world affairs, attitudes toward Canadian mainline denominations, and habits of personal piety. Despite some rallying around the popular Canadian "crusades" of Graham and his sometime Canadian colleague Charles Templeton, more formal and institutional cooperation would emerge only in later decades.

Evangelical developments, to be sure, affected a minority of Canadian Protestants. Yet as problems appeared in mainline Protestantism during this era of apparent success, so did the prospect of the so-called "third force" of evangelicalism. It was to become an increasingly important part of the Canadian Protestant experience.

III

As historian John Webster Grant has remarked, the state of the church in the later 1940s and 1950s was not exactly what it seemed to be. For one thing, traditional emphases of some churches were moderating. The United Church of Canada, for instance, reflecting especially its Methodist tradition, had long opposed alcohol, but in this era it continued to ease its stricture on temperate drinking, letting those who engaged in it continue as members in good standing while maintaining voluntary total abstinence as an ideal and often housing Alcoholics Anonymous meetings in its buildings.

Some were disheartened by the weakness of prominent ecumenical projects. The Canadian Council of Churches, for instance, failed to establish itself as an innovative and forceful representative of the mainstream of Canadian Protestantism. As well, the dialogue towards union between the United and the Anglican churches suffered from the denominationalism prominent at the time to the point that the general council of the United Church challenged the Anglicans in 1958 to declare whether they truly wished to continue this sort of conversation any longer.

Most telling, however, was the fact that the Protestant churches in general and most of the mainline churches in particular were declining in terms of their percentage of total Canadian population even though their actual numbers were increasing (see Figures 1 and 2). The numbers of immigrants contributed to increases for the Roman Catholic, Lutheran, Orthodox, and other churches and a declining total share of the population for the Mainline Protestant groups. Some small conservative groups were growing too, notably the Pentecostals, who increased by more than a third in the 1950s, but their numbers were so relatively tiny at this point that few paused to analyse possible reasons for their growth.

The main factor besides immigration in the actual failure of the Protestant mainline churches to keep up with population growth seems to have been the increasing secular preoccupations of the Anglophone population. For not only were the numbers of Canadians declining who declared to census-takers their allegiance to the mainline churches, so too were the numbers declining of Canadians, who actually attended Anglophone Protestant church services. In 1946, some 60% of Canadian Protestants told the Canadian Institute of Public Opinion that they had gone to church "in the last seven days." Ten years later, this number had dropped by almost one-third to 43%. Some parts of Canada, of course, had been left almost untouched by the affluence and materialism of the 1950s, and church attendance patterns remained much the same. Among those who had more choices of leisure-time activities, however, church adherence was less important. Canadians joined with most other Western nations in viewing ecclesiastical involvement as being part *only of* leisure-time activities.

Despite the call of some Canadian Protestant leaders for a thorough-going improvement of the church, as in R.C. Chalmers's well-balanced *See the Christ Stand!* (1945), it seems that there was less of a revival of genuine and lasting spirituality in the post-war boom than of a revival of general cultural conservatism and consumerism of which church involvement was a component. So when events and personalities of the 1960s challenged this traditional orientation, they challenged the traditional churches as well. The widespread lack of commitment to those churches became much more clear — and, for some, deeply distressing.

Break-up: The "Sixties"

Canadian history, like any other kind of history, rarely jolts from one clearly-defined era to the next. Instead, history is a current which flows variously, sometimes slowing and broadening over flat areas, sometimes accelerating through narrows, sometimes plunging over falls. Tributaries join, alternative channels lead away only sometimes to rejoin the mainstream later. The "Sixties" in Canadian life and in Canadian Protestantism in particular, therefore, did not arrive on the morning of 1 January 1960. Instead, trends from the previous era continued into the next decade, albeit with sometimes surprising results which would encourage observers to conclude that something clearly new had come.

The late 1950s and early 1960s were unhappy times for many Canadians. Buoyed by the nationalism and populism of John Diefenbaker, who presided over a huge majority since the election of 1958, areas of Canada not much improved by the post-war boom hoped for much better. They were disappointed as recession swept much of Canada during this time: unemployment, for instance, reached 11.2 per cent by 1959.

Some turned for help to the nascent social-democratic New Democratic Party, which arose in 1961 out of the Cooperative Commonwealth Federation with support from the Canadian Labour Congress. Others remembered that there was at least *some* truth to the party slogan that "Liberal Times are Good Times," and the Liberal party under Lester B. Pearson gained strength. Still others, however, remembered those Liberal "good times" as happening to *other* Canadians, in *other* parts of the country, and maintained allegiance to the Conservatives as their best hope. The different experiences of Canada's regions in the 1950s were reflected in the election of 1963: the Conservatives dominated the West and the Liberals were strongest in Quebec. The other regions elected some of each party and several Social Crediters/Creditistes and New Democrats leavened the results across the country. The Liberal Party under Pearson, however, was now in power.

Pearson's government did not always make the best of its slim majorities in the 1960s, beginning with two years of embarrassments instead of its promised "days of decision." Nonetheless, Canadians appreciated the returning prosperity and the expanding social services offered by the government, like a national pension plan, a Canada Assistance Plan for the poor, and federally-funded health insurance. Unemployment fell to the low single digits, and increasing American investment, in particular, furthered expansion of the economy.

The nationalism which Diefenbaker had articulated took on a decidedly less English tinge in the 1960s. Earlier in the decade, Diefenbaker had been hurt by Canadian infatuation with John F. Kennedy. Canadians chose the American president against their own prime minister on several issues regarding joint defense, notably support of the U.S. during the Cuban missile crisis of 1962 and the arming with nuclear warheads of U.S. missiles stationed on Canadian soil. As the decade went on, however, Canadians, if unconsciously, reflected America's own questioning of itself and developed a nationalism which in many respects was simply "not British and not American." The adoption of the new Canadian flag in 1965 symbolized the distancing from things British and the establishment of a sort of independent Canadian identity. Canadians determined to show themselves off to the world at the world exposition in Montreal in 1967.

A different sort of nationalism brewed in Quebec during the Quiet Revolution. With prosperity came increasing secularity and independence. Quebeckers became disenchanted with traditional politics, traditional religion, and traditional relationships with the rest of Canada. Sensitivity to the place of Quebec and of Francophones across Canada within Canadian society was manifested in the establishment in 1963 of the Royal Commission on Bilingualism and Biculturalism. The "two solitudes" were still separate, but the character of each was changing in the 1960s and some saw improved prospects for bringing them into more substantial contact even as radicals threatened to tear Confederation apart.

As John Webster Grant has put it, Canadians and their churches emerged late out of the Victorian era. It was in this time of upheaval that the traditional dominance of mainline Protestantism in Anglophone Canadian life finally and obviously began to break up. Some relished what they saw to be new freedom for all those outside the Christian mainstream. Others bemoaned the loss of beneficial restraint the churches had exercised on some of the less noble tendencies of Canadians. Still others saw opportunity for new roles for Canadian Protestants in society and for new relationships among Christians themselves. For with break-up comes both destruction of a previous order and the arrival of a new, and sometimes vital, situation.

I

In this time of the dissolution of traditions and the emergence of new options, the Protestant churches did well simply to hang on for the ride. The mainline churches in particular attempted to keep up with the changes in Canadian life, only to meet with ambiguous success.

The most obvious ambiguity was in membership and church attendance statistics. Mid-decade saw the membership rolls reach all-time highs for the United, Anglican, and Presbyterian churches. In 1966 the United Church reported membership of just over 1 million, the Anglicans reported just under 1.3 million; and the Presbyterians reported 200,000. Of the four large Protestant churches, however, only the Lutherans added numbers beyond the mid-decade "crest." By 1971 the Lutherans collectively had eclipsed the Presbyterians as the third-largest Protestant tradition in Canada, with 200,000 members over against 183,000 Presbyterians. Membership in proportions to the Canadian population at large continued to decline for the United, Anglican, and Presbyterian churches with the Lutherans just maintaining their share (see Figure 1). Furthermore, church attendance for all Protestant churches, which had declined from 60 per cent in 1946 to 43 per cent in 1956, continued to drop steeply so that by 1965 just over one-third of Canadian Protestants reported that they had gone to church in the last week. With the widely-recognized tendency of members of smaller denominations to attend church more regularly than those of the larger ones taken into account, the decline of traditional adherence to mainline Protantism in Canada was unmistakeable.

Statistical fingers began to write on the ecclesiastical wall, and some church leaders drew deeply of the spirit of the time, criticizing their churches in the name of radical change. At the turn of the decade, for instance, the Very Reverend Angus MacQueen, moderator of the United Church, declared that the Canadian church was merely "the feeble guardian of personal decency and the fount of tranquility and optimism." and therefore "too pietistic and irrelevant in the face of the real stuff of life and great issues of our day." He was not alone: a sampling of religious leaders by *Maclean's Magazine* published early in 1961 demonstrated that many already recognized, beneath the ostensible health of Canadian Christianity, what one journalist called "the hidden failure of our churches."

No critique from within, however, had the impact of the critique from without solicited by the Anglican Church of Canada from one of its most distinguished expatriates, Pierre Berton. Encouraged by the bold questioning of the international Anglican Congress held in Toronto in 1963, the leaders of the Canadian church asked Berton to represent the religiously disaffected members of Canadian society in a little book which could be used for study by concerned Anglicans across Canada. The Anglicans got their little book, and considerably more.

The Comfortable Pew (1965) essentially challenged the church to be true to its own principles. Far from a call to be or do something new, Berton's book held the church to its own standards and found it sadly wanting. As he put it elsewhere: "I say the time has come for the Church to put up or shut up." Worship, social outreach, evangelism, preaching, and fellowship all came in for serious and provocative criticism.

Berton's book itself, naturally, came in for criticism as a result. Peter Berger, the prominent American sociologist of religion, dismissed the book and the controversy around it as "the relevance bit comes to Canada." Another reader called it " an ecclesiastical *Fanny Hill*, the product of a mediocre mind." A more biblically-minded person compared Berton himself, in a double-edged simile, with the prophetic ass of Balaam. Others, however, apparently thrilled to find someone publicly endorsing opinions they had held themselves — and on the church's invitation to boot! One priest described it "as possibly the most important document since Martin Luther nailed up his ninety-five theses." Other readers compared Berton to the prophet Amos and John the Baptist, and one even punned, "Thou art Pierre, and upon this rock will I build my Church."

Between these two extremes raged debates in circles everywhere. The book easily met Canadian standards for best-seller status. It provoked comment on talk-shows, in newspapers, in sermons, in religious study groups, and at denominational headquarters. Berton himself soon afterward evinced astonishment at the reaction with the statement: "I thought most of what I said was self-evident." Perhaps, he mused, "[the book's] content wasn't as important as the *event* of its publication."

A national event it surely was, but measuring its importance is very difficult. For all the apparent soul-searching, one might ask, were the Protestant churches, Anglican and otherwise, much improved a year or a decade later? Some church people clearly took seriously the criticisms of Berton's book and the many other current tracts and attempted to reform their churches. The United Church, always quick on the draw, devised a new creed to be used as an

alternative to the Apostle's Creed for various services. The
adopted in 1968, bears some marks of its predomi...
Presbyterian heritage. Nonetheless, observers have judged it to be
noticeably un- Reformed in some respects and, instead, too much
the product of the narcissism of the sixties. The most obvious area
of scrutiny was the very beginning of the creed. Some saw it to
center not upon God, as classical creeds do, or upon the Scriptures,
as some evangelical confessions do. Rather, it seemed to focus upon
humanity: the first three clauses begin, "We are . . ., we live . . .
[and] we believe . . ." For its part, the drafting committee was aware
of its departure from traditional patterns and defended the creed as
an attempt "to make contact with contemporary persons beset by
questions about man, lostness and loneliness on the one hand and
man's self- sufficiency in world affairs on the other." The arguments
could go back and forth, but clearly the creed suited a number of
United Church people for it was adopted and printed in service
books beginning in 1969.

Reforms took place in other aspects of worship as well, with more
popular music and musical instruments taking the place of
traditional hymns and pipe organs. Folk music and guitars were
especially common: one wit suggested that at this time "Pete Seeger
added his name to the roster as a composer of sacred music."
Dialogues and "multi-media presentations" replaced sermons:
doctrine was discussed rather than merely taught and received. Less
radically, the Anglicans issued a revision of the *Book of Common
Prayer* in 1959, although to some it resembled the conservatism of
the post-war era more than the innovation of the era to come. After
considerable disagreement, the Presbyterians agreed upon a new
Book of Common Order in 1962. Some observers wondered if too
much experimentation was being attempted: "Folk music was
invading the choir, psychiatry the pulpit, journalism the text."
Extremes, unfortunately, received disproportionate notice. A
Vancouver pastor invited a local go-go dancer to perform in what he
hoped would be a service so spectacular that it would rival
psychedelic drugs for young people's attention: it wasn't, it didn't,
and he never tried it again!

Other reforms reflected other trends in the larger culture. The
increasing emphasis of innovation in education showed up in the
United Church's introduction of its "New Curriculum" in 1962. The
result of deliberations going back as far as the General Council of
1952, the curriculum attempted to teach Christian truth to laypeople
in lessons which would be informed by the higher criticism of the
Bible which had dominated mainstream academic theology for
decades. Despite its rather "neo-orthodox" interest in increasing the

biblical content of Sunday school teaching, the curriculum looked to many readers disturbingly "modernist" and antagonistic to traditional Christianity. By questioning commonly-held assumptions about the authorship and dates of composition of biblical books, the curriculum was seen to dispute the authority of the Bible itself. Opposition mounted for other reasons, as well. Some, who had no trouble with its theology, thought it demanded too much preparation on the part of teachers despite the apparently wide welcome given to the curriculum the first year or so it was offered; orders tailed off by the mid-1960s.

On another front, the major Protestant churches to some extent stood in the vanguard of the increasing criticism of social policies and attitudes. Inspiration from contacts with Roman Catholics since Vatican II prompted new concern among mainline Protestants; contacts through the World Council of Churches and other agencies with churches involved in social and political struggles in other parts of the world pricked other consciences. As well, the Canadian government's review of certain sections of the Criminal Code (dealing with such issues as contraception, homosexuality, divorce, and abortion) sparked widespread interest. The United Church maintained its traditional engagement in social action but now much more frequently enjoyed the company of the Anglicans and Presbyterians in speaking to a variety of concerns. These concerns covered a wide range including: the plight of the disadvantaged (e.g., senior citizens, the unemployed), bigotry (interracial marriages, treatment of Canadian Indians and Inuit), bilingualism and biculturalism, and violence (whether pornography, suicide, or capital punishment). A sign of the times was the first ordination of an Inuit in the Anglican Church in 1960. This event was at least as much an embarrassment to the church in that it had taken so long to occur, given the history of Anglican missions in the North, as it was a positive omen of increased stature for native peoples in Canadian churches.

The mood of experimentation and innovation in order to "catch up" with and "relate" to contemporary society was prompted by both criticism and a sense of new possibilities and responsibilities. The mainline ecumenical movement, for example, showed new vigour at this time in several respects. Several Lutheran groups amalgamated in the early 1960s as did their American parents, the Lutheran Church of America and the American Lutheran Church. In 1966 the three major Lutheran denominations in Canada formed the Lutheran Council in Canada, becoming operative the next year. United and Anglican church leaders took up their strained conversation with new dedication and produced in 1965 a statement of principles upon which the long-sought union could take place. Delays inherent in large ecclesiastical machinery followed, and murmurs of opposition began to grow. Nonetheless, the decade would end with the expectation that the plan would succeed. The inclusion of the Christian Church (Disciples of Christ), who joined in the deliberations in 1969 even looked possible. A portion of the much smaller Evangelical United Brethren Church joined the United Church in 1968.

Theological education also reflected changes in Canadian church life. One important development occurred in the secular world itself, as departments of religious studies were founded as early as 1960 at public universities. "From divinity to religious studies" marked the change from the "religious" teaching of religion to its secular study, a change manifest also in the cessation of the *Canadian Journal of Theology* (founded in 1955) in favour of the new journal *Studies in Religion/Sciences religeuses* (founded in 1971). This change reflected several things: the continuing interest in matters religious; the new interest in a *variety* of religions; and the lessening of confessional, traditional approaches to religion generally in Canadian society. "Professional," "scientific," "objective" investigation of religion grew. This interest was manifest also in the establishment or further growth of professional societies for religious studies, like the Canadian Society of Biblical Studies, the Canadian Society for the Study of Religion, the Canadian Theological Society, and the Canadian Society of Church History. All these societies were recognized by the Canada Council as "Learneds" by 1971. Indeed, while the departments of religion were growing, most seminaries were shrinking: a mid- 1960s survey of twenty-three "mainline" theological schools revealed that 123 full- and part-time faculty were teaching only 667 students.

The shrinking numbers by no means meant that contemporary theology was dull. Canadians continued to join with other English-speaking scholars, for instance, to study the prominent German theologians Karl Barth, Emil Brunner, Dietrich Bonhoeffer, Rudolph Bultmann, and Paul Tillich. Some in the avant-garde also reflected upon the Christian and atheistic varieties of existentialism coming over from Europe: Gabriel Marcel, Jean-Paul Sartre, and Martin Heidegger were all influential. As well, the American version of neo-orthodoxy associated with Reinhold Niebuhr contributed to the agenda of academic theory in Canada. No identifiably Canadian theology was worked out, however; no Canadian Protestant theologian came to national, much less international, attention. From the first responses of the dialectical theologians to liberalism after World War I to the radical theologies of the 1960s, Canadians followed the arguments and responded generally with characteristic moderation. As Gerald R. Cragg has put it, "In many ways Canada is a vigorous country; theologically it has been a diffident one." What generally filtered down into seminary teaching and from thence to the pew was theological liberalism "corrected" from "excesses" by neo- orthodoxy. Outright "modernist" denials of key orthodox doctrines, therefore, were relatively rare in mainline Protestantism outside intellectual circles.

The lack of candidates for pastoral ministry coincided with greater ecumenical openness to prompt several denominations to pool their resources. Lutheran groups, for instance, began negotiations to operate a seminary jointly in Saskatoon. More radically, by 1967, a report on theological education in Canada had recommended the concentration on four regional study centers to be sponsored by the mainline churches, especially the United and Anglican. Partly in response, the Toronto School of Theology began in 1969: several seminaries cooperated with each other and with the University of Toronto in joint programs. This pattern was soon emulated on both coasts in the Atlantic and Vancouver Schools of Theology.

The most dramatic change in ecumenical relations, though, was prompted by what was perhaps the most important event in twentieth-century Roman Catholic history, the Second Vatican Council (1962-65). This exercise by Catholic leaders in criticism, revision, and re-affirmation of central emphases had at least two effects on many Canadian Protestants. First, it confirmed and encouraged some Canadian Protestants in the pursuit of their similar agendas, and second, it opened the door to dialogue between Catholics and Protestants. This latter development was of course all the more remarkable given the "two solitudes" of Canadian church life.

"Two solitudes" is not an entirely accurate representation of the relationship between Canadian Catholics and Protestants since the Second World War. During the war, the Canadian Protestant League formed to protest what it saw to be lack of patriotism on the part of French Catholics on the one hand and special treatment by Ottawa of Catholics on the other. Though the League diminished greatly in both size and importance after the war, Catholic-Protestant relations continued to be marked by cold isolation, flaring at the borders in the 1940s as Jehovah's Witnesses and evangelical Protestant missionaries attempted to proselytize Quebeckers. The non-Catholic evangelists were repelled sometimes violently, by priests supported by police and other government authorities under the notorious Padlock Law of 1937. The tension was even more obvious as Quebec's censorship board banned the film *Martin Luther* in the mid-1950s. When Roman Catholic bishops at several junctures asked for further support from various provincial governments for their separate school systems, they received strong opposition from a variety of Protestant directions. The mainline Protestant Inter- Church Committee on Protestant-Roman Catholic Relations, which had been founded in 1944 to research areas of possible conflict, was the most notable opponent to Roman Catholic Separate School support in the 1950s and 1960s.

Even this traditionally volatile issue, however, was handled in the 1960s more by direct encounter, as John Webster Grant observed, and "not made [an occasion] for appeals to popular prejudice." With Rome's window opened by Pope John XXIII for some fresh air, as he himself put it, and with at least mainline Protestant leaders as well as Roman Catholic clergy less moved to declaim and more disposed to listen, significant conversations began at various levels. Priests began to attend local ministerial association meetings, joint services (including marriages) were held, and Catholic professors participated in the nonconfessional theological societies.

To be sure, not all ecumenical ventures prospered during this time. Partly because of the increasing openness among many denominations, the Canadian Council of Churches was seen by some as superfluous in its intended role as bridge among groups. In response, it shifted its emphases toward research.

Many of these changes, of course, characterized changes in church life throughout the West and especially in the United States. Part of the continuing British influence on Canadian Protestantism was exemplified in Canadian debate of Englishman J.A.T. Robinson's *Honest to God* (1963). The increasing American influence, however, was clear in theology also as Canadians wondered about Episcopalian James Pike's radical questions and Harvey Cox's "secular city." Many Canadian clergy and seminary professors continued to graduate from American theological colleges and universities while the Canadian institutions considered economic innovations to keep their doors open. Some of the best Canadian theological talent remained south of the border, following the greater pattern in Canadian intellectual history. Developing Sunday school and other educational curricula for a specifically Canadian audience frequently was judged to cost too much, and so they were imported from the United States. Trends, therefore, in all aspects of Canadian Protestant church life came mostly from the United States.

The questioning, the criticism, the new theologies, and the ecumenical spirit of the 1960s came together for mainline

Protestantism at a nationalistic event: the Montreal world's fair in 1967. Roman Catholic, Protestant, and Orthodox churches sponsored a pavilion that offered some disturbing reflections upon their fair's theme "Man and His World." Pictures and words combined to plunge visitors into a kaleidoscope of contemporary experiences with celebrations of the possibilities of the "secular city" but also with poignant reminders of how badly so many men, women, and children were faring in their world. The displays offered no traditional religious cure-alls, no explicit promise of divine salvation, no diversion of attention from this world to the next, and no direct attempt to proselytize. This was the era for dialogue, for questioning of tradition and authority, for exploring other options, for cooperation with seekers of any faith, and the Christian Pavilion at Expo powerfully reflected the attitudes of many Canadian Protestants.

It by no means, however, reflected the attitudes of *all* Canadian Protestants. Conceived as a venture which would unite all Canadian Christians, the Christian Pavilion served instead as one-half of a pair of Christian pavilions, the other half of which served notice that at least some Canadian Christians had emerged from this period of upheaval with very different concerns and were supporting a growing set of institutions and alliances to further them.

II

Smaller Canadian denominations and other Protestant organizations responded to the challenges of the 1960s in different ways. The concrete results were often not apparent until later, but those results were often important and are worth tracing back to this time of new options. Conversations began in the early sixties, for instance, towards the formation by mid- decade of a small group of clergy and laity. Mostly from the mainline churches, with Presbyterians dominating, the Evangelical Fellowship of Canada was established. This group held annual conferences and regional seminars and published a magazine of small circulation, but came to national attention only in the 1980s.

Perhaps the most important activities were in the spheres of both denominational and transdenominational education. As their sense of alienation from the mainline denominations increased, evangelicals supported a number of educational alternatives. They founded or expanded Bible schools and colleges. At a different level, Mennonites, for instance, established Conrad Grebel College in 1961 as an affiliate of the University of Waterloo. Conrad Grebel

offered a distinctively Mennonite education environment wh
contributing to the pluralism of the secular campus following
model common in Canadian higher education. Evangelicals c
various sorts supported Inter-Varsity Christian Fellowship, which
only in this decade began to serve the Atlantic provinces with
steady, full- time staff, thus becoming truly a national organization.

The experimental mood of the times was reflected quite
differently among different evangelicals. The leaders of the Prairie
Bible Institute, for instance, decried the disrespect for authority of
so many young people while praising the godly dedication of their
own students. They warned against the dangers of cozying up to the
Catholics, and basically continued their program of training youth
in the fundamentals of evangelical belief, life, and witness in the
confidence that the terrible tides of modernity would scarcely reach
rural Alberta.

National leaders of Inter-Varsity, on the other hand, confronted
the sixties in downtown Toronto, and encouraged the rest of the
Fellowship to consider new options of Christian service. Informed
especially by Reformed theology, these leaders, especially General
Director H.W. "Wilber" Sutherland, called on evangelicals to
embrace a broader and more thorough view of vocation than full-
time missionary work or personal evangelism. All of one's life and
work was to be seen as service to God. IVCF, Youth for Christ, and
other evangelical student groups maintained their traditional
emphases on a personal spiritual growth and the proselytizing of
peers, but now often added to them a new awareness of modern
social issues, noting the variety of opportunities for service open to
the Christian. To some extent echoing techniques employed by
campus denominational chaplains or by their American
evangelical counterparts, these "parachurch" groups sponsored
coffee houses, folk and rock concerts, "rap sessions," and other
"happenings." However, the evangelical version had a much more
obvious evangelistic emphasis than one would find at similar events
sponsored by the United Church student groups, for example.

Not too much, however, should be made of these developments.
Most Canadians naturally were unaware of anything much
happening beyond the Roman Catholic-United-Anglican-
Presbyterian mainstream. Not only were the numbers of
evangelicals relatively small, but the mass media were not very
interested in what was "old," "conservative," "traditional," and
"unsecular." As one observer put it, "the People's Church [Toronto's
large independent evangelical congregation founded by Oswald J.
Smith] and the Pentecostals were there, but they were not to be
noticed by polite society except when their behaviour found a place

in a newspaper's morning or afternoon 'smile.'" Baptists did not prosper numerically or in any other way during this time, notwithstanding the pleasure of the Fellowship of Evangelical Baptist Churches in adding churches in Quebec and the Atlantic provinces to their fold. Pentecostals were regarded by mainstream Protestants and most evangelicals themselves as both troubled and troubling enthusiasts, denizens of what historian Arthur R.M. Lower once acidly called the "nether world of Protestantism." Mennonites and Christian Reformed were coming off the farms and into the cities in steadily increasing numbers, but most maintained strong ties to ethnicity and religion.

Their common convictions and common alienation from the mainline denominations did bring together evangelicals across Canada to support the construction of an alternative to the mainline Christian Pavilion at Expo 67. "Sermons from Science" presented cinematic and live demonstrations of intriguing scientific phenomena which suggested theological points. The presentation culminated in a direct appeal for conversion or spiritual renewal to those who opted to leave the main theater for a counselling room off to the side. Despite the widespread ignoring of it by the secular and mainline denominational presses in favour of the "other" Christian Pavilion. "Sermons from Science" was one of the most popular pavilions at Expo. It clearly offered visitors an alternative in at least several aspects. Most obviously, it differed from the other display by concentrating not on "Man and His World" but rather on *God* and *his* world. This in turn reflected the more direct nature of its appeal: while the mainline Christian Pavilion asked "Seeing all this, what shall we then do?" the "Sermons from Science" concluded with the proclamation "Seeing all this, ye must be born again." Finally, and most importantly, the presence of two pavilions pointed to an emerging consensus among some Canadians that a different kind of ecumenism was emerging. It was an evangelical alliance which spoke for those in a wide variety of denominations whose concerns, they believed, were not articulated by the leaders of mainline denominations.

At the start of the 1970s, and indeed the 1980s, most Canadians would continue to tell census-takers that they "belonged" to the same large denominations the majority of Canadians had for generations (see Figure 2). But for all the innovation, for all the attempt to be "relevant," for all the efforts at dialogue and responsiveness and flexibility, mainstream Protestantism lost its hegemony over church-going Protestants in this era. The 1970s and 1980s instead would demonstrate that the alternative posed by "Sermons from Science" at Expo 67 would subsequently be posed

more powerfully than perhaps even evangelicals themselves would
have guessed. These decades would also show, though, that however
much evangelicals might congratulate themselves on their growing
presence in Canadian religion, especially in relation to the mainline
denominations, the Canadian society which celebrated its coming
of age at Expo 67 was steadily becoming more secular and less
interested in *either* option.

Fragments: The 1970s and 1980s

Canadians in the 1970s and 1980s supported successively two
apparently contradictory philosophies in national government. The
first, a determined federalism verging on socialism, characterized
the long tenure of Pierre Elliott Trudeau and the Liberal party. The
second, a strong defense of free-market economics and less
governmental shaping of society in general, characterized the
majority governments of Brian Mulroney and the Progressive
Conservatives.

One might presume that the majority governments of both
Liberals and Conservatives had national mandates and reflected
national consensus on important issues, but election returns
throughout this era, as well as inter-provincial and federal-
provincial disputes showed the continuing influence of regionalism
in Canadian life. In at least some important cases, furthermore,
policies of both governments led to ironic results which
underscored the presence of divisions in Canadian society.

First, for example, Trudeau's government attempted to bring the
country together, but with the Official Languages Act (1969) one
essential division in Canadian society was further entrenched.
Second, under Trudeau most Canadians might have enjoyed
together the national event of the patriation of the constitution
(1982) but the process alienated many in Quebec whose government
did not agree to the proceedings. Finally, Mulroney hoped that the
Meech Lake Accord (1987) would bring Quebec on board, even if it
meant increased provincial autonomy at the expense of Trudeau's
federalist dream. Indeed, Trudeau publicly opposed it for this
reason, and others saw too that his idea of a bilingual, bicultural
Canada would be compromised by the granting of special privileges
to Quebec. The prospect of such privileges, however, upset many in
other regions across Canada for a variety of reasons. Some
observers saw inconsistency in Mulroney's Progressive
Conservatives explicitly allowing so much power to a provincial
government to shape the life of its people.

The threat of the Parti Quebecois to split apart Confederation, therefore, perhaps was only the most obvious example of the fragmentation of Canadian society in this era. The fragments could be as large as whole provinces, or even regions, but also as small as the individual, whose increasing importance in Canada was recognized nowhere more clearly than in the controversial Charter of Rights and Freedoms established with the new constitution.

Fragmentation characterized Canadian Protestantism in particular. With what one might call the "final disestablishment" of the old United-Anglican-Presbyterian hegemony, with traditional patterns of church membership eroding, and with sociologists noticing discernible traces of individualistic "pick-and-choose" religious practice, the character of Canadian Protestantism was continuing to change in some fundamental ways. The period saw not only disintegration, however, in the nation as a whole and particularly in the Protestant churches. Instead, some fragments combined in new ways to produce new arrangements, communities, and forces that shaped Canadian life in both new and traditional directions.

I

The basic statistics of mainline Protestant church life in Canada in the 1970s and 1980s continued to reflect a general decline (see Figures 1 and 2). In 1961, Canadians had told census-takers that just over 40 percent of them "belonged" in some way to one of the United-Anglican-Presbyterian-Lutheran mainstream churches. In 1981, only 32 per cent reported the same allegiance, a decline of one-quarter in just two decades. The more problematic measurement of church "membership" told much the same story: only the Lutherans had improved their total numbers relative to those of 1961, barely holding their own relative to the increasing size of the entire Canadian population. Lutheran leaders themselves criticized their flock for their continuing insularity from Canadian society, their preoccupation with themselves, and their weak efforts in evangelism; all of which spelled trouble down the road, they believed. The Presbyterians, for their part, were characterized in 1976 as a "smouldering bush" by their most prominent historian, John S. Moir. They perhaps faced the bleakest future as they had clearly the oldest population and the lowest fertility rate with little apparent prospect of change. Between 1960 and 1985, for instance, the number of students enrolled in their church schools decreased by two-thirds (from 112,000 to 38,000). In recognition of this fact, and in the face of a 2 per cent *decline* in church membership between 1979 and 1985, the Presbyterians' optimistic goal to "double in the eighties" was scaled back in 1986 to simply growing at all. Furthermore, with the decline in numbers of people in mainline churches came declines in numbers of dollars, leaving the denominations often in precarious financial straits. The United Church, for instance, lost 100,000 indentifiable contributors between 1961 and 1975, and its Mission and Service Fund reported dramatic shortfalls in the later 1980s.

As is to be expected, the statistics of Canadian Protestant experience were not even across the country. The "Atlantic high, Pacific low" pattern of religious adherence continued to characterize Canadian Protestantism. The Atlantic provinces maintained the most traditional religious patterns. Ontario and the prairies were lower and about even with each other, and British Columbia was clearly the most secular. Indeed, those claiming "No Religion" in the 1981 census constituted the largest religious grouping in British Columbia — larger than Roman Catholic, United Church, or any other religious group. This national pattern was most often explained in terms of secularization theory: the Atlantic region, for instance, experienced the least industrialization and urbanization and so was touched by modernity and secularization the least. At the other end of the scale and country, some explained that the culture of "beautiful British Columbia" was the most individualistic, hedonistic, and experimental in Canada and so the least open to traditional religious patterns. As one observer put it, in British Columbia "Sunday mornings are for the worship of nature and the cultivation of [a] healthy body, rather than for the worship of God." The latter "explanation," of course, was not an explanation at all but a tautology: British Columbian culture was not as traditional as elsewhere in Canada and so people were relatively less inclined toward traditional activities like churchgoing. In terms of secularization theory, why was more heavily urbanized and industrialized Ontario not more secular still? Some speculated instead that British Columbia's climate and geography, and their attraction for highly mobile young adults, were the most important factors in the tone of its culture. Moreover, data collected in 1985 indicated that religious commitment in Canadian rural areas was only slightly stronger than in urban centers and this was true in British Columbia itself. The analysis was complicated further by the observation that while evangelical Protestantism continued to be proportionately stronger relative to mainline Protestantism in the Atlantic region than anywhere else in Canada, British Columbia for its part had seen evangelical Protestantism grow significantly in the 1970s and 1980s while mainline Protestantism steeply declined. Nonetheless, while the sociologists and historians continued to seek for explanations, the overall pattern was indisputable.

Turning back to the national picture as a whole, decline in these national numbers slowed noticeably in the 1980s and aggregate church attendance among all Protestants actually rose slightly between 1975 and 1986 (25 per cent to 27 per cent — versus 32 per cent in 1965). The churches now faced the new problem of overabundance of clerical candidates: Canadian colleges affiliated with the Association of Theological Schools increased enrollment by almost 50 per cent between 1975 and 1981. This increase was due in no small measure to the welcoming of women into the pastoral ministry, and in the 1980s women often made up half or more of the students in these colleges.

Church life continued, though not necessarily in response to the decline in numbers. Ecclesiastical leaders, for instance, often put forward controversial views which risked alienating substantial parts of their churches' membership. Sometimes these views took the form of social and political critiques with which Christians of more conservative views vociferously disagreed. The ordination of women to pastoral ministry in the Anglican, Presbyterian, and some Baptist and Lutheran churches continued to prompt considerable debate, only to be overshadowed in the late 1980s by the decision to allow the ordination of practicing homosexuals in the United Church. This decision saw some congregations split, others actually leave the denomination, and still others reconsider their future in it.

Some of these controversies affected interdenominational relations as well. The United and Anglican churches produced a popular hymnbook together in 1971 and a general commission agreed on a Plan of Union in 1972. Nonetheless, negotiations between the United and Anglican churches finally fell through in 1975, and the conversations between the United Church and Church of Christ (Disciples) ended a decade later. One well-positioned observer attributed the breakdown to fear in different quarters of "unwelcome innovation": especially among Anglicans. Anglo-Catholic and evangelical Anglicans were deeply concerned that denominational distinctives important to them would be lost in such a union. When this concern coincided with trouble over so many other controversial issues facing Canadian Anglicans in the early 1970s, therefore, the prospect of wholesale change was just too much for too many to countenance.

The Lutherans did not entirely unite either, but in 1986 the Lutheran Church of America, Canadian Section, and the Evangelical Lutheran Church of Canada joined to form the Evangelical Lutheran Church of Canada. Furthermore, their solidarity with their Missouri Synod counterparts was confirmed as the Missouri Synod branch became officially independent on 1 January 1989.

This failure to unite "fragments" of the church at one level, however, was mitigated by the continuing cooperation among several churches at other levels. In 1975, for instance, the Anglican, Lutheran (except Missouri Synod), Presbyterian, Roman Catholic, and United churches agreed to recognize one another's baptisms. On a different level, a somewhat bewildering alphabet soup of organizations sprang up to deal with a wide range of issues: Project North, for northern native Canadian affairs; Association to Promote Justice in Canada (also known by the initials of the sponsoring denominations, Presbyterians, Lutheran, United, Roman Catholic, and Anglican, as PLURA); GATT- Fly for issues of international trade; Inter-Church Consultative Committee on Development and Relief (ICCCDR) for co-ordinating a variety of projects overseas; and Inter-Church Committee on Human Rights in Latin America (ICCHRLA). These groups and dozens of others presented briefs before government inquiries and courts as well as information to churches in order to bring Christian principles to bear on questions of public policy. Sometimes, too, they and the sponsoring churches themselves took more direct action as the sponsorship of "Boat People" from Vietnam and Kampuchea in 1979 and 1980 and Central American refugees a decade later. Some observers believed these church actions shamed the federal government into increasing its immigration quotas for such refugees. In general, however, the effects of these coalitions are impossible to measure, even if the efforts were considerable.

Critics within and without the supporting denominations, however, frequently saw these agencies to be disturbingly consistent in their disapproval of capitalism and their leanings toward socialism. This discomfort again reflecting a recurring pattern in mainline Canadian Protestantism in which ecclesiastical leaders maintained positions not shared by large portions of the churches they purported to represent. Some voiced their disaffection through church courts; others formed organizations to try through publications, conferences, and other means to persuade the churches to change their minds. The first of these groups was the Confederation of Church and Business People, begun in 1977, and another was the Centre for the Study of Economics and Religion, part of the Vancouver-based Fraser Institute economic thinktank.

These tensions, however, had at least in theory a better chance of being resolved than previously because of another new front of initiative. For a number of reasons, emphasis upon lay leadership and general involvement in the churches increased in some quarters. Perhaps it was because of the continued lack of well-qualified clergy in some denominations to serve outside the cities, despite the influx of new theological students; perhaps it was a result of the questioning of traditional authorities so current in the 1960s; perhaps it was encouraged by Vatican II and World Council of Churches initiatives in this direction; perhaps with so many nominal members no longer regularly participating, those who remained were more determined to be involved.

Whatever the reasons, the mainline churches increasingly welcomed lay initiative. Centers opened to train laypeople, expanding a form of ministry which began in the United Church, for instance, as early as 1947 in British Columbia. In the later 1980s the United Church discussed suggestions by one of its exploratory committees to adjust its education of professional clergy to better emphasize the personal experience and growth of the lay centers rather than, say, to make the lay centers more demanding of theological and historical competence. The General Council did not support these suggestions, but clearly the training of laypeople figured largely in the minds of many leaders. Laypeople were elected to the highest offices in the United Church and to the faculties of its theological colleges. Similar influence was wielded in the other major denominations. Some well-positioned critics doubted that all of this "activation of the laity" had produced a measurably greater witness to the world and wondered if it had instead amounted merely to "play musical chairs in church." By the end of this period, it was unclear how much change the old, clerically-dominated ecclesiastical wineskins could or *should* accommodate.

Charismatic renewal stretched several of those wineskins in other ways. Beginning on this continent among American Episcopalians and Roman Catholics in the 1960s, the movement spread to Canada and blossomed in the 1970s, with the "Jesus People" being only the most spectacular manifestation. All major denominations were touched, most obviously the Roman Catholic and Anglican. The fresh emphasis upon vital personal piety, transforming spiritual experience, and spectacular supernatural gifts brought enthusiasm and vigour to some congregations and bitter divisions in others. No respecter of clerical orders, the charismatic experience threatened established authority; strongly emotional, the movement threatened traditional emphasis upon right doctrine; focused upon experience, it threatened social action and evangelism.

In this way, at least, some of its opponents saw it. Others saw the dangers but worked to keep "the fire in the fireplace," to direct the excitement into traditional channels. In turn it could purify and transform those channels to some extent. Not all of the channels, it should be noted, were traditional. Parachurch groups formed across the continent, with the Full Gospel Business Men's Fellowship and Women Aglow perhaps the most prominent. Nonetheless, these Protestants generally retained their membership in traditional denominations, hence the term "charismatic renewal" distinguished this movement from denominational Pentecostalism. All of the major denominations, as well as many non-Pentecostal evangelical groups, had to deal with the phenomenon. After considerable deliberations most public statements were cautiously affirmative, with the Presbyterians the most cautious of all. Some small evangelical groups, by contrast, rejected it out of hand as inconsistent with their understanding of the New Testament. For example, the transdenominational evangelical revival of the early 1970s arising out of the ministry of the Sutera brothers on the prairies, institutionalized in the Canadian Revival Fellowship, explicitly distanced itself from things charismatic. By the late 1980s, the Charismatic renewal was no longer news, but the fires continued to burn across Canada, sometimes opening new doors to cooperation in worship and service among congregations in the same locality of different denominations.

The overall pattern of decline, however, continued through the 1980s. The mainline churches simply were no longer the powers in Canadian society they once were. Some wondered if religion itself were terminally ill in Canada. Others, however, thought Dean M. Kelley of the National Council of Churches in the U.S. had asked a good question when he inquired into *Why Conservative Churches Are Growing* (1972). In the 1970s and 1980s, conservative evangelical churches in Canada, as in the United States, did emerge into greater prominence. This prominence, however, was ambiguous: were conservative churches growing merely in relation to the decline in mainline force? Were they actually increasing their influence upon Canadian life? There was little question that evangelicalism was becoming a more clearly defined, integrated, and vigorous part of Canadian Protestantism. Measuring its importance, however, was another matter.

II

The 1970s and even more the 1980s saw the emergence of a growing evangelical network in Canada. An interlocking set of institutions, many of which predated this era but were only at this time linking up in official and important ways, manifested a transdenominational alliance of Protestants concerned chiefly with the traditional evangelical emphases upon orthodoxy founded on the authority of the Bible, personal piety, and evangelism. These evangelicals increasingly, however, broadened the scope of their common interests to include social matters, such as Sunday closings, civil rights for homosexuals, and abortion. To a lesser extent, economic issues united them, generally, along free-enterprise, anti-socialism lines. Politics, of course, is connected to these concerns, and evangelicals clearly sought to use the political process more effectively to champion their interests. Most dramatically, not one but *two* political parties (Reform and Christian Heritage) were formed with evangelical support in the late 1980s and fielded dozens of candidates in the federal election of 1988. These candidates did not win any seats until an Alberta byelection in 1989. Apparently, they siphoned enough votes away from the predominant choice of evangelicals, the Progressive Conservatives, that, ironically, sometimes other parties' candidates won instead. As the 1980s ended, therefore, it seemed that a new force in Canadian Protestantism, of a sort not seen before, was poised to take an important place in Canadian religious life.

Changes among the generally evangelical denominations themselves, however, deserve note in their own right. Several of them withdrew from American parent bodies and became autonomously Canadian in this era. The Baptist General Conference of Canada in 1984 and the Evangelical Free Church in 1985 are two examples. Both denominations are centered in the west with strong American connections.

The Pentecostals continued their path of growth so that by the mid-1980s their reported membership exceeded that of both the Canadian Baptist Federation (the Baptist Federation of Canada re-named in 1983) and of the Presbyterian Church in Canada (see Figure 1). It can be said that Pentecostals now joined the mainstream of Canadian evangelicalism, if not Canadian Protestantism as a whole. Nevertheless, significant numbers of evangelicals, especially those influenced by dispensational theology, maintained that the Pentecostal/charismatic emphasis upon spiritual gifts of "tongues," healing, and prophecy was at least dangerous, since it could lead to neglect of what these critics understood to be more important gifts like preaching and administration. Some even surmised that the whole phenomenon was in fact a distraction perpetrated by the devil himself. Transdenominational evangelical institutions, however, generally welcomed those in the Pentecostal and charismatic movements. Pentecostals for their part began to support such institutions outside their own denomination. For example, the PAOC sent students to Ontario Theological Seminary and Regent College. Prominent Pentecostals were in turn recognized in positions of leadership. In the 1980s, for instance, Pentecostal pastor David Mainse presided over Canada's most popular religious television program, *100 Huntley Street*, and Brian C. Stiller, also ordained in the Pentecostal Assemblies of Canada, was the dynamic leader of the Evangelical Fellowship of Canada. The presence of Pentecostals in public life was no longer remarkable as it had been in the 1950s. Pentecostals themselves observed more ambiguous changes in their movement as they moderated "separatistic" or "sectarian" patterns of belief and practice: divorce, for instance, under certain circumstances was allowed by the early 1970s: it had previously been categorically forbidden.

A similar, if more modest, pattern was seen among Canadian Mennonites. Darlings of sociologists, the growing urbanization, wealth, and sophistication of Mennonites since 1960 and the resulting strains on their traditional ethnicity and religion were well-documented. With the retention of some Mennonite beliefs and ways and the discarding of others, many more Mennonites than previously began to see evangelicals of other denominations as kindred spirits. Consequently, they began to participate significantly in transdenominational ventures like Inter-Varsity Christian Fellowship, the Evangelical Fellowship of Canada, and transdenominational schools.

A shift toward evangelicalism was discernible as well among Baptists associated with the Canadian Baptist Federation. This trend worried at least some Baptists who were concerned about jeopardizing broader alliances. By 1980 all of the Baptist conventions but the Baptist Convention of Ontario and Quebec opposed belonging to the Canadian and World Councils of Churches. Others worried about the erosion of denominational distinctives as Baptists became more "generically" evangelical. Acadia Divinity College became noticeably more conservative theologically under the principalships of Abner Langley, Harold Mitton, and Andrew MacRae, and controversy over the theological pluralism and future direction of McMaster Divinity College simmered in Ontario. Baptists in western Canada explicity linked up with transdenominational evangelicalism in the 1980s as they sponsored pastoral training at Carey Hall jointly with Regent College in Vancouver. The Baptist Union of Western Canada also officially joined the Evangelical Fellowship of Canada in 1986. Many Baptists welcomed these trends, seeing only much-needed reinforcement from the broader evangelical community for the Canadian Baptist Federation's goal of growing to 200,000 by the year 2000. Others saw this goal to be utterly unrealistic since these Baptists in the 1980s were about the same size as they were after the schisms of the 1920s and 1930s.

For the Fellowship of Evangelical Baptist Churches, however, the Canadian Baptist Federation was by no means evangelical enough. The legacy of the Baptist struggles of the 1920s was continued antipathy and separation between Fellowship and Federation Baptists. Some observers puzzled over this: since there was considerable evidence that most Federation Baptists were very largely orthodox on virtually every significant doctrine, why was there not more interest in rapprochement? Was there something other than theological rectitude at stake? Indeed there was: the dividing issue seemed to be the Fellowship's characteristic fundamentalist attitude of separation from everything that was impure, including not only heresy by also those who hold to it. Fellowship Baptists, that is, generally continued to see the Federation Baptists as dangerously tolerant of theological pluralism. For proof, they could turn to a number of prominent Baptists who could not meet the Fellowship's standard of orthodoxy and yet were quite welcome in the Federation. For their part, reflecting precisely this basic difference, Federation Baptists continued to see the Fellowship as inflexibly intolerant of pluralism. The separatism of T.T. Shields lived on in the Fellowship of Evangelical Baptist Churches so that it was the most important of the few evangelical denominations which remained wary of transdenominational evangelicalism, even if some of its leaders and ranks frequently participated in these projects.

On its own, nonetheless, the Fellowship continued to lead other evangelicals in establishing churches among quickly- secularizing Quebec, founding over fifty in the 1980s alone. The Baptist work begun at Grande Ligne among Francophone Catholics a hundred and fifty years earlier, therefore, continued in this mode and was bolstered by efforts notably of the Christian Brethren and Pentecostals. Yet, the numbers of the uniformly evangelical denominations in Quebec remained well below the totals for the Anglican and United churches, let alone the Roman Catholic church. Indeed, one evangelical source declared in 1989 that the success of evangelicals in winning converts had diminished since the 1970s and that still only one out of every two thousand Quebeckers was what it would call "evangelical."

Even as some of these evangelical denominations were entering more fully into Canadian society at large, they also were extending themselves northward into new missions among the Indians, Metis, and Inuit. Much of what remained of centuries of mainline missions was giving way to government agencies although various innovative ways of fostering and cooperating with native leadership were attempted in the churches. One milestone was reached as Charles Arthurson was consecrated the first Indian bishop of the Anglican Church of Canada early in 1989. He was to be responsible for the Saskatchewan diocese which covered the northern half of the province and included 15,000 church members who spoke primarily Cree. Some mainline Protestants, however, questioned whether the traditional aim of converting native Canadians away from tribal beliefs to Christianity was ethnocentric and misguided. At the same time, though, they continued to sponsor agencies which sought natives' social welfare. For their part, evangelical denominations grew in their recognition of a concern for the social needs of the natives. Generally untrammelled by a burden to "civilize" the natives and characteristically concerned with a simple gospel presented by white or native leaders trained in Bible schools, Mennonites, Baptists, and especially Pentecostals made significant inroads into this field of mission.

While not influencing their denominations along the same path as the Baptists, some evangelicals within the United, Anglican, and Presbyterian churches joined together in denominational fellowships to protest what they saw to be threats within the churches to biblical Christianity. The Baptist Convention of Ontario and Quebec, the most theologically pluralistic of Canadian Baptist groups, had its own Renewal Fellowship, and the Atlantic Baptists for a time had a similar small group as well. The ordination of women and homosexuals stirred up special concern, as did the question of continuing membership in the World Council of Churches when the WCC was viewed as supporting violent political revolutionaries in Africa. Some also objected to the increasing use of inclusive language that avoided terms attributing masculinity to God, like "King," "Father," and so on. Beyond protest, however, these groups often spoke positively as well of the renewal of what they saw to be the best parts of their traditions, which were generally a higher view of the inspiration and authority of Scripture, a return to expository preaching, a fresh emphasis upon vital personal and congregational piety, and new initiatives in evangelism to complement the existing efforts in social ministry. It should be noted that some evangelicals within these denominations did not join these fellowships, seeing them to be too strident, conservative, or divisive. Partly out of sensitivity to these criticisms as well as from a desire for a more positive focus, the renewal groups increasingly manifested the pluralism of evangelicalism itself and moderated earlier stands on certain issues like the ordination of women. If they could not include all evangelicals, much less direct their denominations, then these fellowships acted at least as a stimulus to raise the concerns of at least some members of these pluralistic churches.

In other cases, congregations of some small Canadian denominations sponsored schools, which drew support from evangelicals across denominational lines. These private religious elementary and secondary schools were often sponsored by the Christian Reformed with their long-standing interest in confessionally-based education. Others were established increasingly by Pentecostal and other evangelical churches concerned about what they saw to be growing secularism in the public schools. These latter schools often received inspiration and curricula from the burgeoning parallel movements in the United States. Between 1971 and 1985, according to one evangelical source, the number of independent schools and students in Ontario doubled, with more than 82,000 students in 1985 opting out of the public system.

Most prominent, though, of these education efforts were the three well-known liberal arts colleges in Canada. Redeemer College, outside Hamilton, Ontario, and the King's College, in Edmonton, were founded by members of the Christian Reformed Church and by the late 1980s were awarding provincially- sanctioned degrees. Trinity Western University, south of Vancouver, was begun in 1962 with seventeen students. By the 1980s it was the largest of the evangelical liberal arts colleges, with an enrollment of well over one thousand students. Begun by the Evangelical Free Church, a group of Scandinavian origin and prominent in Canada especially on the prairies, the original junior college grew to become the first of these colleges to win full standing with the Association of Universities and Colleges of Canada. St. Stephen's University in New Brunswick was a fourth, lesser known and much smaller liberal arts college belonging to this type of educational effort.

Ontario Bible College, formed out of London Bible College and the much older Toronto Bible College in 1968, led the way in offering a Bible school education more fully rounded out with liberal arts courses. A bachelor's degree could be earned, though it was not a B.A., but a degree nonetheless. Other schools, responding to the desires of their supporters for more thorough and more respectable education for their leaders, increasingly adopted this Bible *college* model, and some went the next step to offer graduate training in new seminaries. Briercrest Bible College and the Christian and Missionary Alliance's schools in rural Saskatchewan and Regina respectively, were among the leaders of this movement on the prairies. Whether they "upgraded" their programs or not, however, a 1985 survey of 76 Canadian Bible schools by the Evangelical Fellowship of Canada listed a combined full-time equivalent enrollment of 8,300 in these schools, not counting their graduate division, outstripping any other kind of religious education in Canada.

The desire for graduate theological training prompted two other important new initiatives. Ontario Bible College began Ontario Theological Seminary in 1976, and by the mid-1980s its enrollment had surpassed that of the largest denominational college in Canada, Emmanuel of the United Church in Toronto. Its leadership dominated by Presbyterians and Baptists, it nonetheless strove to meet the needs of other constituencies, most notably the Pentecostals and the expanding oriental churches of Toronto. Recognition of its maturity came from its peers as it received full accreditation by the Association of Theological Schools in 1989.

More unusual, perhaps, was the academic institution founded on the campus of the University of British Columbia in 1970, Regent College. Begun by Plymouth Brethren as an institute to train church leaders who had secular jobs as well as those engaged in full-time pastoring, the school from the start was transdenominational and enrolled evangelicals from a variety of denominations and nationalities. With a faculty that included high-profile authors such as Canadian Clark H. Pinnock and Englishmen J.I. Packer and Michael Green, the college steadily grew, obtained full accreditation from the Association of Theological Schools, and became Canada's largest seminary as well as its largest lay-training center in the mid-1980s. In 1985, the Evangelical Fellowship of Canada listed seventeen Canadian seminaries which identified themselves as "evangelical" and which enrolled a full-time student equivalent enrolment of 1,350. This total was one-half to two-thirds of what mainline theological colelges enrolled that year, allowing for several relatively large schools such as Wycliffe, Acadia and McMaster being listed in both categories.

By the 1980s several institutions began to link up these schools and the proliferating variety of other Canadian evangelical denominational and para-church organizations. Inter-Varsity Fellowship obviously contributed in this regard, but most important perhaps was the Evangelical Fellowship of Canada (EFC) under the leadership of Brian Stiller. The EFC sought to sign up as members individuals, congregations, and whole denominations, and claimed an aggregate membership of well over a million Canadians by the mid-1980s. Its budget increased from about $60,000 in 1983 to $1.3 million in 1987. For all those people and with all that money the EFC did several things. It conducted seminars and published newsletters presenting evangelical analysis and response to trends in Canadian society. It submitted briefs to governments at various levels on issues for which its leaders could discern a predominant evangelical response: for example, against abortion, against full Sunday retailing, for increasing maternity and paternity benefits to strengthen families, and for acknowledgement of God in the new constitution. It managed the Canadian arm of World Relief, the relief agency of the World Evangelical Fellowship of which the EFC was a member. It also published Canada's most important transdenominational evangelical magazine, *Faith Today,* which clearly sought to play the role in Canadian evangelicalism that *Christianity Today* played in the United States. The journal offered timely comment on contemporary issues but, at least as importantly, also informed Canadian evangelicals about *each other* through its copy and perhaps no less through the advertisements it carried. A similar function, as it happened, began to be exercised in 1987 by *Christian Week*, a biweekly tabloid out of Winnipeg. The EFC, more than anything else, symbolized the emerging network of Canadian evangelical institutions which fostered, even as it manifested, the growing consolidation of evangelicals across denominational lines.

Estimates of the strength of this grouping of Protestants varied, due partly to the problem of defining both "strength" and "evangelical" no less than to the difficulty of applying these terms to a grouping which included many Christians within pluralistic denominations. Furthermore, despite the obvious growth of many congregations, it remained unclear how well evangelical churches were drawing in those from outside the evangelical fold. Several sociologists found that those evangelical churches that grew did so mainly by attracting evangelicals from other churches, by immigration, by a higher- than-average birth rate, and by a better-than-average ability at retaining children and geographically mobile members. This produced what one study called "the circulation of saints," rather than growth mainly through the evangelization of non- evangelicals.

Some other observers of Canadian evangelicalism, as well as participants themselves, could not shake the conviction that there were more real conversions here than the sociologists were finding. No matter how one accounted for church growth, some measurements, although rough, indicated beyond doubt that evangelicals were not to be ignored as a group in Canadian religious life. While there was evidence that, proportionately speaking, there were not many more evangelicals in Canada in 1985

than in 1945, the 1980s especially saw among these Protestants
considerable increase in "morale, efficiency, visibility, technique,
group identity, and expressiveness," as one writer characterized the
American parallel.

This vitality was all the more conspicuous in comparison with
mainline Protestantism. Several responsible estimates, for instance,
saw more evangelicals in church on a typical Sunday morning than
Christians attending the services of the largest Protestant
denomination, the United Church. Evangelicals ran the two largest
seminaries in Canada, and the Bible schools and colleges far outdid
the relatively pale efforts of the mainline churches to educate their
laity. For decades the smaller evangelical denominations had sent
out and supported many more foreign missionaries than had the
large pluralistic ones: in 1985, for instance, any one of several very
small denominations, including the Associated Gospel Churches,
Christian Brethren, and Christian and Missionary Alliance, sent
out by themselves more missionaries than did the United, Anglican,
and Presbyterian churches *combined*. This commitment to
supporting missions was part of a larger pattern of dramatically
higher financial contributions per member among evangelical
churches than among the mainline denominations. Sociologist
Reginald W. Bibby found what he termed "Conservative
Protestants," which would not include in this case evangelical
members of mainline churches, led both Roman Catholics and
other Protestants in all of his measurements of traditional religious
belief and practice; from knowledge and private reading of the
Bible to church membership and attendance.

By the late 1980s, then, the growth curve of evangelical
institutions, denominations, and cooperative ventures had not
flattened out. Evangelicals looked toward new possibilities for
influencing both the mainline churches and Canadian society. For
a book published in 1963, the eminent historian H.H. Walsh wrote
that "the sectarian groups are a diminishing influence in Canadian
national life," but a quarter-century later this epitaph seemed
premature indeed.

For all the apparent success, however, some observers wondered
what was the real significance of Canadian evangelicalism and
what were its prospects. Was H.H. Walsh in fact so far wrong?
Charles Templeton, formerly a prominent Canadian evangelical
himself but for some time since a critic of it, wrote in 1984 of what
he called "the fundamentalist wing" of the church, by which he
meant this broad group of evangelicals: "It is, for all it claims, of
little influence on the day-to-day life of the world. . . One can go for
months without ever meeting a 'fundamentalist' or seeing evidence

of any altering of the fabric of the society by his or her ideals."
Templeton's conclusion was direct: "We are not, as is loudly
trumpeted, on the verge of a great revival."

Whatever one made of Templeton's judgement, even those loyal
to the evangelical movement could see that bigger churches, better
schools, higher-tech mass media, and increased access to the
corridors of power had all been enjoyed before by others —precisely
by those mainline denominations suffering a decline and with
whom evangelicals sometimes favourably compared themselves. If
evangelicals now were solidly, if not uniformly, members of the
middle class, now had gained a measure of prominence, wealth, and
respectability in modern Canadian society, did this indicate that
they were influencing that society more than they had before, or that
instead that society had in fact co-opted them? And what price
might evangelicals have to pay to maintain, let alone increase, their
new status?

III

Reginald Bibby contributed an important metaphor to the
discussion of Canadian religion in the 1970s and 1980s in the title of
his book, *Fragmented Gods* (1987). While the aptness of the plural
"gods" is debatable, the idea of "fragments" clearly is not.

To change the image, what Bibby meant is that Canadians in the
1970s and 1980s increasingly saw religion to be a smorgasbord of
dishes from which an individual might select what and as much as
one wanted. That is, rather than an integrated world-and-life view
centered in a life of discipleship to God and manifested in a
particular community to which one belonged and with which one
importantly identified oneself, Christianity was reduced to more-
or-less interesting and useful bits in such areas of liturgy, music,
counseling, preaching, social clubs, service, and rites of passage.
From these one chose what suited one's taste and needs. So while
close to 90 per cent of Canadians identified themselves with Roman
Catholicism or Protestantism in the 1981 census, less than one-third
said that they regularly prayed even once a day and less than 10 per
cent regularly read the Bible privately even once a *week*. As Bibby
noted, "horoscope readers easily [outnumbered] the nation's Bible
readers." Furthermore, despite God's appearances in the new
English-language version of "O Canada" and the new constitution,
and despite a few clergy in public office, Canadian public life was
less affected by Christianity than at any time since the first coming
of Europeans to this land. Even the issue of state funding for
separate Roman Catholic schools, formerly guaranteed to arouse

powerful Anglo-Protestant feelings, failed to ignite Ontario as it had in the past; in the early 1980s William Davis's government extended its level of financial support to the Roman Catholic system and allowed its schools to offer a full secondary curriculum over only limited protests and with the agreement, in fact, of some conservative Protestants who aspired to the same privileges for *their* independent schools.

Bibby's metaphor has been extended considerably here to deal with other developments in late twentieth-century Protestantism in Canada. For instance, the dominance of the mainline Protestant churches in many respects broke up; attempts to unify some denominational traditions failed; certain denominations tolerated and even encouraged internal diversity of theology and practice; traditional patterns of alliance were modified as evangelicalism rose to some prominence as a new religious network; and increasing numbers of people identified themselves as having "no religion." The list could go on.

Fragmentation, however, is only part of the story. Various parts of Canadian Protestantism in this era reconfigured themselves into new aggregates, whether mainline coalitions, interfaith premarital counselling, parachurch student groups, women's fellowships, and — still! — the sponsorship of Billy Graham crusades. Indeed, the Graham crusades were one instance of several in which evangelicals joined with other Protestants in joint ventures; the Community of Concern within the United Church to protest the ordination of practicing homosexuals was another, as was "Vision TV," a multi-faith television channel begun in 1988.

Some wondered, in fact, if new coalitions, whether organized along evangelical, social action, or other lines, would replace the denominations as the important bodies in Canadian church life. Such organizations as were visible in the late 1980s, however, did not seem to constitute such a strong alternative to the traditional organization of Canadian Protestantism, even as some of them supplemented, modified, and actually competed with the denominations in various respects.

Other observers considered whether the fragmentation of religion in Canada, along with the decline of the mainline churches and the rise of evangelicalism, were reflections of the "Americanization" of Canadian society in general. Clearly there were connections in the religious evolution of the two countries. Mainline and evangelical organizations in Canada obviously drew ideas, personnel, training, and other resources from their American counterparts. On the other hand, the traffic was by no means entirely one way. For example, numerous Canadian scholars and other leaders were prominent in

American religious institutions. Influential religious publications read in both countries, like *The Christan Century* and *Christianity Today*, included Canadians on their editorial boards and attempted at least intermittently to take Canadian Christianity into account, even though they were based in America and were preoccupied with things American. So too American professional organizations like the American Academy of Religion, the Society of Biblical Literature, and the Evangelical Theological Society included a number of Canadian scholars and other religious leaders in their ranks, while Americans and American concerns understandably dominated the conferences, journals, and the agendas. Only one of the most obvious connections, therefore, was the prominent presence in Canada of American religious broadcasting. Enough Canadians, at least before the scandals of the later 1980s which hurt many American religious broadcasters, were avid supporters of American religious television to donate an estimated $19 million in 1984 to such programs. They also contributed about $21 million to home-grown ministries like those of David Mainse and Terry Winter. For their part, both Mainse and Winter broadcasted also on American television stations. These various connections, then, naturally led to significant and increasing homogeneity in the religious character of the two countries.

On the other hand, however, some Canadian denominations, like the larger Lutherans and the smaller Evangelical Free Church, had been dominated from the start by their closer American relations while the decades especially since the Canadian centennial saw many of them grow more autonomous, if not always distinctly more Canadian. Other Canadian institutions, whether magazines, professional societies, or broadcasting; not to mention historically independent denominations, schools, and missionary also had their own lives and voices.

The most obvious differences, though, had to do with the character and status of evangelicalism in the two countries. By the late 1980s, evangelicalism clearly was still a substantially less powerful force in Canadian society than in the United States even as the Canadian version was less diverse with fewer and less important eccentric groups. This was connected to the fact that Canadian evangelicals could be seen as being at least a full generation behind the Americans in erecting what one scholar called "an evangelical denomination" of transdenominational agencies and identity. Finally, the relative position of respect and acceptance of the mainline churches in Canada vis-a-vis evangelicals was not paralleled in the United States in which evangelicals were more nearly on equal terms with mainline

Christianity. This was true not only in certain regions, like the South, in which the revivalist tradition really *was* the mainline, but also in the national consciousness at large, as American mass media and politics demonstrated.

Further and longer-range analysis would be necessary, therefore, to distinguish between what was distinctly "American" in the similarities between late twentieth-century Canadian and American Christianity and what was more generically "modern." The older model of "secularization" seemed to describe well enough the apparent steady evacuation of Christianity from Canadian life since 1945 as simply part of the story of the waning of Christianity's influence in modern western societies in general. The Canadian habit of continuing to identify with Christian denominations at census time and for rites of pasage vis-a-vis the substantial decline in most other kinds of religious practice was a pattern common enough throughout the west.

Evangelicals who would protest against this general picture by pointing to the vitality in their own ranks yet had to contend with newer models of secularization which recognized the maintenance and even growth of vigorous religion but only as relegated to the private sphere of life. This compartmentalization of religious experience and commitment, according to these models still represented the deterioration of Christianity. After all, Christianity, according to most of its exponents, is supposed to strive in Christ's name to transform the whole world, not just private individual experience. Some evangelicals, particulai y through organizations like the Evangelical Fellowship of Canada, seemed more determined in the late 1980s than they had been for some time to bring Christian principles to bear on public life, but it was too early to tell whether these incipient efforts represented a considerable force which could help effect important changes in Canadian society.

A generation after the Second World War, therefore, two observations at least seemed valid about the Canadian Protestant experience. One was that some superficial patterns were the same as they had been in 1945. The second, though, was that beneath the surface important new patterns were forming as many of the old patterns faded and disintegrated. Vital new forces were coming to the fore even as formidable new challenges also emerged. All of this appeared to portend new varieties of experience for Canadian Protestants. The more things had apparently stayed the same, the more they surely had changed.

FIGURE 1

Population of Canada and Reported Membership
of Select Denominations
1941-1985
in thousands of persons
(percentage of total population)

Year	Total	United	Ang.	Luth.	Pres.	Bapt[1]	Pent.
1941	11,507	717 (6.2)	861 (7.5)	n.a.	174 (1.5)	134 (1.2)	n.a.
1951	14,009	834 (6.0)	1096 (7.8)	121 (0.9)	177 (1.3)	135 (1.0)	45 (0.3)
1961	18,238	1037 (5.7)	1358 (7.5)	172 (0.9)	201 (1.1)	138 (0.8)	60 (0.3)
1971	21,568	1017 (4.7)	1109 (5.1)	200 (0.9)	183 (0.9)	132 (0.6)	150 (0.7)
1981	24,343	900 (3.7)	922 (3.8)	218 (0.9)	165 (0.7)	128 (0.5)	125 (0.5)
1985	25,174	881 (3.5)	856 (3.4)	208 (0.8)	163 (0.6)	130 (0.5)	179 (0.7)

[1]Groups affiliated with Canadian Baptist Federation

FIGURE 2

Population of Canada and Religious Affiliation
With Select Denominations
1941-1981
in thousands of persons
(percentage of total population)

Year	Total	United	Ang.	Luth.	Pres.	Bapt[1]	Pent.
1941	11,507	2209 (19.2)	1754 (15.2)	402 (3.5)	831 (7.2)	484 (4.2)	58 (0.5)
1951	14,009	2867 (20.5)	2061 (14.7)	445 (3.2)	782 (5.6)	520 (3.7)	95 (0.7)
1961	18,238	3664 (20.1)	2409 (13.2)	663 (3.6)	819 (4.5)	594 (3.3)	144 (0.8)
1971	21,568	3769 (17.5)	2543 (11.0)	716 (3.3)	872 (4.0)	667 (3.1)	220 (1.0)
1981	24,343	3798 (15.6)	2463 (10.1)	706 (2.9)	820 (3.4)	706 (2.9)	341 (1.4)

SUGGESTIONS FOR FURTHER READING

Three recent works provide good summaries of the general history of Canada in this period: Robert Bothwell, Ian Drummond, and John English, *Canada since 1945: Power, Politics, and Provincialism* (Toronto: University of Toronto Press, 1981); Desmond Morton, "Strains of Affluence (1945-1987)," in *The Illustrated History of Canada,* ed. Craig Brown (Toronto: Lester & Orpen Dennys, 1987), 467-543; and Kenneth McNaught, *The Penguin History of Canada*, rev. ed. (London: Penguin, 1988).

Overviews of the church history of the period come in different shapes and sizes. The relevant sections of H.H. Walsh, *The Christian Church in Canada* (Toronto: Ryerson Press, 1956), John Webster Grant, ed., *The Churches and the Canadian Experience: A Faith and Order Study of the Christian Tradition,* with a Foreword by David W. Hay (Toronto: Ryerson Press, 1963), and Douglas J. Wilson, *The Church Grows in Canada* (Toronto: Ryerson Press, 1966), are still useful as far as they go, but they have been superceded by two other works: Robert T. Handy, *A History of the Churches in the United States and Canada* (Toronto: Oxford University Press, 1976), and John Webster Grant, *The Church in the Canadian Era,* rev. ed. (Burlington, Ont.: G.R. Welch, 1988).

Portraits of Canadian religion in general in the second half of the twentieth century have come more frequently from sociologists than historians. The section on Canada in David B. Barrett, ed., *World Christian Encyclopedia: A Comparative Study of Churches and Religions in the Modern World AD 1900-2000* (Nairobi, Oxford, and London: Oxford University Press, 1982), 211-217, contains a wealth of data in a small space. Harold Fallding attempts a brief overview in his chapter on Canada in *Western Religion: A Country by Country Sociological Inquiry,* ed. Hans Mol (The Hague and Paris: Mouton, 1972), 101-115. Hans Mol himself goes on more ambitiously in *Faith and Fragility: Religion and Identity in Canada* (Burlington, Ont.: Trinity Press, 1985), a book which bites off rather more subject matter than it thoroughly chews in interpretation but which nonetheless provides a good start for further inquiry. Probably his generation's most prolific sociologist of Canadian religion, Reginald W. Bibby sets out the fruit of considerable research in *Fragmented Gods: The Poverty and Potential of Religion in Canada,* with a Foreword by George Gallup Jr. (Toronto: Irwin, 1987). This book's bibliography guides the student to the many studies Bibby has conducted which lie behind it.

Surveys of the contemporary state of religion in Canada have come at different times from historians, sociologists, and journalists, and these surveys have rarely come unaccompanied by criticism. Ralph Allen, "The Hidden Failure of Our Churches," *Maclean's Magazine* (25 February 1961): 11-50 passim, was one of the first in this era. Pierre Berton's *The Comfortable Pew* (Toronto: McClelland and Stewart, 1965), of course, was the best known, and helped to spark at least two responses: Arthur Brydon, Warren Bruleigh, and Gordon K. Stewart, eds., *Why the Sea Is Boiling Hot: A Symposium on the Church and the World*, with a Foreword by Ernest Marshall Howse (Toronto: Ryerson, 1965), and William Kilbourn, ed., *The Restless Church: A Response to The Comfortable Pew* (Toronto: McClelland and Stewart, 1966). William Kilbourn, ed., *Religion in Canada: The Spiritual Development of a Nation* (Toronto: McClelland and Stewart, 1968), is an appealing journalistic presentation, while Stewart Crysdale and Les Wheatcroft, eds., *Religion in Canadian Society* (Toronto: Macmillan, 1976), contains a miscellany of scholarly articles. A brief look at Christianity in the 1980s is provided in John G. Stackhouse, Jr., "Canadian Church in the '80s: Dismay and Promise," *Christian Week* 3 (16 May 1989): 10-12.

More statistically minded are the following studies, Douglas W. Johnson and George W. Cornell, *Punctured Preconceptions: What North American Christians Think about the Church* (N.p.: National Council of Churches, 1972), in fact deals only with the United Church when it deals with Canada. Charles A. Tipp and Terry Winter, *The Christian Church in Canada: A Survey of Protestant Churches and Organizations* (N.p.: Canadian Congress on Evangelism, 1970), provides a wealth of data on organizations, especially evangelical ones, many of which were previously unaccounted for in serious scholarship. The *Yearbook of American and Canadian Churches,* ed. Constant H. Jacquet, Jr. (Nashville: Abingdon Press), provides several reflections on the religious data of Canadian censuses over the years. Finally, Dennis Mackintosh Oliver, "The New Canadian Religious Pluralism" (paper delivered to the Canadian Society of Church History, Saskatoon, Saskatchewan, 1 June 1979), is the first study of which I am aware which suggests that more evangelicals attend church than do Christians of any of the major denominations.

More personal, if sometimes idiosyncratic, reflections on religion in Canada often set out points of departure for the scholar. Arthur R.M. Lower, "Religion and Religious Institutions," in *Canada* ed. George W. Brown (Toronto: University of Toronto Press, 1950), and Harold A. Innis, "The Church in Canada," in *Essays in Canadian Economic History,* ed. Mary Q. Innis (Toronto: University of Toronto

Press, 1956), 383-93, reflect the cast of mind of many Canadian intellectuals toward religion, as does Robertson Davies, "Keeping Faith," *Saturday Night* 102 (January 1987): 187-92, a generation later. Characteristically more moderate and better informed is an essay by John Webster Grant, "The Churches in Canadian Space and Time," *Mid-Stream* 22 (July/October 1983): 354-62.

Canadians in a variety of fields since 1945 increasingly studied their culture with reference to the United States. Examples abound in the fields of religious studies: John Webster Grant, "'At Least You Knew Where You Stood with Them': Reflections on Religious Pluralism in Canada and the United States," *Studies in Religion/ Sciences Religeuses* 2 (1973): 340-51; Harold Fallding, "Mainline Protestantism in Canada and the United States of America: An Overview," *Canadian Journal of Sociology* 3 (Spring 1978): 141- 60; and Kenneth Westhues, "Religious Organization in Canada and the United States," *International Journal of Comparative Sociology* 17 (September-December 1976): 206-25. For that matter, American scholar Robert T. Handy made a specialty of American-Canadian comparisons: beyond his book-length history, he published several articles, such as "Protestant Patterns in Canada and the United States: Similarities and Differences," in *In the Great Tradition: In Honor of Winthrop S. Hudson, Essays on Pluralism, Voluntaryism, and Revivalism,* ed. Joseph D. Ban and Paul R. Dekar (Valley Forge, PA: Judson Press, 1982), 33-51; "Dominant Patterns of Christian Life in Canada and the United States: Similarities and Differences," *Religion/Culture: Comparative Canadian Studies* 7 (1985): 344-55; and "The 'Lively Experiment' in Canada," in *The Lively Experiment Continued,* ed. Jerald C. Brauer (Macon, GA: Mercer University Press, 1987), 203-18.

Articles which dealt with questions of nationalism and Canadian identity usually had American in mind: four prominent examples are John Webster Grant, "The Church and Canada's Self-Awareness," *Canadian Journal of Theology* 13 (1967): 155-62; idem, "Religion and the Quest for a National Identity: The Background in Canadian History," in *Religion and Culture in Canada,* ed. Peter Slater (N.p.: Corporation Canadienne des Sciences Religieuses/ Canadian Corporation for Studies in Religion, [197], 8-21, N. Keith Clifford, "His Dominion: A Vision in Crisis," *Studies in Religion/Sciences religeuses* 2 (1973): 315-26; and Paul R. Dekar, "On the Soul of Nations: Religion and Nationalism in Canada and the United States," in *In the Great Tradition: In Honor of Winthrop S. Hudson, Essays on Pluralism, Voluntaryism, and Revivalism,* ed. Joseph D. Ban and Paul R. Dekar (Valley Forge, PA: Judson Press, 1982), 53-72.

A variety of smaller subjects in Canadian religion as well were studies in direct reference to things American. Handy again was involved, with "The Influence of Canadians on Baptist Theological Education in the United States," *Foundations* 23 (1980): 42-56, and the same issue included Winthrop S. Hudson, "The Interrelationships of Baptists in Canada and the United States," *Foundations* 23 (1980): 22-41. G.G. Harrop had come earlier with his setting of "Canadian Baptists in Their North American Context," *Foundations* 4 (1961): 216-224. Harry H. Hiller looked at "Continentalism and the Third Force in Religion," *Canadian Journal of Sociology* 3 (Spring 1978): 183- 207, and John Simpson published the only study of "Federal Regulation and Religious Broadcasting in Canada and the United States: A Comparative Sociological Analysis," *Religion/Culture: Comparative Canadian Studies* 7 (1985): 152-63. Conspicuous by its interest in things *European* was Gerald R. Cragg, "The European Wellsprings of Canadian Christianity," *McMaster Divinity College Theological Bulletin* 3 (January 1968): 4-14. Students of Canadian Protestantism in particular seemed by the late 1980s overdue to consider other obvious comparative contexts, whether the British Isles (again) or Australia and New Zealand.

The larger Canadian denominations in general lacked surveys of the recent history. Neil Semple's pamphlet, *The United Church of Canada: The First Sixty Years, Living and Risking* (Toronto: United Church of Canada [1985]), was a helpful little history complemented by Ralph Milton, *This United Church of Ours* (Winfield, B.C. and Toronto: Wood Lake Press, 1981), a personal portrait of the contemporary church. In the 1960s, Stewart Crysdale was a one-man information center on the United Church: see, for example, his *The Changing Church in Canada: Beliefs and Social Attitudes of United Church People* (Toronto: United Church of Canada, n.d.); and *Churches Where the Action Is!: Churches and People in Canadian Situations* (Toronto: United Church of Canada, 1966). Studies of changes in the ethos of the United Church usually prompted suggestions for improvement as well. Randolph Carleton Chalmers championed a well-balanced, fully biblical identity and mission in *See the Christ Stand!: A Study in Doctrine in the United Church of Canada* (Toronto: Ryerson Press, 1945); years later he joined with John Webster Grant to discuss "The United Church of Canada: Its Way of Experiencing and Expressing the Ultimate Reality and Meaning," *Ultimate Reality and Meaning* 1 (1978): 100-14. Grant wrote on his own about "The United Church and Its Heritage in Evangelism," *Touchstone* 1 (October 1983): 6-13; Henry Gordon Macleod sounded concerns about "The Transformation of the

United Church of Canada, 1946-1977: A Study in the Sociology of the Denomination" (Ph.D. diss., University of Toronto, 1980); and N. Keith Clifford posed theological questions in "The United Church of Canada and Doctrinal Confession," *Touchstone* 2 (May 1984): 6-21, and in "Which Way Will the United Church Be Taken by *Learning on the Way?*" *Touchstone* 5 (January 1987): 4-15.

The Anglicans had no general survey. Philip Carrington's standard *The Anglican Church in Canada* (Toronto: Collins, 1963) awaited updating. Beyond it lay narrowly focused studies like those by W.S.F. Pickering and J.L. Blanchard, *Taken for Granted: A Survey of the Parish Clergy of the Anglican Church of Canada* (Toronto: Anglican Church of Canada, 1967); Reginald W. Bibby, *Anglitrends: A Profile and Prognosis* (Toronto: Anglican Diocese of Toronto, 1986); and Edward Pulkner, *We Stand on Their Shoulders: The Growth of Social Concern in Canadian Anglicanism* (Toronto: Anglican Book Centre, 1986).

The Lutherans were in much the same position, as Carl Raymond Cronmiller, *A History of the Lutheran Church in Canada* (N.p.: Evangelical Lutheran Synod of Canada, 1961), and George O. Evenson, *Adventuring for Christ: The Story of the Evangelical Lutheran Church of Canada* (Calgary: Foothills Lutheran press, 1974), remained the main sources for Lutheran history. These were supplemented, however, by the essays in Norman J. Threinen, ed., *In Search of Identity: A Look at Lutheran Identity in Canada* (Winnipeg: Lutheran Council in Canada, 1977).

Finally, the Presbyterians were well served by John S. Moir, who added a new chapter to his history of Canadian Presbyterianism, *Enduring Witness: A History of the Presbyterian Church in Canada,* 2nd ed. (n.p.: Presbyterian Church in Canada, [1988]), the text which largely replaced the briefer study by N.G. Smith, A.L. Farris, and H.K. Markell, *A Short History of the Presbyterian Church in Canada* (Toronto: Presbyterian, 1965). Moir's new chapter was a more dispassionate portrayal of the Presbyterian Church in Canada than his earlier article, "The Smouldering Bush: The Presbyterian Church in Canada Faces Its Second Century," *Chelsea Journal* 2 (March-April 1976): 97-99. Moir's work was complemented by a couple of other works of different sorts: T.M. Bailey, *The Covenant in Canada: Four Hundred Years History of the Presbyterian Church in Canada* (Hamilton, Ont.: The MacNab Circle, 1975); Joseph W. Reed and William Klempa, "An Enduring Witness: The Work and Outreach of the Presbyterian Church in Canada," *International Review of Mission* 71 (July 1982): 287-94; Ian S. Rennie, "Conservatism in the Presbyterian Church in Canada in 1925 and Beyond: An Introductory Exploration," *Canadian Society of*

Presbyterian Church History Papers, 1982; and "Profile: 'Median Street' Presbyterian Church," *The Presbyterian Record* (October 1984): 22-23.

Perhaps no Protestants in Canada since 1970, however, were as busy in the examination of their history than were those of the Canadian Baptist Federation. Several important collections of essays were published, each of which contained studies pertaining to this period: Jarold K. Zeman, ed., *Baptists in Canada: Search for Identity amidst Diversity* (Burlington, Ont.: G.R. Welch, 1980); Murray J.S. Ford, ed., *Canadian Baptist History and Polity* (Hamilton, Ont.: McMaster University Divinity College, n.d.); Paul R. Dekar and Murray J.S. Ford, eds., *Celebrating the Canadian Baptist Heritage: Three Hundred Years of God's Providence* (Hamilton, Ont.: McMaster University Divinity College, n.d.); and Jarold K. Zeman, ed., *Costly Vision: The Baptist Pilgrimage in Canada* (Burlington, Ont.: Welch, 1988). Books, articles, and other works, scholarly and popular, examined a number of aspects of Baptist life and work: Walter E. Ellis, *Can the God of the Desert Grow Grapes?: A Study of Toronto Baptists* (N.p., n.d.); idem, "A Place to Stand: Contemporary History of the Baptist Union of Western Canada," *American Baptist Quarterly* 6 (March 1987); 31-51; J.E. Harris, *The Baptist Union of Western Canada: A Centennial History,* 1873-1973 (Saint John, N.B.: Lingley Printing, n.d.); William H. Jones, *What Canadian Baptists Believe* (Niagara Falls, Ont.: JBTS, 1980); I. Judson Levy, "Canadian Baptist Ecumenical Relationships," *Foundations* 23 (1980): 84-96; Gordon H. Pousett, "A History of the Convention of Baptist Churches of British Columbia" (M.Th. thesis, Vancouver School of Theology, 1982); Margaret E. Thompson, *The Baptist Story in Western Canada* (Calgary, Alta.: Baptist Union of Western Canada, [1974]); and Jarold K. Zeman, *Baptist Roots and Identity* (N.p.: Baptist Convention of Ontario and Quebec, 1978).

The Fellowship of Evangelical Baptist Churches devoted less attention to history, but still produced some useful work. Leslie K. Tarr, *This Dominion His Dominion: The Story of Evangelical Baptist Endeavour in Canada* (Willowdale, Ont.: Fellowship of Evangelical Baptist Churches in Canada, 1968) and J.H. Watt, *The Fellowship Story: Our First 25 Years* (n.p.: Fellowship of Evangelical Baptist Churches in Canada, 1978), were the most important surveys, complemented by several other studies: Kenneth R. Davies, "The Struggle for a United Evangelical Baptist Fellowship, 1953-1965," in *Baptists in Canada: Search for Identity amidst Diversity,* ed. Jarold K. Zeman (Burlington, Ont.: G.R. Welch, 1980), 237-65; Gordon H. Pousett, "The History of the Regular Baptists of British Columbia" (B.D. thesis, McMaster University, 1956); and John B. Richards,

Baptists in British Columbia: A Struggle to Maintain "Sectarianism"
Vancouver: Northwest Baptist Theological College and Seminary,
1977). Charles A. Tipp, "Objections to Unity," in *One Church, Two
Nations?* ed. Philip LeBlanc and Arnold Edinborough (Don Mills,
Ont.: Longmands, 1968), 54-68, purports to speak for evangelicals in
general but is read better as a sounding of the Fellowship Baptist
mind.

If the Federation Baptists had rivals in studying their own
tradition, they would have been the Mennonites. Analyzed for some
time by sociologists from the outside, they increasingly produced
scholarly studies of their own. One important collection of articles
in fact emerged from a joint project with Baptists and others: Jarold
K. Zeman and Walter Klaassen, eds., *The Believers' Church in
Canada* (N.p.: Baptist Federation of Canada and Mennonite
Central Committee [Canada], 1979); another, earlier volume deals
with Mennonites only: Henry Poettcker and Rudy A. Regehr, eds.,
Call to Faithfulness: Essays in Canadian Mennonite Studies (Winnipeg,
Man.: Canadian Mennonite Bible College, 1972). These volumes
can serve as good introductions to the abundance of sociological
literature on Mennonites and other Anabaptists, as does Peter M.
Hamm, *Continuity and Change among Canadian Mennonite Brethren*
(Waterloo, Ont.: Wilfrid Laurier University Press, 1987). Examples
of such literature follow: Frank Epp, "The Mennonite Experience in
Canada," in *Religion and Ethnicity,* ed. Harold Coward and Leslie
Kawamura (Waterloo, Ont.: Wilfrid Laurier University Press, 1978),
21-36; William Klassen, "Mennonites in Canada: Taking Their
Place in Society," *International Review of Mission 71 (July 1982): 315-
19;* and Rodney J. Sawatsky, "Domesticated Sectarianism:
Mennonites in the U.S. and Canada in Comparative Perspective,"
Canadian Journal of Sociology 3 (Spring 1978): 233- 44. A helpful
series of essays sociological and theological is presented in Rodney
J. Sawatsky, *Authority and Identity: The Dynamics of the General
Conference Mennonite Church* (North Newton, KS: Bethel College,
1987).

Other smaller denominations had much less to offer themselves
or others. As the most vigorous of these denominations, the
Pentecostals did produce some accounting in the midst of their
other activities. Gloria G. Kulbeck, *What God Hath Wrought: A
History of the Pentecostal Assemblies of Canada,* ed. Walter E.
McAlister and George R. Upton, with a Foreword by A.G. Ward
(Toronto: Pentecostal Assemblies of Canada, 1958), was the only
published attempt at a comprehensive history, but it was joined by
Paul Hawkes, "Pentecostalism in Canada: A History with
Implications for the Future" (D.Min. diss., San Francisco

Theological Seminary, 1982); Ronald A.N. Kydd, "The Pentecostal Assemblies of Canada and Society," *Canadian Society of Church History Papers* (1972-73): 1-15 + i-viii; Erna Alma Peters, *The Contribution to Education by the Pentecostal Assemblies of Canada* (Altona, Man.: By the author, 1971); and an editorial, "Growing Churches in the Sixth Decade 1968-1978," *The Pentecostal Testimony* (September 1978): 4-7. Two different portraits were painted of the Salvation Army, the first a fine scholarly history and the second a winsome journalistic impression: R.G. Moyles, *The Blood and Fire in Canada: A History of the Salvation Army in the Dominion 1882-1976* (Toronto: Peter Martin Associates, 1977); and Robert Collins, *The Holy War of Sally Ann: The Salvation Army in Canada* (Saskatoon, Sask.: Western Producer Prairie Books, 1984).

From here, however, resources are scant for other denominations: Arthur Garratt Dorland, *The Quakers in Canada: A History* (Toronto: Ryerson Press, 1968); David Goa, "Secularization among Ethnic Communities in Western Canada," in *Religion and Ethnicity,* ed. Harold Coward and Leslie Kawamura (Waterloo, Ont.: Wilfrid Laurier University Press, 1978), 1-19; Muriel Hanson, *Fifty Years and Seventy Places: The Story of the Evangelical Free Church in Canada* (Minneapolis: Free Church Publications, 1967); R. Wayne Kleinsteuber, *More than a Memory: The Renewal of Methodism in Canada* (N.p.: Light and Life Press Canada, 1984); Thomas Peake, "Fifty Years of Gospel Witness: The Story of the Associated Gospel Churches of Canada 1920-1970" (Research paper, Bob Jones University Graduate School, 1970); A. Ronald Tonks, "The History of the Christian and Missionary Alliance with a Brief Summary of the Work in Canada" (B.D. thesis, McMaster University, 1958); W.W.J. Vanoene, *Inheritance Preserved: The Canadian Reformed Churches in Historical Perspective* (Winnipeg: Premier Printing, 1975); and the pertinent sections in James W. St.G. Walker, *A History of Blacks in Canada: A Study Guide for Teachers and Students* (Hull, Quebec: Minister of State Multiculturalism, 1980), and Robin W. Winks, *The Blacks in Canada: A History* (New Haven: Yale University Press and Montreal: McGill-Queen's University Press, 1971).

Religion in certain regions in Canada has been studied better than it has been in others. Charles P. Anderson, Tirthankar Bose, and Joseph I. Richardson, ed., *Circle of Voices: A History of the Religious Communities of British Columbia* (Lantzville, B.C.: Oolichan Books, 1983), is an unparalleled and quite useful set of sketches. Bob Stewart, "That's the B.C. Spirit!" Religion and Secularity in Lotus Land," *The Canadian Society of Church History Papers* (1983): 22-35, gives a strong sense of contemporary developments. Other regions have received less attention per se: Harry H. Hiller, "Alberta and the Bible Belt Stereotype," in *Religion in Canadian Society,* ed. Stewart Crysdale and Les Wheatcroft (Toronto: Macmillan, 1976), 372-83; Benjamin G. Smillie, ed., *Visions of the New Jerusalem: Religious Settlement on the Prairies* (Edmonton: NeWest Press, 1983); Stewart Crysdale, "Supplement II: The Place of Religion in Ontario in the Twentieth Century," in *The Conservation of Ontario Churches: A Programme for Funding Religious Properties of Architectural and Historical Significance,* by Harold D. Kalman (Toronto: Ministry of Culture and Recreation, Province of Ontario, 1977); and John R. Williams, "Religion in Newfoundland," in *Religion and Culture in Canada* ed. Peter Slater (N.p.: Corporation Canadienne des Sciences Religieuses/Canadian Corporation for Studies in Religion, [1977]), 96-116; despite its title, this article focuses almost entirely upon the social action policies, or the lack of them, of Newfoundland denominations. Donald R. Whyte, "Rural Canada in Transition," in *Rural Canada in Transition,* ed. Marc-Adelard Tremblay and Walton J. Anderson (N.p.: Agricultural Economics Research Council of Canada, 1966), deals with the question of "regions" in an obviously different way.

Ecumenical relations during this period of various kinds have received some treatment. Roger Cann, "What is the CCC?" *International Review of Mission* 71 (July 1982): 312-13, asks a question many Canadians, even churchgoers, would have had trouble answering. John Webster Grant presents one of the latest installments in the continuing Canadian church union serial: "Leading a Horse to Water: Reflections on Church Union Conversations in Canada," in *Studies of the Church in History: Essays Honoring Robert S. Paul on His Sixty-Fifth Birthday,* ed. Horton Davies (Allison Park, PA: Pickwick, 1983), 165-81, a summary which furthers Randolph Bruce Scott's "History of Church Union Conversations between the Anglican Church of Canada and the United Church of Canada" (M.Th. thesis, Toronto Graduate School of Theological Studies, 1966.) David M. Heer studied a different kind of ecumenical movement in "The Trend of Interfaith Marriages in Canada: 1922-1957," *American Sociological Review* 27 (April 1962): 245-50; and so did Margaret Beattie, whose work was used to produce the *Brief History of the Student Christian Movement in Canada 1921-1974* (N.p.: Student Christian Movement, 1975).

A number of authors have discussed the churches' attitudes toward involvement in social issues, particularly via the various coalitions: Stewart Crysdale, *The Industrial Struggle and Protestant Ethics in Canada* (Toronto: Ryerson, 1961); D.J.M. Heap, "The Church and the Workers," *Canadian Journal of Theology* 10 (1964):

132-38; Roger Hutchinson, "Ecumenical Social Action in Canada: Selected Documents: (Manuscript, [1983]); idem, "Ecumenical Witness in Canada: Social Action Coalitions," *International Review of Mission* 71 (July 1982): 344-52; William Webster Sherwin, "The Church and Penal Reform in Canada" (M.Th. thesis, Victoria University, 1963); and John R. Williams, ed., *Canadian Churches and Social Justice* (Toronto: Anglican Book Centre and James Lorimer, 1984).

Interest in Protestants in Quebec, Catholic-Protestant relations in general, and the contact between Francophone and Anglophone Christians have naturally gained a good deal attention since the Quiet Revolution and Vatican II: Robert Choquette, "Religion et rapports interculturels au Canada," *Religion/Culture: Comparative Canadian Studies* 7 (1985): 198-211; Ramsay Cook, "Protestant Lion, Catholic Lamb," in *One Church, Two Nations?* ed. Philip LeBlanc and Arnold Edinborough (Don Mills, Ont.: Longmans, 1968), 3-7: H. Fines, *Album du Protestantisme francais en Amerique du Nord* (Montreal: l'Aurore, 1972); Donald M. Lewis, "Evangelical Renewal in French Canada, *His Dominion* 9 (May 1983): 3-12; Brent Reilly, "Baptists and Organized Opposition to Roman Catholicism, 1941-1962," in *Costly Vision: The Baptist Pilgrimage in Canada*, ed. Jarold K. Zeman (Burlington, Ont.: Welch, 1988), 181-98; J.-P. Rouleau with J.-P. Montminy and L. Painchaud, "Religion in Quebec: Present and Future," *Pro Mundi Vita Dossiers* no. 3 (November- December 1977); Glen G. Scorgie, "Twentieth-Century Evangelistic Renewal in French Canada" (Guided study report, Regent College, 1980); and Henry Warkentin, "A History of the Protestant Church in Quebec" (B.D. thesis, Waterloo Lutheran Seminary, 1963). See also the entire November 1977 issue of *Faith Today* for evangelical work in Quebec, and an update from Christian Direction, the organization that administered the "Sermons from Science" pavilion at Expo '67, "How Not to Think about Quebec," supplement to *Christian Week* 22 (7 March 1989). On the "separate schools" question, see among other sources J. Bascom St. John, *Separate Schools in Ontario* (Toronto: The Globe and Mail, 1963), and Theodore Elia Thomas, "The Protestant Churches and the Religious Issue in Ontario's Public Schools: A Study in Church and State" (Ph.D. diss., Columbia University, 1972), although the story has advanced considerably since then.

The scholarly study of evangelicalism in Canada lags well behind that in the United States. A guide to evangelicalism in Canada since World War I is John G. Stackhouse, Jr., "Proclaiming the Word: Canadian Evangelicalism since World War I" (Ph.D. diss., University of Chicago, 1987). Robert K. Burkinshaw, "Strangers and

Pilgrims in Lotus Land: Conservative Protestantism in British Columbia, 1917-1981" (Ph.D. diss., University of British Columbia, 1988), sums up Burkinshaw's several helpful studies of evangelicalism in that province. Lloyd Mackie, "Spreading the Gospel," *Vancouver* 14 (April 1981): 66-103 passim, separates the various strands of lower mainland evangelicalism — although the author does have the distressing problem of confusing "evangelicalism" with the action of "evangelism" and even a non-word, "evangelicism." Judith Haiven, *Faith, Hope, No Charity: An Inside Look at the Born Again Movement in Canada and the United States,* with a Foreword by Charles Templeton (Vancouver: New Star Books, 1984), is a decidedly uncharitable look at evangelicalism. The book's bitterness threatens to obscure some important insights. A much briefer and more forgiving view of evangelicalism in the early 1980s is Brian C. Stiller, "Evangelical Megatrends: Major Influences Shaping the Canadian Church," *Faith Alive* 3 (April 1985): 14-24.

Other studies of evangelicalism have a variety of focuses. Reginald Bibby's several studies of evangelical church growth which dispute the thesis of Dean M. Kelley, *Why Conservative Churches Are Growing: A Study in Sociology of Religion* (New York: Harper & Row, 1972), are confirmed in Ken Little et al., "Are the Conservative Churches Reaching Canada?" *His Dominion* 4 (Spring 1977): 12-13. Erwin W. Lutzer, *Flames of Freedom* (Chicago: Moody Press, 1976), describes the prairie revival of the early 1970s whose reverberations were still felt two decades later. John H. Simpson questions whether a "New Religious Right" could thrive in Canada in "The Politics of Morality in Canada," in *Religious Movements: Genesis, Exodus, and Numbers,* ed. Rodney Stark (New York: Paragon House, 1985), 221-35. John G. Stackhouse, Jr. outlines approaches to the controversial issue of women in church leadership among evangelicals in "Women in Public Ministry in Twentieth-Century Canadian and American Evangelicalism: Five Models," *Studies in Religion/Sciences religeuses* 17 (1988): 471-485. Brian C. Stiller surveys evangelical mass media in "Canadian Evangelicals: A Changing Face," *Faith Alive* 3 (Septmber 1985): 10-17. David Mainse tells his own story with David Manuel in *100 Huntley Street* (Plainfield, NJ: Logos International and Toronto: G.R. Welch, 1979). Canadian religious television broadcasting is briefly profiled in Wendy Nelles, "Canadian TV Ministries: Higher on Hope than Hype," *Christianity Today* 33 (17 March 1989): 46-47.

The Canadian movement of charismatic renewal, which overlapped with evangelicalism, has only one account: Al Reimers, *God's Country: Charismatic Renewal* (Toronto: G.R. Welch, 1979).

Frederick B. Bird, "A Comparative Analysis of the Rituals Used by
Some Contemporary 'New' Religious and Para-Religious Move-
ments," in *Religion and Culture in Canada*, ed. Peter Slater
(N.p.: Corporation Canadienne des Sciences Religieuses/Canadian
Corporation for Studies in Religion [1977]), 448-69, and Frederick
Bird and William Reimer, "New Religious and Para-religious
Movements in Montreal," in *Religion in Canadian Society*, ed.
Stewart Crysdale and Les Wheatcroft (Toronto: Macmillan, 1976),
307-20, discuss a Charismatic Renewal group in Montreal, but the
national phenomenon still awaits scholarly examination. Ronald
Kydd has looked recently at "Pentecostals, Charismatics and the
Canadian Denominations," *Eglise et Theologie* 13 (1982): 211-31.

Missionary work in the second half of the twentieth century is
also a field largely unexplored by scholars. The new standard on
domestic missions in John Webster Grant, *Moon of Wintertime:
Missionaries and the Indians of Canada in Encounter since 1534*
(Toronto: University of Toronto Press, 1984). A history of foreign
missions supported by Canadians — a story of considerable
importance, given the magnitude of the effort —has never been
written.

Religious scholarship and education in Canada are multi-
faceted things, but more and more facets are receiving attention.
Several works attempt to present a survey of Canadian theological
scholarship's history and state-of-the-art: N. Keith Clifford,
"History of Religion in Canada," *The Ecumenist* 18 (July-August
1980): 65-69; idem, "Religion and the Development of Canadian
Society: An Historiographic Analysis," *Church History* 38 (1969):
506-23; Stewart Crysdale and J.-P. Montminy et al., *La Religion au
Canada/Religion in Canada: Annotated Inventory of Scientific Studies of
Religion 1945-1972* (Downsview, Ont.: York University and Quebec:
Les Presses de l'Universite Laval, 1974); Harry H. Hiller, "The
Sociology of Religion in the Canadian Context," in *Introduction to
Canadian Society: Sociological Analysis*, ed. G.N. Ramu and Stuart D.
Johnson (Toronto: Macmillan, 1976), 349-400; John S. Moir, "The
Canadian Society of Church History: A Twenty-Year Retrospect,"
Canadian Society of Church History Papers (1980): 76-98; idem,
"Coming of Age, but Slowly: Aspects of Canadian Religious
Historiography since Confederation," *Canadian Catholic Historical
Association Study Sessions* 50 (1983): 89-98; idem, *A History of Biblical
Studies in Canada: A Sense of Proportion (Chico, CA: Scholars Press,
1982); D.C. Masters, Protestant Church Colleges in Canada* (Toronto:
University of Toronto Press, 1966); idem, "The Rise of Liberalism in
Canadian Protestant Churches," *Canadian Catholic Historical
Association Study Sessions* (1969): 27-39; Terrence Murphy, "The

Religious History of Atlantic Canada: The State of the Art,"
Acadiensis 15 (Autumn 1985): 152-74; Roger O'Toole, "Some Good
Purpose: Notes on Sociology of Religion in Canada," *Annual Review
of the Social Sciences of Religion* 6 (1982): 177-217; and F.A. Peake,
"Reflections on Canadian Church History," *Journal of the Canadian
Church Historical Society* 22 (April 1980): 46-50.

Theological education is part of many of the immediately
preceding stories, but is discussed also in the following: Arnold
Edinburgh, *The Enduring Word: A Centennial History of Wycliffe
College* (Toronto: University of Toronto Press, 1978); Ben Harder,
"The Bible Institute-College Movement in Canada," *Journal of the
Canadian Church Historical Society* 19 (April 1980): 29-45; Oswald
Howard, *The Montreal Diocesan Theological College: A History from
1873 - 1963* (Montreal: McGill University Press, 1963); George
Rawlyk and Kevin Quinn, *The Redeemed of the Lord Say So: A
History of Queen's Theological College, 1912-72* (Kingston, Ont.:
Queen's Theological College, 1980); Ian S. Rennie, "Theological
Education in Canada: Past and Present," (paper presented at
Ontario Bible College, January 1974); and S.A. Witner, *The Bible
College Story: Education with Dimension* (Manhasset, NY: Channel
Press, 1962). In addition to these, see the recurrent articles on
theological education in Canada in the *Yearbook of American and
Canadian Churches*, ed. Constant H. Jacquet, Jr. (Nashville:
Abingdon) for schools belonging to the Association of Theological
Schools and in *Faith Today* for institutions which have identified
themselves as evangelical.

Finally, the literature on secularization is immense. Most helpful
for general categories in framing the few comments above in this
regard were the following: Peter L. Berger, *The Sacred Canopy:
Elements of a Sociological Theory of Religion* (Garden City, NY:
Anchor, 1969 [1967]); Os Guinness, *The Gravedigger File: Papers on
the Subversion of the Modern Church* (Downers Grove, IL:
InterVarsity Press, 1983); David Lyon, *The Steeple's Shadow: On the
Myths and Realities of Secularization* (Grand Rapids, MI: Wm. B.
Eerdmans, 1987 [1985]); David Martin, *A General Theory of
Secularization* (New York: Harper & Row, 1978); and Martin E.
Marty, *The Modern Schism: Three Paths to the Secular* (New York:
Harper & Row, 1969). Lyon in particular is a good guide to the
current state of the question.

Index

Aberhart, William, 142,
183-185,
Alline, Henry, 15, 21, 22,
25, 27, 29, 31, 32, 34, 35,
36, 37, 38, 40, 43, 65,
183,
Anglicans, 9, 10, 11, 14,
15, 16, 17, 18, 19, 20, 21,
29, 30, 40, 60, 65, 66, 67,
86, 87, 88, 91, 100, 106,
107, 120, 121, 124, 126,
140, 151, 161, 189, 191-
192, 200, 209, 222,
Asbury, Francis, 21, 23,
Bailey, Jacob, 39,
Bangs, Nathan, 11, 22, 23,
24, 29, 31, 32, 33, 40, 41,
43,
Baptists, 10, 15, 21, 24, 35,
42, 65, 66, 67, 91, 99,
100, 106, 107, 120, 140,
159, 161, 191-192, 202,
203, 222, 226-228,
Berton, Pierre, 210,
Bethune, A.N., 86,
Bibby, Reginald, 233, 234,
Bible College and
Schools, 164-165, 204-
205, 230-231,
Black, William, 37,
Bland, Henry, Flesher, 75,
84,
Bland, Salem, 112,
Brooke, John, 81,
Bryden, W.W., 179,
Buchman, Frank, 173,
174-177,
Burns, Nelson, 110,
Burns, Robert, 79, 80, 82,
84,
Burwash, Nathanael, 109,
112,
Campbell, John, 112,
Carman, Albert, 110,
Case, William, 22, 30, 32,
33, 40,
Chalmers, R.C., 206,
Chiniquy, Charles, 113,
Chipman, Thomas H., 39,
Chown, S.D., 130,
Clarke, J.C.D., 14, 90,
Coate, Samuel, 31,
Congregationalists, 9, 20,
21, 100, 140, 151,

Cooperative
Commonwealth
Federation (CCF), 177,
178, 181, 189, 190-
Crossley, G.T. and
Hunter, J.E., 117, 118,
Cramp, John, Mocket, 51,
52, 53, 57, 72, 83,
Dimock, Joseph, 34,
Douglas, T.C., 189-190
Dow, Lorenzo, 22,
Errington, Jane, 13, 14, 43,
Evangelical Fellowship of
Canada, 231-232,
Expo Christian Pavilions,
216, 218,
Fellowship for a Christian
Social Order, 177-178,
180-181,
French, Goldwin, 28, 52,
66, 67,
Fundamentalism, 157-171,
Garrettson, Freeborn, 21,
29, 30, 35,
Gatchell, Joseph, 29,
Grant, George Munro,
100,
Grant, J. W., 58, 101, 205,
208,
Hague, Dyson, 161,
Hatch, Nathan, 14, 20, 27,
Hay Bay, 12, 13, 39,
Holiness Movement, 109,
110, 163,
Horner, Ralph Cecil, 109,
Inglis, Charles, 11, 12, 14,
15, 16, 18, 19, 30,
I.V.C.F., 165-166, 204-205,
216-217,
Jackson, George, 112, 123,
Jehovah's Witnesses, 143,
163,
Kagawa, Toyohiko, 173-
174,
King, Mackenzie, W.L.,
148, 149,
Langhorn, John, 17,
Lord's Day Alliance, 123,
Losee, William, 22, 23, 31,
Lutherans, 20, 100, 107,
141, 162, 191-192, 202,
209, 212,
McColl, Duncan, 25, 29,
McCulloch, Thomas, 62,
63, 68, 69, 73, 76, 77, 78